Elizabeth Wright

MILLER FREEMAN

MAN OF ACTION

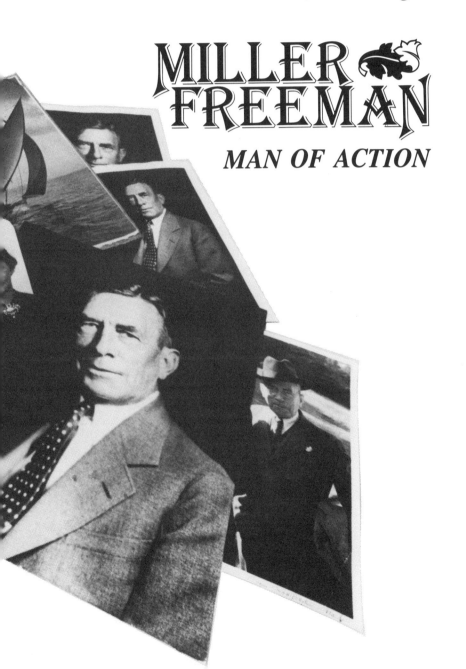

This book is dedicated to

DeWitt Gilbert

*a close friend and business associate
of Miller Freeman's. DeWitt Gilbert's outstanding
work in completing Miller Freeman's unfinished
Memoirs, provided an
invaluable guide and foundation for
his biography.*

EW

Contents

Acknowledgments

The author and her publishers wish to acknowledge the assistance of the following organizations and publications in compiling this book:

As the Valley Was, ed. Jeanne R. Crawford (Yakima, Washington: Yakima Federal Savings and Loan Association, 1968). Illustrations from this publication appear on pages 28 and 29. Photographs are by Frank Lanterman.

Seattle Historical Society; U.S. Army Corps of Engineers, Seattle District; University of Washington School of Fisheries Library; Yakima Valley Museum, Yakima, Washington.

Bellevue American; *Coast* Magazine; San Francisco *Bulletin*; Seattle *Daily Journal of Commerce*; *Seattle Post-Intelligencer*; *Seattle Star*; *Seattle Times*; Spokane *Spokesman-Review; Spokane Daily Chronicle; Victoria Daily Times;* Walla Walla *Union-Bulletin; Yakima Herald*.

Some persons should be singled out for special thanks:

DeWitt Gilbert, longtime associate of Miller Freeman, whose section of the original *Memoirs* provided the basis for much of the historical material in this book, has kindly furnished additional information and patiently answered many questions posed by both the author and the publishers.

Dr. David B. Charlton, who lent early reports of the International Fisheries Commission and the International Pacific Salmon Fisheries Commission from his file of material relative to the Pacific Northwest.

Janet Breuner, talented artist and friend of the author, who produced the fine oil painting of Miller Freeman reproduced on page 10 of this book. Janet worked from a studio photograph of Miller Freeman taken in Seattle just a few years before his death.

Many members of the publishers' staff contributed much to the book, but the author wishes to express special thanks to Peggy Boyer for her expert assistance in expanding and editing the text. The association with Peggy gave the author much pleasure and benefited the book greatly. The author also appreciates the care and talent with which Peter Tucker, also of the publishers' staff, handled the book's design and production.

Elizabeth Wright (Freeman)

Preface

The intent of this book is to trace the career of Miller Freeman—a publisher and journalist—the scope of whose interests and activities went far beyond the boundaries of his chosen occupation. His many campaigns in the public interest, and the often unique manner and methods he employed in realizing his goals merit this account.

Miller Freeman/Man of Action together with its predecessor, *Independence in all Things/Neutrality in Nothing*, comprise the saga of two early western publishers. The two books together tell the stories of the lives and careers of a father and his son.

The first book, *Independence in all Things/Neutrality in Nothing*, deals with the career of pioneer Legh Richmond Freeman, who blazed a publishing trail with his newspaper, the *Frontier Index*, literally following the Union Pacific Railroad as the tracks were laid westward across Nebraska and Wyoming. With the railroad completed, Legh Freeman then continued subsequent publishing ventures in Utah, Montana, and, finally, the state of Washington.

Miller Freeman, Legh Freeman's son, steeped from earliest childhood in the essence of pioneer publishing, emerges in this book to make his own notable contribution to twentieth century industrial magazine publishing and leave his mark on a broad spectrum of activity at regional and national political and social levels.

Miller Freeman was, above all, a West Coast industrial magazine publisher; a deeply concerned conservationist whose efforts were responsible for bringing about effective measures for the preservation of the Pacific Coast fisheries and timber resources; and a participant in the writing of international fisheries treaties and subsequent national and international regulation.

Miller Freeman was a political force; a Washington state legislator; a persistent fighter against foreign aggression and intrusion into West Coast territorial fishing waters; a campaigner for sound United States immigration policies fairly administered; a delegate to three Republican Party nominating conventions and chairman of the Washington

State Republican delegation in 1940; a member of the Washington State Planning Council; and a friend and correspondent of many national political figures.

Miller Freeman was a recognized civic leader of the Northwest. He was commander of the Naval Reserve Training Station at the University of Washington during World War I. He was a strong supporter of the Lake Washington Ship Canal; chairman of the House Harbor and Waterways Committee which helped to bring about Seattle's waterfront development. He was largely responsible for the establishment of the School of Fisheries at the University of Washington and was active in efforts to secure approval for the planning and eventual construction of the Lake Washington floating bridge. He was also actively involved in establishing the Bellevue Shopping Square at Bellevue, Washington.

The facts for this biography of Miller Freeman were drawn primarily from his *Memoirs*, which he had partially finished at the time of his death in 1955 and which were later completed by his longtime business associate and close friend, DeWitt Gilbert. A limited number of the *Memoirs* were published for family and friends soon after Miller Freeman's death. The author felt, however, that this record, although reasonably complete, could be reorganized in a manner that would make for easier reading, better continuity in the progress of his career, and with greater appreciation of him as a man of exceptional ability and accomplishment.

In addition to the *Memoirs*, sources used by the author include Miller Freeman's personal files of correspondence; published material dealing with his activities; the records of his career as publisher of a group of Western industrial journals, as preserved by his family and the company he founded; and the recollections of his sons and of those who worked in close association with him.

June 1976   *Elizabeth Wright (Freeman)*
                                               Moraga, California

Prologue
The MYTHICAL INDIAN

I T MAY HAVE BEEN THE EERIE RED GLOW of the embers on which Chief Saluskin danced one moonless night—or it may have been the wild glint in the old Indian's eyes as he stepped on the burning coals to prove his stoicism—that seared an indelible impression on the young boy's mind and, somehow, even on his features. Perhaps its was the cherished potlatch* given him by an Indian friend and carried in his grubby pocket; the occasional chilling report of an Indian massacre; or the vivid memory of listening wide-eyed to the steady rhythmic beat of distant tom-toms which carried far into the hot summer nights—all these realities of his eastern Washington boyhood influenced the man and may have etched the spirit of the Indian on his soul, and so on his face.

Quite probably it was only chance that made Miller's cheek bones high, his face long and his skin mahogany. As a boy whose features were yet shaping, the comparison was not distinct. As the boy turned to young manhood, the features strengthened and firmed so that there was noticeable resemblance to the Indian. In the older man the likeness was startling.

Whatever the reason for this resemblance, it gave birth to a myth which Miller carried with him through the years. It was never long before a friend or acquaintance learned that Miller Freeman was "a full-blooded North American Indian, born on the Yakima, Washington, Indian Reservation."

Miller's second self, his Indian, bore surprising likeness to Horatio Vattel, Lightning Scout of the Mountains, a mythical character with whom his pioneer father, Legh Richmond Freeman, had consorted many years before. Father and son used these imaginary beings with the same deep-rooted, whimsical humor. Each spoke inner thoughts through these unseen brothers.

Looking back into the pioneer past, it must have been Horatio, the Lightning Scout, who lured Legh always westward in restless wandering from place to place and tempted him, too, toward strong jour-

---

Chinook Jargon meaning "gift," as used here.

nalistic stands, throwing in a dash of raucous humor to lighten the frequent diet of heavy words so often used by Legh in his papers.

Miller's Indian served him in a different way from his father's Horatio, for Miller was above all a practical man of action who could not tolerate false postures. He therefore used the Indian to mock pretense, because in those days, if you were an Indian you *must* be humble. For Miller, the mythical Indian epitomized humility and encouraged the search for the real friend rather than the vain and pompous one. The myth laughed, too, at the man who paled at the thought of Indian blood.

Father and son were much alike in many ways—and at the same time strikingly different. Each became a publisher, each had fire and imagination, each was strong willed and possessed exceptional determination. But, where the father's emotions often ruled him and overrode wisdom, the son made the visions fit logically into the reality of life around him.

Miller's Indian myth lay dormant during the early years of his career. With gained assurance which came with his success later in life, he more often jokingly referred to his Indian ancestry. So, Miller's claims of Indian connections finally became his stock in trade to his own waggish delight and the amusement of his friends.

I
The Early Years
1875-1897

1
FOCUS on BEGINNINGS

T
O FOCUS on Miller Freeman's beginnings, it is necessary to go back to Ogden, Utah, in the summer of 1875. His birth on July 20 of that year occurred little more than a month after issuance of the first edition of the *Ogden Freeman,* a biweekly newssheet published by his mother and father, Ada Miller and Legh Richmond Freeman. As Legh Miller (so he was christened) grew from babyhood to childhood, Ada Freeman bore a multiple role as manager of her home, mother of three small sons, and overseer of the printing and publishing plant. Thus, the child's earliest recollections were of the life surrounding the operation of a newspaper office.

It is easy to visualize the little boy who was frequently with his mother as she worked. He played and watched the varied activities of a publishing office. To him, his mother's part in these procedures seemed a natural addition to her household duties. He observed her as she managed the office, gathered the news, wrote editorial material, directed typesetting, and took part in the final crescendo of activity preceding the issuance of the paper. This swirl of movement, including the accompanying sights, the sounds of the press, and the smell of ink, were a deeply imprinted part of Legh Miller's earliest memories.

By 1879, after four years of publishing their independent paper in hectic competition with the Mormon-controlled press of Ogden, and with the loss of their fourth and youngest son of two years, the husband and wife publishing team looked forward eagerly to new and freer frontiers in Montana. Therefore, when he was four, Legh Miller moved with his family to Butte by covered wagon.

Legh Richmond, anxious to make advance preparations for his family's arrival, was the first to leave for Butte. Ada, a dauntless woman, accustomed to pioneer hardships, soon set out with her sons to follow him. As the party left Ogden one morning in early August of 1879, Legh Miller rode with his mother in the lead wagon. The printer

Ada Virginia Miller Freeman grew up in Strasburg, Virginia, where she and Legh met as children. Her father was Dr. Thomas Jefferson Miller, a community leader.

and the two older boys followed in a buckboard loaded with the press and a few household belongings.

But fate soon intervened to alter the lives of each member of Legh's family for it was on this trip to Montana, at a spot just past Red Rock Creek on the dusty, bumpy road, that Ada Freeman was mortally wounded when a shotgun suddenly broke loose from its mooring and discharged as it fell into the spokes of the turning wheel below her.

A moment of stillness followed the vicious blast before Ada's startled cry of pain. The acrid odor of gunsmoke filled the warm air as the travelers, in shocked disbelief, gradually began to comprehend what had happened. As the children looked on in terror, the printer rushed to Ada and helped staunch the flow of blood from the deep wound torn in her hip by the shot. As she was helped to lie down in the back of her wagon, Ada calmly talked to her boys and assured them that all would be well. Legh, alerted to the accident, raced south to meet the party and with them hurried the last long miles to Butte where Ada was placed in a small hospital.

Legh Miller, who was sitting with his mother on the driver's seat at the time of the accident, remembered vividly the tragic event, the terror of the moment, the dash to Butte with his mother in desperate need of medical help. The days that followed were filled with confusion and fear for the little boy as his mother's life hung in the balance while she gave birth to a stillborn daughter and fought the spreading infection from her wound.

Out of the misty fog of childhood memories, Legh Miller was to clearly recall the day he was led by his father to the hospital to stand by his dying mother's bedside. And he was never to forget the weight of

16

Legh Richmond Freeman, photographed with his sons: Legh Miller, left; Hoomes Kemper, seated; and Randolph Russell, standing at right.

her loving arm on his shoulders and the sound of her voice as she said, "Legh Miller, I know you will always be a good boy."

Soon after these events the furor seemed to end in sudden stillness more terrifying than all that had gone on before. All at once, he was with a strange and silent father. He was cared for by those unknown to him. His world of happy security had disintegrated in a blinding flash.

Plans for the care of Legh's sons were quickly made. Randolph, Hoomes, and Legh Miller were placed in a Catholic boarding school in Ogden, Utah. Then, with heavy heart after months of paralyzing grief, Legh established himself in Butte to continue his now lonely career with the publication of the *Butte Inter-Mountains Freeman.*

For the next four years, the three brothers lived under the benevolent protection and able tutelage of the Catholic sisters, first in Ogden's Sacred Heart Academy and later in Catholic schools in Salt Lake City and in Missoula, Montana. The kindly disciplines, the strictly regulated life, the good education for their day that these schools provided, benefited the three boys in all ways. The love and warmth the nuns bestowed upon the motherless boys were to provide the basis of security which was of greatest value to each of them.

In the spring of 1883, Legh brought his boys home to live with him in Butte. At ten and thirteen years of age, the older boys were put to work in their father's printing office, while Legh Miller was left largely to his own devices. It was here that the small boy, wanting desperately to be part of his father's business operations, one afternoon asked his father for a stack of papers just off the press. Setting out in high enthusiasm to sell them, he ended his business venture soon thereafter in forlorn dejection, having sold none.

17

REFLECTIONS OF YAKIMA'S PAST—Mirrored the windows of the Star Clothing Company 66 years ago and preserved for a later day are a horse and buggy and buildings across the street, the faces and names of which have been changed. Adults shown standing on the boardwalk are, from left, Fred Rowe, Frank Snipes and the proprietors and founders of the company, William Lemon and I. H. Dills. The small boy is the late Miller Freeman, Seattle editor and publisher nd proprietor of a printing shop. The men in the doorway are unidentified. The building where the shop was located in 1895—110 E. Yakima Ave.—was recently razed by the Yakima branch of the National Bank of Commerce.

As he sat on the plank walk which bordered the dusty main street of Butte, tears rolled down his cheeks. To return to his father and brothers, having failed, seemed degrading. At that moment, an older newsboy, tough and knowledgeable in the ways of selling, stopped to view the small child and asked in some disgust what his troubles were. Legh Miller's teary look toward his pile of unsold papers indicated the source of his grief. The older boy emitted a snort of derision and said, "Hell, don't you know you can't sell no papers unless you *holler*?"

Legh Miller opened wide eyes as he watched his benefactor disappear down the street; then with the back of his hand he wiped a lingering tear from his cheek, rose, hitched his papers under his arm, and began to shout his wares. Within a short time he had sold every paper. Triumphantly clutching in his small, hot fist the valued coins, he ran as fast as short legs would take him to his father's office to recount his success.

Each of us recalls sharply etched childhood incidents which later seem unimportant and unrelated to other events. But to Legh Miller this encounter became a beacon in an otherwise flat landscape of remembrance. This lesson, casually delivered by an unwitting teacher, fell on receptive ears. Its truth impressed itself indelibly on an eager mind to become for Legh Miller a firmly held operating principle. The words repeatedly flashed through his thoughts during his lifetime: "You gotta *holler* if you're going to sell." Referring to the incident many years later, Miller said, "That was my first lesson in business aggressiveness, a graphic demonstration of the power of advertising, brought to me at an impressionable age. Never for one minute did I forget the lesson, and on the power of advertising, I subsequently built my business."

It was about a year and a half after his boys' return to Butte that Legh once more decided on a move; this time it was to Yakima in Washington Territory, where the Northern Pacific Railroad was extending its line. Opportunity followed the railroad and there, near its

terminus, Legh wanted to be. He moved his printing plant by freight car to Ainsworth, railhead of the Northern Pacific at the time. From Ainsworth, situated on the Snake River about four miles north of Pasco, the plant was taken to Yakima by wagon. The boys rode in a buggy up through the Yakima Indian Reservation.

The family arrived at a time when the Northern Pacific officials, having been unable to purchase the desired land for their station, had decided to relocate it four miles to the north of old Yakima (now Union Gap). As the officials had promised, the railroad company moved the town and all willing inhabitants to the new site, which was known as North Yakima for many years until the word *North* was dropped on January 1, 1918.

In addition to assistance in moving buildings, the railroad had offered each property owner of old Yakima a free piece of ground equal to the size of his holdings in the old town. Legh helped plot the new community and built one of the first buildings—a printing plant with living quarters in the rear—on its main street.

Moving a town was an astonishing undertaking, especially to a nine-year-old boy, but in a few months the job was done. The small buildings and homes were jacked up on timbers and carried on wagon trucks, making the move in one day. Larger buildings were put on rollers, which were run on planks laid down on the flat prairie; progress of these structures was a few hundred feet a day. Legh Miller later described the transport of the Yakima National Bank, vault and all, in this manner. The bank carried a sign, Business as Usual, and customers hitched their horses to the rack on the moving building while they went inside to do their banking.

Legh soon began the publication of *Yakima Farmer* (later the *Washington Farmer*), a journal designed to serve the agriculturalists and ranchers. Again, Legh's older sons worked with their father. Legh Miller was sent to board with the Tanner family on their ranch outside of town and adjacent to the Yakima Indian Reservation.

19

(Courtesy Yakima Valley
Museum, Yakima, Washington.)

These Yakima Indians
on their ponies
are typical of those Miller
met during his boyhood.

Thus, at nine, Legh Miller became a working man as he helped the
Tanners with the many chores pertaining to ranch life. His major job
was to herd cattle on the lands of the Indian Reservation, but he was
also assigned all other jobs that a small boy could handle. The upkeep
of a pioneer ranch entailed endless labor which stretched a working
day from dawn until dark. His days were long and hard for a child, but
he was treated kindly and he happily accepted his new life. With this
move, too, there were many new and exciting interests for him. Herd-
ing cattle on the Indian Reservation, he daily met Indians who roamed
the hills.

His first encounter with a group of mounted braves startled and
frightened him as he came upon them unexpectedly on the rise of a hill.
But, while these Indians looked fierce, Legh Miller soon found them to
be friendly. He frequently visited them at their encampments, played
with their children, and became familiar with their customs and man-
ners. It was during this time that he had the opportunity to watch Chief
Saluskin in a ceremonial dance. He went to the ceremony uninvited
but, as he later explained, "I minded my own business and nobody
objected to my presence."

With the long period of sporadic warfare between the Indians and
white settlers nearly over, the Northwest communities of the 1880s
saw them peacefully intermingling. While the Indians continued to live
on their reservations, preserving their customs and ways of living, they
regularly visited the towns. A familiar sight for Legh Miller was the
Indian riding his plains pony on the dusty streets of Yakima, wearing
his colorful blanket—often with the addition of a white man's large-
brimmed western hat perched high on his forehead, his long black hair
falling straight beneath it. Indian blanket and western hat were, in fact,

The otter-skin braided wraps worn by this Indian show that he is a chief or related to a chief. His wife wears a beaded wool dress and woven basket hat.

symbols of two cultures, proudly and practically worn by the Northwest Indians.

As he came to know many of the Indians and to observe life on the reservation, Legh Miller realized that, despite their legal rights under the treaties, these people were subject to exploitation and injustice. "The lands of the Yakima Reservation were coming to be recognized as exceptionally fine and fertile and the white man coveted them from my earliest recollections," he commented later.

Some of our Congressmen, he recalled, seemed to feel that their first duty to their constituents was to enact laws which would enable the white men to clip off for themselves the richest and best portions of the reservation. Among the most destructive of these laws upon the Indians and their future was one permitting any Indian to own 80 acres of land outright and defining an Indian as anyone with even a little Indian blood in his veins. The result was that some white men married squaws for the sole purpose of acquiring lands in the names of their children. In this way, a white man could build himself an empire in a few years by begetting half-breed children who were entitled to 80 acres each, which, of course, their white father would control as their legal guardian.

"In my observation, the white man has little of which to be proud in his treatment of the Indians and in his too frequent breaking of solemn treaties when it became profitable to do so," he concluded.

It was while Legh Miller was with the Tanners in the bitter cold winter of 1884-85—months of relative inactivity on the ranch—that he had the opportunity to attend a three months' session of the one-room school at Ahtanum. This period, added to his primary schooling at the Catholic boarding schools in Utah and Montana, was to be his total

Chief White Swan of the Klickitats, one of many tribes assigned to the Yakima Indian Reservation, with his wife. The town of White Swan, near Toppenish, Washington, was named for this man.

exposure to formal schooling, amounting, if fairly reckoned, to approximately two years.

While young Legh Miller's stay with the Tanner family had been approved by his father, Legh soon felt that it was time for his youngest son to assume his place and carry responsibility with the rest of his family in the printing office. Therefore, in the summer of 1885, at the age of ten, Legh Miller returned to his father's home and was apprenticed to work by the side of his brothers at all manner of jobs common to a country printing office. He readily accepted his new role with businesslike enthusiasm for he was proud to be included, at last, in the family publishing operation.

A family portrait taken after Legh's marriage to Janie Ward, his second wife. From left: seated, Legh; Janie; Legh Miller; standing, Hoomes Kemper; Florence Freeman, Legh's niece; and Randolph Russell.

2
A CLEAN BREAK

I N THE 1880s it was not unusual for a child to go to work at the age of ten. However, by the time Legh Miller had reached the age of twenty-one, he could look back on nearly eleven years of work in the family publishing office and print shop. He had gradually become an integral part of the working force of the plant and was qualified to assume responsibility in all jobs pertaining to the putting together of his father's publication, the *Washington Farmer*.

Since his nineteenth birthday he had been alone with his father. As they reached maturity, Randolph and Hoomes had, in turn, deserted their father and struck out on their own. But Miller had stuck with his father longer than the others. He knew he had done his jobs well, without wages or share in the business, since he was a small child. He had waited for six months after his twenty-first birthday, hoping his father would open the subject now increasingly important to him and would include him in a fair share in the printing and publishing business, or at least give him a respectable salary. Well, the subject had not been opened and Legh Miller realized it was up to him to broach it.

The results of his request to Legh were as bitter as his worst fears could have predicted. Often in later years he recalled the miserable confrontation when he had met his father's adamant resistance to any proposed change. Yes, Legh Miller himself had angered quickly at the injustice and had not done his cause any good by using harsh words. That he later readily conceded. But Legh, too, had flared in anger at his son's audacity. Whatever chance there might have been to establish some more equitable business arrangement between the two was irrevocably lost in the unreasoned anger of the moment.

Legh Miller reddened and grew coldly silent as his father's words whipped him. His large mouth set in a hard line and his steely eyes glinted. As his father talked, Legh Miller was convinced that their differences were irreconcilable. He turned abruptly, pulled open the office door, stepped through and slammed it behind him, then walked swiftly to his room, collected a few belongings and left the house.

As he pedaled his bicycle furiously down the muddy street through the sharp morning air, he reached his first positive decision, Shedding the name Legh with a sudden angry wrench, he decided to use only his middle name, Miller. At that moment be became Miller Freeman, a young man completely on his own whose only possessions amounted to his valued bicycle, a few clothes, and three dollars. With this meager assortment of worldly possessions, coupled with grim determination born of anger at his father's injustice, Miller faced his future.

He had parted from his father in a clean, hard break. He knew there was no turning back. Overwhelmed with emotion as he left home, he had headed for the outskirts of town and now sat by the railroad water tank to think out his problems.

By degrees, the morning sun in the chilly February air brought an easing of his spirit with a beginning clarification of some ideas for his future. With his sudden freedom, thoughts that had long germinated began to take root. Deliberately, he sorted from the first confusion of mind some clear principles. These he mentally laid out before him and carefully weighed. They followed in a simple, logical pattern. He knew he was too spare and small of build to do hard physical labor. Briefly, he considered other possibilities for many kinds of work but he came back to the unalterable fact that he knew two trades—publishing and printing. He liked both occupations and it seemed wise to stay with them.

He quickly determined that he wanted to publish a farm journal that would serve the farmer and rancher as a purely nonpartisan paper to give these people news and information strictly concerned with their working problems. Yes, his thoughts continued, it would be in direct competition with his father's paper. An angry glint returned momentarily to his eyes as he recalled the injustice of his father's stubbornness. Again, his jaw set hard as he conceded *that* was how it was to be.

While working for his father he had increasingly resented the use of the *Washington Farmer* as a political mouthpiece. He felt that partisan issues had little to do with what the farmer and rancher wanted, and should rightfully receive from a farm paper. Above all, Miller wanted nothing more to do with archaic political issues and useless preoccupation with Confederate stances. To devote space to the propounding of the Democratic doctrines of William Jennings Bryan and concern over the "Crime of 1873" when the Republicans demonetized silver, seemed more than pointless to him. Miller was a young man of the present.

Thinking it over carefully, he decided there was opportunity in a strictly nonpartisan farm journal, concerned with the farmer's technical problems and their solutions. In the 1890s farming was coming to be recognized as a subject for scientific study and improvement. Miller sensed that scientific advance in agriculture was overdue and would certainly move at a quickening pace.

Somewhat later, ending his long thought-out planning session, he mounted his bike and headed back to town to take the first step toward the establishment of his career.

24

II
1897-1910
The Foundations
of a Publishing Career

3
STARTING STEPS with RANCH and RANGE

MILLER PEDALED his way back to town to transact a first business deal on his own. At the Front Street restaurant he invested his entire liquid assets—three dollars—in a week's meal ticket. His second call of the morning was to the office of the *Yakima Republic* where he made a deal to use the paper's printing plant at times when it was otherwise idle. (The rent was not required to be paid in advance.) Having successfully transacted his first business contract, he felt a small confidence which seemed to accelerate action and encourage important decisions. As he walked down the street, he decided he would call his paper *Ranch and Range,* using a part of the name of *The Ranch,* a publication recently discontinued. He wanted his paper to include the vigorous livestock business as well as farming and so decided on a name that would be indicative of its broader field of interest.

At this point he assessed his position and found that he had concrete assets amounting to a bicycle and some sound ideas on which to launch his publishing career. Things could be much worse. The future was beginning to clarify itself, but the concern of the moment was for a night's lodging—elsewhere than in his father's home, for there he would not return. Continuing down the street toward the center of town, he met an acquaintance. When Miller briefly recounted his problem and the fact that he had left home, the young man warmly offered to share his humble quarters with Miller. This satisfactory arrangement left Miller free to make a final call at his father's house to collect the remainder of his belongings. Having done this—luckily meeting no one there—all ties with the past were broken.

In his planning Miller realized that his bicycle was his most precious asset, because it offered him the means to circulate in wide areas through the surrounding countryside. Accordingly, the day after he declared his independence, he set out to sell subscriptions. He was well known and well received by most of the farmers and ranchers he called on. His reputation as an industrious young fellow, earned during the years with his father, now paid off.

For two months he kept "on the go" constantly. The first week he

stayed within range of the Front Street restaurant where his meal ticket was. After it ran out he traveled farther from Yakima, eating and sleeping wherever he could find cheap accommodations. Often, to his advantage, he bedded down in a farmer's barn and was fed from the family kitchen. During this time, he paid his out-of-pocket expenses from advance collections—wherever he could make them—on subscriptions and advertising space to stock breeders, implement concerns, and business houses.

At the end of sixty days of pedaling and well-planned calling, he returned to Yakima to produce his first edition of one thousand copies of *Ranch and Range*. He became an all-in-one publisher: collecting and writing up editorial material; setting type; composing advertisements; making up forms; running the presses (as he could around the business hours of the *Yakima Republic*); wrapping, addressing, and finally delivering the copies to the post office. The first edition of *Ranch and Range* burst on the spring landscape in April 1897, and the young man's pride in accomplishment grew. He had made a first big step. Immediately upon issuance of this first edition, he headed out on his bike to collect on the balance of advertising and subscriptions, which enabled him to pay for the rental of the printshop.

On the completion of these negotiations Miller had a net profit of $100. With this sound starting capital, he immediately hired a printer. He was determined he would never again set a stick of type. And with one exception he never did.* The $100 loomed large and glorious to one who had never before possessed more than a few dollars of his own. But of far greater intrinsic value was his steadily growing feeling of self-adequacy. It seemed as if he had suddenly been released from invisible bonds which had held him while he stayed with his father. He was now free and able to make his own way, and this was powerful wine.

---

*Many years later when driving from California to Seattle, Miller Freeman parked by chance in front of the local newspaper office in the town of Redding, California. Instinctively, he walked into the office, met the proprietor and, as he talked, spotted in the corner a rarity—a box of old type. Almost automatically, he moved to it and, while continuing to talk, dexterously began to set type. When he finished, the line read: "See, after half a century, I can still set type by hand."

First issue of Ranch and Range *was published in North Yakima (original name of what is now Yakima) in April 1897. This early view of the downtown section was taken from the old Sloan building, Yakima Avenue and First Street.*

Northern Pacific's original railroad station in North Yakima was built in 1885, when the company was refused land in Yakima and moved the town.

Ranch and Range turned out to be a good paper, with a fresh, vigorous approach. Armed only with promises, he had, in some mysterious way, convinced the farmer and rancher that he would give them what they needed. Now he had justified their faith in him. The first edition proved that his promises were good.

Shortly after his first edition came out, Miller started to expand his field. He made a trip to Spokane and combed that rich agricultural community, harvesting a pocketful of subscriptions and advertisements. Soon after this trip, he rode the Northern Pacific freight car to Seattle. He had been through Seattle in 1894 when his father returned to Yakima from Anacortes and had been well impressed with the city. At that time he had even thought that his father and brothers should try to publish a daily paper there. His idea had been briefly considered by them but finally rejected as too ambitious.

Visiting Seattle again, he quickly decided that this was where he wanted to have his headquarters. True, it was far removed from the heart of the agricultural area in eastern Washington where the bulk of his business was, but it had the advantage of being farther removed from his father's operation. This seemed a healthy thing to him. As far as he was concerned, he would be on the road most of the time and a little more distance would not make that much difference to the efficiency of his business.

Returning to Yakima a few days after this decision, he prepared for his move. As he looked back over the six months since his declared independence, he experienced a glow of satisfaction. He knew his father would be watching his moves and he paused to wonder quizzically what he was thinking. He would not know because the gulf between Miller and Legh was too deep for either to breach. Anyway, Miller thought a little whimsically, the young Indian was doing pretty well. He resolutely pushed the past farther behind him as he packed his belongings and prepared to leave the eastern Washington of his boyhood and take his chances in a new community.

Within a few days, Miller had settled his affairs in Yakima and was ready to pull up stakes. He boarded the morning Northern Pacific

29

freight train, pulling his bike into the boxcar with him and settling himself in the now familiar surroundings of its interior. The door creaked closed and blackness enveloped him as the train lumbered out of the station.

In the darkened car, Miller sat with his back against his thin roll of personal belongings, his valued bike close beside him. The motion of the train lulled him to relaxation and he dozed. Hours later the train whistle echoed long and mournfully against the cliffs of the western slope of the Cascades as it braked, creaking, down the curving grade. Miller was acutely conscious that this was a turning point in his life, and these lonely hours, as the train pulled steadily toward his destination, provided valuable moments for him to assess his present position and his new direction.

The months since the break with his father had been packed with feverish activity aimed toward the immediate goal of balancing his finances. A small profit had given him a beginning assurance. During this period, however, there was little time for reassessment of his long-range goals. The days had seen him making calls to far-separated rural locations. The physical strain of this life was taxing, even to one in the prime of energetic youth. The nights, spent in whatever economy quarters he could find, or as an occasional guest in a ranch or farm home or barn, had seen him fall asleep in exhaustion from his long, tough days.

These hours of necessary inactivity in the boxcar gave him time for reflection. As he sat in the restful blackness, a strange phenomenon occurred which Miller viewed with amazement. The wonder of it merged with his far-reaching thoughts and imprinted itself vividly on his mind.

A small aperture in the door behind his head allowed a pinprick of bright light to throw its beam on the wall opposite him. Amazing to him was the marvel of watching the passing landscape reflected in the inverted picture—as through the lens of a camera—detailed and sharp. This panorama, together with the peaceful moments given him to face and assess an important juncture of his life, became a crystallization in time which he was to recall in minute detail during his lifetime. It was as though a corner had been turned and the dawn of a new life lay ahead.

When an unsure young man of just twenty-two arrived in Seattle in the summer of 1897, he bore the unmistakable stamp of a country boy. He had gained a certain assurance that he could successfully manage his small business, but that was in the familiar surroundings of rural eastern Washington. Seattle was a big city and, while its bustling vitality attracted him, at the same time it renewed some of his insecurity.

But Miller was pretty busy with the problems of meeting his publication deadline when he arrived in town with his bicycle and few belongings. He had little time to spare for worrying about his feelings. Nor was he, in any event, prone to much introspection. Most important to him was that he had good editorial material, collected on his recent tour of several rich agricultural areas, plus ample advertisements, many of which he had composed himself for his customers. These elements, admittedly the lifeblood of his small publishing venture, gave rise to an enthusiasm which superseded his shyness. He was anxious to start putting together the first Seattle-produced edition of *Ranch and Range*. But, where?

As Miller wandered about the city, preoccupied with a young publisher's problems, luck led him to the door of a second-floor printing office on First Avenue. The proprietor, a young man named William Calvert, was launching his career and was hungry for business. Miller needed a printer to produce his paper. The two lost little time in reaching a business deal, advantageous to each of them. Their meeting began an association, both in business and in personal friendship, which persisted for many years and closed only with William Calvert's death.

Miller had brought all his possessions from Yakima in a canvas telescope-type bag, which could be expanded to hold his personal effects as well as his subscription list, advertising contracts, and a few engravings and other printing accessories. He needed a place to work, he told Calvert, and was offered a plain table and chair in a corner of the office.

The arrangement suited Miller perfectly and he moved in immediately. He obtained some mail sacks from the post office and stowed them under the table ready for use. Then he swung into action to meet his fast-approaching deadline. He worked late the first night without taking time out to find a place to live. In exhaustion, he collapsed on the stack of mail sacks and slept there through the night. The next morning, when Calvert arrived at his office, Miller was washed, combed, and ready for the business day, appearing to have just arrived himself.

This primitive but economical and convenient arrangement for lodging continued for more than a week. Since Miller worked all day and far into the night, he began to slide under the table automatically and go to sleep on the mail sacks. However, one morning Calvert arrived at the office earlier than usual and found Miller still asleep under the table. Sizing up the situation in a hurry, Calvert prodded Miller until he was thoroughly awake, then let him understand that a printing contract with desk privileges did *not* include lodging. In a few vivid phrases, he told Miller that he was thrown out so far as sleeping in the shop was concerned, although they would be glad to keep his printing business.

Calvert's temper heated fast and cooled equally fast. Soon the two men were laughing over Miller's imposition and the episode was to provide mutual entertainment in its retelling during their long friendship. Readily accepting the justice of Calvert's anger, Miller quickly found a room on a nearby street for eight dollars a week.

4
PUBLISHER on the MOVE

MILLER WAS NOT in town much because he kept on the move constantly, visiting strategic points in eastern Washington and Oregon. Loading his bicycle into the baggage car, he now traveled by coach on a pass, bestowed on him as a farm publisher. After an overnight train ride, he unloaded his bike at a planned destination and pedaled in a productive radius, soliciting business throughout the area. Then, after a long day's work, he again loaded his bicycle and rode the coach to the next promising community to repeat the procedure. He was dedicated to the energetic development of his newssheet. He broadened his contacts with farmers and ranchers and businessmen in the rural areas until he was a familiar figure in many parts of the two states.

He was well known as the "little fellow" who became the friend of many farmers. His ease with them was natural, for he was, in fact, one of them. As a product of their rural environment, he was fully at home with them in their setting. But a sharp difference marked Miller from his farm friends. While he slipped into easy camaraderie with these people, passed the time of day naturally with them, concerned himself with their particular problems, and laughed appreciatively at their backwoods humor, he never forgot the purpose of his call. The ad, subscription, or news story required for his journal was the all-important goal of every visit.

Closeness to the people of the farm and ranch country was valuable to Miller. Familiarity with their lives was enriching to him personally and to his business as well. As he was increasingly exposed to city life, he did not lose sight of the outlook of the rural man nor of his basic needs, for it was his recognized job to meet these needs. The earthiness of his contacts with the farmer and rancher during those days remained in Miller's consciousness all his life. The early triumphs were cornerstones of confidence to him. Some experiences remained to haunt him for years, but all were chalked up by him to learning. None was ever forgotten.

One of Miller's first payments in a five dollar gold coin gave him a

THE RANCH

Nineteenth Year   SEATTLE, WASHINGTON, SEPT. 15, 1902.   Subscription, $2 Per Year Worth Two Gold Dollars

Ranch and Range was soon renamed The Ranch, *after its predecessor. The September 1902 cover pictured Perry Polson, founder of Polson Instrument Company, Seattle. His building housed MFP headquarters for many years.*

deep thrill of satisfaction. It was only a single coin but it seemed a golden threshold for him. As he pedaled down the dusty road, following a late afternoon call on a farmer, he was acutely conscious of the money reposing deep in his pocket. A pleasing sensation of success overcame him and he stopped his pedaling, laid his bicycle on the roadside, jumped a fence to mount a low knoll, from which he could look over the rich valley below. The sunset sky was streaked with gold and rose, the earth gave off the summer-sweet scent of dust and sage, and a feeling of well-being engulfed Miller. He held his gold piece in his fist, then he opened the fist and looked long at his prize. He flipped it in the air and caught it successfully a few times. Then he flipped it higher with the added exuberance of a juggler. This time he missed the catch and the gold piece buried itself in the deep dust at his feet. He stooped to retrieve it, thinking he knew exactly where it had fallen. His hand groped in the powder dust without success. His search continued and grew frantic. It was still light, for the August evenings were long; but despite adequate light, youthful energy, and increasing determination to regain his hard-earned gold piece, Miller could not find the coin. His search continued as he became desperate with failure.

At last dark came and Miller's hopes faded. It seemed impossible that his gold piece was lost at his feet—but it was. It was hard to give up but realistic to do so after digging in the dust, seemingly for hours. Miller never gave the story particular significance, except to recount it as an unforgettable experience and a bitter disappointment. Yet, as a wise man and one who learned from experience, he treated money with an even more hard-fisted respect thereafter.

After a business deal was completed, Miller was often asked by his customer to stay for a meal. Those home-cooked dinners were special treats to one accustomed to restaurant meals.

33

A JOURNAL OF THE LAND A

One such day etched itself in his memory. The farmer whom he visited had given him a subscription and the feeling was good between the two men. When he was asked to remain for the noonday meal he gladly accepted, knowing it would be satisfying and filling. The meal was especially good, and the farmer's daughter reasonably attractive. As the hearty meal progressed and his wineglass was filled and refilled—the first wine he had ever had—the farmer's daughter became increasingly the object of his rosy admiration. Suddenly, the room began to spin and he saw his surroundings through a fuzzy fog. Still retaining surprising presence of mind, he paid a hasty thanks to his host and beat a fast retreat. The power of alcohol to befuddle the mind was sharply illustrated to him that day, and the lesson was never forgotten. During his later life, while he did not unduly censure the other fellow for "partaking," he assiduously kept his head clear and was well known as an abstainer.

V.OL. XXII. NO. 5.   SEATTLE, WASI

Nor did he ever lose the vivid recollection of the day he paid a call on an old farmer who gave him a subscription and then, as they visited in a friendly manner, suddenly slumped toward Miller and died in his arms. The young man was shocked and saddened. Surely, in retrospect he must have mused over his ability to put on a hard sell. He prided himself on an aggressive approach, but had it been too much for this fellow? Who could know?

The humor of those times in the country area emerged from the life experiences of the people there. Their stories combined the grim with the ludicrous. The extremes of climate to which these areas were subject gave rise to tragic stories of hardship and death to men and animals. Typical of these was the tale of the windstorm so violent and long-lasting that a rancher's sheep were blown high against his barn wall and there impaled to die of starvation before the wind let up. Horrifying or humorous, these chronicles fascinated Miller.

, MARCH 1, 1905.   50c per Year; 5c the Copy.

THE RANCH

A Journal of the Land and the Home in the New West.

With which is consolidated
The Washington Farmer,
The Pacific Coast Dairyman,
The Farmer and Dairyman,
The Farmer and Turfman.

Official organ of the State Dairymen's Association and the State Live Stock Breeders' Association.

MILLER FREEMAN, - Editor and Manager.

Editorial Offices: - - Seattle, Wash.
Tel. Main 1265—Long Distance Connection.

BUSINESS OFFICES:
Seattle - - Metropolitan Bldg.,
Cor. Third and Main Sts.
Spokane - Alexander & Co., 521 First Ave.

Subscription (in advance) $1.00 per year.
Agents wanted in every town to solicit subscriptions. Good commission and salaries paid.

The paper is sent to each subscriber until an order to discontinue is received from the subscriber. We must be notified in writing, by letter or postal card, when a subscriber wishes his paper stopped. Returning the paper will not answer, as we cannot find it on our list from the name alone on the paper. We must have both name and address, and all arrearages or dues must be paid as required by law.
Date of expiration of subscription is shown on your paper by address label containing your name. Failing to receive the paper regularly you should notify the Seattle office at once, when mistakes, if any, will be corrected.
Address all communications to THE RANCH, 104 W. Washington St., Seattle, Washington.

1902 FAIRS.

Salem ....Sept. 15 to 20
Portland ....Sept. 22 to 27
Wenatchee ....Sept 24 to 27
North Yakima.......Sept. 29 to Oct 4
New Westminster ..Sept. 30 to Oct 4
Victoria ....Oct 7 to 11
Spokane ....Oct 6 to 14
Lewiston ....Oct 13 to 18
Boise ....Oct 20 to 25

Read what a White river farmer has to say about the Kent condensery, and then you will agree with us that that institution has had more to do with transforming that section into its present exceptionally prosperous condition than any other one cause or condition. And right here we want to say that it would behoove some of the other dairy sections of this state to endeavor to have such plants established in their midst, instead of having capital go off down into Oregon for investment in condenseries.

James Hart gives us an excellent road talk in this issue. The statements therein made are applicable to about nine-tenths of the road districts of this state. What is needed is organized effort for intelligent expenditure of the road fund.

Those pure-food commissioners who met at Portland show that they are a mighty shortsighted lot in asking the next session of congress for a national pure food law. Once such a law is enacted, and its enforcement placed in the hands of Uncle Sam, the commissioners will all lose their jobs!

The June number of the Bulletin issued by the State Agricultural college is just at hand. A singular error occurs, in that it gives W. J. Spillman as the professor of agriculture. He resigned some months ago to take the position at Washington City of chief of the division of grasses and forage

A TEN-DOLLAR BOOK FREE.

We have received a supply of the 1901 Yearbook of the Department of Agriculture, one copy of which will be mailed free to every subscriber in good standing who asks us for it.

This valuable book contains 846 pages. There are 143 illustrations.

The report of the secretary is a comprehensive resume of the work of the department and shows the scope of this institution.

A valuable feature of this book is that the addresses of all experiment stations are given, so that one can write any of them for special information, bulletins, etc. Also a directory of officials is given of every live stock and dairy association in the United States.

The latest information regarding orchard and garden pests, insect ravages, fruit growing, road building, etc., is given.

Considerable space is given to the range question, irrigation, drainage, etc.

The reports of the last census upon crops and agricultural industries of the Union is presented in the form deemed best adapted to the requirements of the Yearbook and easy use by its readers.

If you want a copy, write us, and we'll mail to you. At the same time, see how your subscription stands, and mail us enough to date your label ahead another year. And you'd better write at once, as the number is limited.

DR. ANDREWS' DON'TS.

Dr. E. Benjamin Andrews of the University of Nebraska says:

"Don't teach the children to fear God.

"Don't teach them the doctrine of eternal damnation.

"Don't muddle their brains with the theory of original sin.

"Don't scare them with the devil.

"Don't worry them about baptism.

"Don't terrorize them with the mental picture of an avenging God."

Grand advice if it is only followed. There are trouble and sorrow enough in life, anyway, without forcing the little children to grow up in an atmosphere of terror. Let their young lives be bright with hope, not dark with fear.

Teach them the same things that are good for ourselves. In the words of Dr. Andrews, "Teach them ethics. Teach them right and wrong." Teach them to speak the truth, to keep their word, to be loving and pure and gentle and just.

"Tell the children the simple facts of the story of Christ."

Secretary Wilson says Americans are becoming the greatest beef eaters in the world. They must be or they wouldn't pay the prevailing price.

Some one who has the money to pay a reasonable price can get about fifty head of good dairy stock from B. L. Reber of Sunnyside. Read his classified advertisement on page 11.

The few who oppose the construc-

Kansas is worrying over a decr in population. So many of her [...] ers are touring in Europe.

Room rent at the State Agricul college is only $24 per year and b $2.75 per week. That's cheaper most students than staying at h

Fred Benoit, North Yakima, from Crookston, M brought with him a herd of ten of Polled Angus cattle. He wil hibit at the state fair.

The showing of stock at the fair, North Yakima, will be cons ably increased this year.

"Want any pertaters terday?" a a macaroni as he pulled up in of a house in the village.

"No," replied the housekeeper; last lot we bought from you wa satisfactory."

"What was the matter with ' asked the son of toil.

"The potatoes at the top of the ket were nice and large," replie woman, "but at the bottom they tiny things."

"That was no fault of mine," re ed the honest farmer. "It wa cause of the good growin' wea we've been havin'. Pertaters are growin' so fast lately that by the I get a basketful dug, the last are ever so much bigger'n the 'uns."—Submarine.

Rural free mail delivery is a [...] convenience and benefit to far [...] We want a convenient fractional [...] rency to remit by mail; a parcels [...] a safe government savings bank; phones and electric railroads in a rections. Give us these and co-o [...] tion among farmers and we will [...] pretty near depopulating the citi [...] the scramble by people to own and [...] on farms. We don't think these th are far off.

"How is Ann Matilda making as postmistress at Elm Crossroad "Getting along fine. To-day read twenty postals, held nine le up to the light, and opened four r papers."—Chicago News.

GOOD LIVING ON THE FAR

"Talk about living high," sa [...] thrasher at the Whatcom fair, " we thrashed for a farmer at La [...] ner last week, and for dinner [...] chicken, roast beef, pickles, pota

He was also absorbed by the vicissitudes in the daily lives of his farm and ranch customers. Recounted again and again, the individual stories varied only in minor detail. Sometimes, too, through the repetition of these tales, Miller was made acutely conscious of the unmet needs of these people in their jobs and of the necessary corrections indicated for better and more efficient farming.

During this beginning period, Miller was developing a journalistic style entirely different from that of his father. His editorial style, as well as his writing, was simple, clear, and direct. Abhorrent and grueling as the years of typesetting may have been, it is reasonable to assume that his adeptness and agility in the use of uncomplicated English was attributable, at least in part, to those boyhood years of practice. His publication and its content never diverged from—nor did the publisher ever lose sight of—its originally stated purpose. He gave his advertisers and subscribers what he had pledged and what they had paid to get. His concept for a paper like *Ranch and Range* (the name of which he soon changed to *The Ranch)* covered the activities and problems of people in a whole agricultural area. This coverage made the paper a highly valued organ for the industry.

What was most important to him was that he was generally known and liked by his customers as the energetic young fellow who was doing the job he had promised to do for them. And with few exceptions, he knew he satisfied his rural patrons. The exceptions he received with open-minded earnestness in a desire to correct errors. In a few cases, complaints provided uproarious fun for the young man.

A few letters typical of the ones he received during his early publishing days were kept in his files. A turning point in a man's career may sometimes come from what seems at the time a minor incident. Looking back, Miller counted as such an omen the receipt of the letter from a Lewiston, Idaho, subscriber, signed A. H. Stevenson. It played a part in encouraging him to continue his career. The letter is among those reproduced in this chapter.

With his close contacts among farmers and ranchers, Miller was well equipped to serve as deputy dairy commissioner for the state of Washington when he was appointed to that post in 1897. The salary—ninety dollars a year—was not much, but the position gave him, as a young publisher, a status not without value to him. He became a traveling monitor for dairy farm standards, and reported conditions to a central agency. With increasing public consciousness of quality and content of foods, the state was building standards to which the dairyman must adhere. Largely due to Miller's energy, the sale of the newly developed dairy substitute, oleomargarine, was controlled to avoid market competition

Page three of this 1902 Ranch, *at left, gave its readers fair dates, homely philosophy, jokes, and offered all subscribers in good standing a ten-dollar book free.*

Garfield Wash.
May 6th 1907

Mr Miller Freeman
        Sir I Subscribed
for your paper The Ranch
one year and I hav
notifyed you once before to
stop sending it to me
now I will notify you the
second time to stop sending
it to me and if you dont
you will never get a red sent
out of me any way for I am
under age and you cant take
Blood out of a turnip
hoping you will take
warning in time I ame
        Resp=
address. Samuel D. Clark
        Garfield,
        Wash=

Letters from early-day subscribers.

Porter, Wash.
Jan. 29. 1907

Dear Sir
        I sent you 50¢ cents
last year and tole you not
to sent it to me any
more and dont send it
this year
        I dont think I owe you
this year for the paper
but if you contilly say
that I owe you fifty cents
I can send it but I wont
do it last I haft to
        I. B. Moore

Jan 4 1901 Lewiston Idaho

Ranch And Range
Please find inclosed
in pament for the
Valebel Farmers Paper $3.00
I would not be without it
If I hed to pay you dollars
a yeare for it

The Laide that induced me
To take the Ranch and Range
I think She liver in
Spokane God Bless
her Sweet Sole
I would like to see her
Again
        A. H. Stevens

Cedar Mountain Wash
April 24th 1906
Mr Miller Freeman
    Dear Sir
    I notice The Bull of
mine in the Ranch
and with great sidesfactery
the only mistack I see
are that You said
the half=tone printed on this page
if you had said the nerly one Tone
as hi waightet abaut 1,800 lbs.
    I asks You in a Letter
sum times a gow about sending
me a halfe a Dozen of the
numbers of the Ranch that my
Bull was Printit and I would
Pay for sam, I wishes to send them
sum of my Eastern Friendes

    I have not Jet received them
but hoping that I will
if You poseble have them
And hoping that you Dow

        Yours Respettfully
        Phillep B. Peterson

Following the publication of this item and photograph, Miller received this comment from Philip B. Peterson.

The half-tone printed on this page shows the pure-bred Red Polled bull General 3930, owned by Phillip B. Peterson, of Cedar Mountain, Wash. The bull is a finely-bred animal, from the best strains of that breed to be found in America, and Mr. Peterson, who is a lover of good stock, takes considerable pride in him. In the picture Mr. Peterson himself is included, just as he appears around the farm.

General, 3930, and his owner, P. B. Peterson.

with butter. For many years, the sale of butter substitutes in the state of Washington was all but eliminated.

As mentioned earlier, it was a time of fast-increasing awareness of scientific improvements for the farmer and rancher. Agricultural colleges at Pullman, Washington, Moscow, Idaho, and Corvallis, Oregon, were developing farming methods and new machinery of tremendous help to the farmer—and to Miller. He sold more advertising pages and he used his news columns to pass along vital information to his readers.

During the late 1890s, Miller also served a term as secretary of the Northwest Fruitgrowers Association—without salary. He kept on the road constantly, regularly attending farm meetings. It continued to be his pattern to travel by night, sleeping in the coach car, getting off the train in the morning, pulling his bike out of the baggage car, and going to work. In this manner Miller covered nearly every section of rural Washington and Oregon and talked to hundreds of farmers. He was usually received well as an association official and when promoting his paper as an organ of up-to-date farming methods. Sometimes he received a setback, however. On one such occasion a farmer said he didn't think *The Ranch* was worth a dollar a year. Replying earnestly that reading the paper would make him a better farmer, Miller was considerably taken aback when the man said, "Oh heck, I *know* how to be a better farmer than I am now."

Molson, March 18. 1902.

Dir Sir do not send your Ranch no mor Mr Zange is in jail.
yours truly.

Mrs Margaret Zange

In 1901, Miller was challenged by the colorful Dr. N. G. Blalock of Walla Walla, president of the Northwest Fruitgrowers Association, to devise a plan to rid his island in the Columbia River of its overpowering jackrabbit population and thus make the land salable farm property. Dr. Blalock's island property included about 4,000 acres which he proposed to develop as soon as he was assured of public interest and support.

Miller soon conceived a way of achieving Dr. Blalock's two objectives. His plan called for a giant picnic to be held in March on the banks of the Columbia for the avowed purpose of a massive shoot to wipe out the jackrabbits and, at the same time, to expose the attractive land to large numbers of prospective buyers.

With remarkable effectiveness, Miller carried on a publicity campaign in preparation for the affair. Excursion rates were arranged with the railroads, and posters in all eastern Washington and Oregon railway stations advertised the jackrabbit shoot. Every paper in the two states carried announcements. A carnival atmosphere marked the coming event, and the jackrabbit safari became the topic of conversation weeks before it was to take place.

The day before the scheduled event dawned clear and hot. Some reports estimated that more than 2,000 enthusiastic participants and spectators from a wide geographic radius were gathered on the banks of the Columbia River opposite the island. As dusk came, the glow from myriad fires lit up the darkening star-studded sky as the participants prepared meals and set up their camps.

Dr. Blalock, mingling happily with the multitudes, was overjoyed at the turnout. He was reminded, too, of his Civil War days when fighting men bivouacked, resting between battles. He trudged from group to group and fire to fire instilling these troops with ever greater enthusiasm for the coming hunt and for the potential real estate bonanza surely imminent for Blalock Island.

Early on invasion day the army crossed to the island to charge against the unsuspecting jackrabbits. As the armed hordes advanced in relentless waves, blasting the enemy with the deafening noise from a thousand guns, the rabbits suffered a horrible defeat. Their annihilation was complete and the Northwest hailed the affair as one of the most memorable sporting events in its history.

With this goal accomplished, the doctor still had problems, however. The island needed a water system. Blalock asked Miller to obtain machinery which would lift the river water for irrigation, taking stock in the development company to cover its cost. Undaunted, the latter successfully obtained this equipment from a San Francisco farm machinery outfit in return for $1,500 worth of advertising in *The Ranch*. As agreed, Miller received $1,500 worth of stock in the Blalock Development Company.

Expectations were bright for the development of the island after the installation of a giant waterwheel. It worked excellently until a calamitous spring flood washed out the valuable machinery in a few bitter moments. The developers of the project were stunned by the disaster.

Miller suddenly received a shock. Upon reading the fine print on his stock certificate, he discovered that the stockholders were assessable. Rushing to Spokane, he visited a friend and a major stockholder who, to his immense relief, offered to buy Miller's shares for $1,500 par value. Miller exhaled a thankful breath, and, clutching his first sound capital, resolved to stick exclusively to publishing in the future.

During Miller's term as secretary of the Northwest Fruitgrowers Association, he regularly attended state fairs. These popular events also offered fine opportunity to publicize his magazine to potential advertisers and to sell subscriptions. For this purpose he often set up booths in order to do business with the public. An imaginative lure to enlarge his subscription list proved highly successful. Buying gross lots of Ingersoll watches for sixty-two cents each, he offered a watch retailing for one dollar with each new one dollar subscription, thereby netting thirty-eight cents—not a bad profit in 1900.

Things seemed to break well for Miller. His luck, if it was that, could be partly attributed to the fact that he was where the action was, alert to all opportunities and not reticent about accepting advantages when they opened up. But, if he took advantage and prospered on some luck, his code was to give himself in full measure to the industries he served.

In a colorful two-page account, the Seattle P-I *of March 10, 1901, reported a successful rabbit shoot. The paper informed its readers that Miller Freeman "although burdened with three weighty cameras . . . killed his share and was a mainstay of the expedition when it came to making noise. His friends said he was the [Teddy] Roosevelt of jackrabbit hunting."*

GREAT RABBIT DRIVE on Blalock Island

THE START

THE greatest rabbit drive of recent years in the Northwest was held on Blalock island, in the Columbia river, last Tuesday morning. It was memorable not only for the number of the little pests killed, more than 1,000, but also for its social features. Business men and sportsmen from Seattle, Portland, Walla Walla and Spokane were present for the purpose of having a good time, and none were disappointed. The ranchers of the neighborhood, who looked upon the drive as a serious business enterprise and entered into it as

Spokane. It was, as one of the wags said, "a gathering of the anti-jackrabbit clans, and out for blood."

The first detachment arrived Sunday afternoon and was followed by many others. Unchecked hilarity prevailed. The hunters brought their own blankets and war clubs. Some of the more fastidious had tents, but it was felt by the majority that this savored too much of civilization. They camped on the beach, and in the night a long line of twinkling camp fires told the passengers in the passing trains and steamers that the hosts had assembled to war on poor Brer Rabbit. The next day, last Monday, saw the largely increased, was

5
YOUNG MAN of SEATTLE

A FURTHER STROKE of good fortune is found in the story of Miller's first office in Seattle. Shortly after his arrival in the city, he had become acquainted with W. L. Benham, general manager of the Great Northern Railway's Western operations. It was not long before Benham asked Miller if he would like to take over the offices of the defunct Washington Immigration Association and liquidate the organization.

This body had been set up originally to attract immigrants from eastern states to settle the lands along the railroads. The plan had operated for several years and had served its purpose. The railroads were looking for a way to wind up the venture. Miller agreed to do the job and was astonished to find himself the possessor of a suite of five rooms, complete with office furniture. Opportunity had knocked firmly on his door and he moved to avail himself of its beneficent fruits. Thus, four rooms in the Pioneer Building at First Avenue and Yesler Way became his first office, and the fifth room was converted into living quarters—his first home in Seattle.

As Miller moved farther away from ties with his father, he developed an individual manner by which he was soon recognized. The patterns of his personality, which had been controlled and directed in his boyhood by a dominant and overbearing father, were now being channeled into distinct individuality. The stranger saw him as an alert young fellow, somewhat short of stature, slight, but of muscular build. His head seemed unusually large for his body. His face was long with the cheek bones noticeably high. With maturity his large mouth had become a more dominant and expressive feature. It mirrored his feelings, as did his steel gray eyes.

A most distinctive mark of the young man was his manner of walking, which indicated a directness of purpose with a complete lack of wasted motion. His step was steady and solid and it propelled him firmly toward his goal. Customarily, he looked neither right nor left—he proceeded—for his mind was always totally occupied with other matters.

While his whole manner could be summed up as abrupt but friendly, those who came to know him recognized firmness that warned of a toughness at first easily missed. But along with these qualities he combined a boisterous sense of humor which, since release from his father's domination, seemed to be developing more surely. His frequent laugh was sudden and resounding.

In these early days, as a young bachelor with little money or security to worry about in any event, Miller was able to indulge in a certain deep-rooted urge to gamble. His friends in Seattle, too, were struggling along with him. Most of them did not have much money either and, like Miller, were ambitious and willing to take long chances to get ahead in the business world. At one time, however, Miller stretched his bank account beyond its capacity in order to pump life into his infant publishing business. He was not comfortable in this situation for, above all, he was seeking to establish good financial standing.

One morning, burdened with financial worries, and with head bowed, he strode along the avenue to the steps of his bank. A passing friend nearly collided with him. He also looked burdened. The two stopped to greet one another. Pleasantries passed between them and the perennial question followed, "How are you doing?" And the answer, "Oh, pretty good, but I've got my problems." Each secretly thought he was worse off than the other fellow.

After commiserating a few minutes, one of them remarked that they would only know who was in worse financial straits if they switched bank accounts. This seemed like a sporting idea. One fellow would obviously come out better than the other and Miller, feeling that his overdraft probably exceeded that of his friend, hoped the gamble would pay off well for him.

The two entered the bank and made the exchange, each with considerable anticipation. Moments later, bank clerks and customers were startled by the uproarious laughter of two young men who were studying slips of paper. Miller had lost. His friend's bank overdraft was greater than his. Each, however, found he had greatly enjoyed the gamble. The friend had bettered his situation and Miller had found, to his relief, that some were worse off than he!

Miller adapted well to city life. While his business took him away from Seattle much of the time, he entered enthusiastically into social life when he was in town. He joined the Seattle Athletic Club and became an expert handball player, winning the club's championship in 1903.

Although this picture of Seattle's Second Avenue, looking north from Yesler Way, was taken about 1912, it shows the area much as it was during Miller's early days in the city. Excavation for the Smith Building, lower right. (Courtesy Seattle Historical Society.)

The game suited his energies and his purse and offered him good opportunity to widen his friendships.

As Miller increasingly became a part of Seattle's social life and was associating with friends of some sophistication, he began to think more of his appearance. As a boy brought up in a cattle raising and farming area, largely in male company, he had had little chance for exposure to social graces or fine dress. His whole existence had been devoted to serious work from earliest boyhood. The eastern Washington of his day, and Yakima specifically, was a rough pioneer section of the country. His father's interests, too, centered on simple, unadorned living, and whatever social life there might have been in Yakima at the time of Miller's boyhood would not have included a young man who worked in a print shop from dawn until dark under a father's stern eye.

When he was much older, Miller often thought back to his late teens when his future wife, Bessie Bogle, also lived in Yakima. Her family had moved from their Seattle home to a drier climate east of the mountains for her father's health. Miller had heard about Judge William H. Bogle*, Bess' father, and had become acquainted with his son, Max Bogle. Beyond that casual brush with his future wife's family he had lived in a world apart from the people in the Bogles' end of town. He had been a dedicated working man from the time he had reached his tenth year.

But things were changing rapidly for Miller after his move to Seattle and he was soon ready to assume the role of an urban dweller and the respectable dress of a city businessman. When he contemplated the purchase of a new suit of clothes, however, it was with considerable ignorance and no particular talent for such things. What a man wore had never seemed particularly important up to that time in his life. As far as he was concerned, there were only two specifications for a garment: First, it must be cheap, and second, it must be durable. However undeveloped his tastes were, they must have been strongly influenced by the bright colors and daring designs of the Yakima Indian blankets to which he had been exposed from earliest childhood. The purchase of his first suit from a Seattle clothier proved this.

When Miller entered the sanctum of Julius Rudelsheimer, First Avenue clothing merchant, he did not trust his own taste. He was willing to abide by the store owner's recommendation. Rudelsheimer chose for him a natty blue-gray suit with a stripe down the pantleg. Miller surveyed himself critically in the long mirror and, liking what he saw, paid ten dollars and promptly left the shop. Proceeding down the street a few minutes later, he was shocked as he passed a mailman wearing an identical suit. He stopped abruptly, turned back to the clothing store to accost Julius Rudelsheimer. He didn't want to look like a public servant, he said. The merchant was understanding and, with exceptional generosity, offered to take back the suit and find

*W. H. Bogle was appointed to serve on several Yakima trials in the 1890s as a judge pro tem and was thereafter always referred to as "Judge."

another more distinctive one for his young customer. Together, Miller and he next chose one of a new design and cut, made of a colorful patterned material. Putting it on, Miller again looked himself up and down. The effect was striking and pleasing to both men. This one, they decided, was much more distinctive than the first suit. So delighted was the store owner that in his enthusiasm he threw in a cap to match the new outfit.

Thus newly attired and very pleased, Miller made his way to the *Post-Intelligencer* office where he had business. Upon entering, he was met by a business acquaintance who suddenly let out a roar, yelling so that all could hear, "Lord-a-mighty, *where* did you get that outfit?"

The suit caused such a stir that, quickly transacting his business, Miller retreated in surprise and dismay. *He* liked the outfit, but reactions like this were disturbing—and he must consider his customers.

Hurrying back to the clothing store he explained to Rudelsheimer what had happened. The clothing merchant once more proved himself exceptionally generous and again agreed to exchange the suit—this time for one more subdued. Together the two men chose a conservative suit. It did not gladden the hearts of either man but its drabness assured them of its acceptance in the world of urban sophistication.

In the early part of the new century land fever continued to provide dazzling and attractive opportunity for making a speedy dollar, and there were those in Seattle who were making fortunes in real estate. Acquainted with some of these men, Miller was attracted to their ventures and not adverse to the idea of trying a little speculation himself on a scale commensurate with his resources.

In one of his first tries at real estate he invested $2,000 in two lots on the tidelands of Seattle's Fourth Avenue. He asked for and was given four years' time in which to pay off on the investment. A tough pull he thought, but worth a gamble. Miller blinked in amazement when, six months later, the lots were sold at exactly double the price he had contracted to pay for them.

It was natural that his first success led to other transactions. In late 1905 Miller went to his good friend, Frank Case, a young man from Kansas, who had recently become a member of the McGraw Kittinger realty firm. He asked Case if he had any promising realty property that he could recommend as an investment. Frank consulted with his partners and, poring over city maps, came up with the recommendation to buy a piece of property on Sixth Avenue. Miller offered to buy two lots—if the realtors could give him good terms. They offered him a four-year deal with an $11,000 down payment. To firm the contract, he put down $100 which he had in his pocket. He then left with considerable to worry about.

Miller walked down the street solemnly contemplating his commitment, wondering how he would raise the tremendous sum of $11,000. Looking very worried he came upon a dapper young friend, one E. L. Reber, city editor of the *Post-Intelligencer,* who immediately accosted him, remarking on his solemnity. Miller replied that he had plenty to worry about, since he had just bought a piece of property and owed $11,000 on it *right away.*

Reber, a buoyant sort of fellow, said, "Oh, nothing to it. All depends on the way you go about it. You know, if you go to your father and say 'Dad, I need $10 awfully bad; I don't suppose you can give it to me, can you?' you won't get it. But if you go to him and say, 'Father, give me $10,000,' he'll give it to you right away."

Miller paused a minute to contemplate this interesting philosophy. Certainly, his own father did not enter into this category under any conceivable circumstances. Nevertheless, he was one to give things a try and promptly walked across the street to the Dexter Horton Bank. He went to the desk of N. H. Latimer, leaned across the barrier between him and the president's desk and explained that he wanted to borrow $11,000. Latimer was somewhat taken aback by the abruptness of the request, but judging his customer to be a good risk from what he knew of him, recovered quickly. And in ten minutes Miller had the necessary money.

A few months later, this same land was purchased by the railroad for its terminal, and Miller sold the two lots for a net profit of $35,000—an astounding bit of luck. Unfortunately, however, all his experiences in real estate did not end so well, and Miller continued to consider real estate a gamble on which he was willing to invest only reasonable amounts. He liked a moderate gamble—just that and no more. And to emphasize that his approach was a sane one, he often in later years drove past a piece of property on Twelfth and Jackson streets in Seattle. He called it his "dog" and pointed it out as a great failure.

6

PACIFIC FISHERMAN:
JOURNAL for the INDUSTRY

AFTER SEVERAL YEARS of hard slogging, Miller attained a circulation of 10,000 for *The Ranch*. That was "darn good" in his estimation. All of Miller's efforts to establish a good publication were bearing fruit. After five years his paper was on a sound, paying basis. It was well accepted as the leading news organ for the agriculturalist and rancher in Washington and Oregon. And the publisher was known and respected in his field for the workmanlike job he had done for these industries.

But as he reached a sound business footing with *The Ranch*, he began looking beyond the confines of his publishing field. He felt there were inherent drawbacks in agricultural magazines.

Several considerations tempted Miller to change his line of publishing. *The Ranch* served a widely scattered field, required continuous and extensive travel, and necessitated constant personal contact with those in farming and ranching.

There were also wide differences of interest among the cattle and sheep raisers, grain farmers, and orchard men. Individual buying power in these groups was comparatively low, and a large circulation was necessary in order to attract advertising. It was hard sledding, at best, and he looked critically at other fields for industries that might provide better opportunity for healthy profit, without the drawbacks of the agricultural field.

At that time the whole Pacific Coast was tied strongly to a fast-growing fisheries industry, with fish canning becoming increasingly important. This was a more compact industrial field, with a few centers where circulation would be limited but highly selective, where individual buying power would be large, and further industrial growth was probable. It looked good to Miller and he proceeded to make careful studies of the economics of the industry. Gasoline engines were coming into use and Miller sensed that this stimulus would bring a wide expansion in the fisheries industry.

With this background, he and C. M. (Max) Bogle, his former Yakima acquaintance, entered into partnership in the fall of 1902 to establish an industrial publishing business with the magazine *Pacific Fisherman.* (The fact that Judge Bogle, Max's father, was an attorney and a director of an Alaska salmon canning company possibly influenced Miller toward this field.)

In January 1903, while continuing publication of *The Ranch,* Miller got out the first edition of *Pacific Fisherman.* His partner, Max Bogle, became editor of the new journal and Miller devoted himself to advertising sales and management of business affairs.

At that time, San Francisco was the major center of the salmon canning business on the Pacific Coast. It was there that Miller made one of his first calls and accomplished his first real stroke of business. With considerable satisfaction he sold a front cover of *Pacific Fisherman* to Henry W. Phelps, then manager of the newly established American Can Company, later for many years its president, and subsequently a warm personal friend of Miller's. Considering that he set out in almost total ignorance of his new field, this sale was a fine beginning—but Miller had a long way to go before he had a full grasp of the fishing industry. On one of his early junkets down the coast he made some glaring mistakes with his first customers. He suffered keenly over these mistakes, but they served to goad him to learn the facts—fast.

He never forgot one of the first calls he made on the owner of the Portland Fish Company. He met a swarthy man working on a wet dock, surrounded by nets, hooks and appurtenances yet unknown to Miller. To make a pleasant opening, which he hoped would lead to acquiring a substantial advertising contract, he asked how the salmon were running at that time. There was a long and pregnant pause, and Miller thought the man had not heard him. The plant owner, however, finally raised himself from his work, balefully eyed Miller, and scornfully answered, "*Hell,* don't you know this ain't the season for salmon?"

To his embarrassment, Miller didn't know, but the experience galled him sufficiently that he decided to make a full study of the most detailed workings of the industry he now proposed to serve. Proving that he ultimately made good his resolve, he later made a friend of this plant owner, who remained a regular advertiser for many years.

The Ranch

JOURNAL OF THE LAND AND THE HOME IN THE NEW WEST.

50c per Year; 5c the Copy.

SEATTLE, WASHINGTON, MARCH 1, 1905.

PRINCIPLES OF ARID FARMING

DESTROYED BY FIRE MAY 16, 1904.

THE NEW HOME RECENTLY COMPLETED.

PORTLAND WIRE & IRON WORKS, PORTLAND, OR.

(See Page 3.)

eciate the neces-
in arid farming
to know the rela-
the soil and the
the plant obtains
e water is held in
fferent forms, viz:
hygroscopic water,
pillary water which
e of supply for the
water is held as a
und the soil grains.
erizing the soil ren-
for more capillary wa-
Plowing the land has
able influence on the
er that can be held by
s been shown by many
riments. At the Utah
ation at the time of seed-
fall the foremen on the
d the great amount of
esent in the land plowed
but which land had not
ed, as compared with ad-
that had not been plowed.
ars ago members of the ex-
farms took samples of soil
n of five feet on two adja-
es of ground, one of which
r been plowed, while the
d been cultivated for a great
ars and from which a crop had
n removed. Notwithstanding
e that the crop had used con-
le quantities of moisture, there
ill more than 53 tons per acre
water in the ground which had
plowed and cropped, showing
sively that the more cultivation
receives the greater will be the
nt of water that it will hold.
ll plowing is the best in all cases,
t has a very great influence on
per cent of water held in the soil.
ne years ago the Utah station took
nples from adjacent pieces of
ound in the same field, one of which
d been plowed in the fall and the
her in the following spring. The
amples were secured in the middle
f July, and it was found that the fall
plowed land contained a difference of
7.47 per cent of moisture over the
spring plowed land, this difference
amounting to one-third of the average
rainfall of the year, or more than 506
tons of water to the acre in the first
five feet of soil. The greater the
depth in the soil the greater was the
amount of water held. The moisture
will be more effective in plant growth
if found at this point, simply for the
fact that it is less likely to be evapor-
ated than if found in the first one or
two feet of soil. At the deeper point
the plant can obtain the moisture at
_____ it is most needed. The
_____ roots will pene-
_____ upon

the character of the soil, the amount
of water it holds, and the method of
treatment.

Although no data is at hand, it is
believed that in the arid regions the
wheat plant sends its roots in search
of water to more than four or five
feet down. This makes it important
that the preparation of the soil be
done properly, preferably in the fall.
The general consensus of opinion
among arid farmers of experience is
that deep plowing is much more effective than shallow plowing. Th
general practice on the dry farms
to use two teams of horses on a fou
teen-inch sulky plow and turn the s
to a depth of eight to ten inches.
many large farms the practice of s
soiling to a depth of about twe
inches is carried out at least onc
three years. Most farmers, howe
think it very doubtful whether
method of plowing has proved he
enough to warrant the extra ex
Deep plowing is beneficial beca
increases the moisture holding
city of the soil and, as is belie
some, retains not only all the
added to it, but also draws som
ure from the deeper layers
through capillary action.

The practice of leaving
fallow or unoccupied every
son, or on some instances e
season, is followed on most a
It has been discovered that
od results in better yields
the land is continuously cr
on many well conducted fa
sults desired by fallowing
secured through intellige
An intimate knowledge o
habits and needs of vari
ables the wise farmer t
crops in such successi
food will be available
the time most needed.
aimed at in fallowing
tion of troublesome w
be accomplished by re
arid farms, however,
aimed at in fallowin
or conservation of
succeeding crop.
methods of tillage,
of two years may
soil and can be d
crop when needed.
the precipitation
not always suffici
experience has sh
moisture of two
the production of
moisture of thr
two crops, bette
In regard to
seed and seedin

(Continue

Pacific Fisherman, *MFP's first industrial journal, was established in the fall of 1902. The first issue was published in January 1903.* The Annual Number *(renamed the* Yearbook*) was started during the same year. (Courtesy School of Fisheries Library, University of Washington.)*

Pacific Fisherman soon became to the fisheries industry what *The Ranch* had been to the agriculturalist. The paper served as a clearing-house for the new field. Miller offered the fisherman, the canner, and the industry as a whole a strong voice as he had successfully done for the agriculturalist of eastern Washington and Oregon. From the start of the operation he liked his new journalistic endeavor. It seemed tailored to his tastes. It also had the added attraction of keeping his business calls on the West Coast where he wanted to be.

He showed the same dedication to the fishing industry and its people that he felt for the farmer and rancher, and he soon became an integral part of his new field. He lost no opportunity to make himself known and helpful to all those involved in the industry's offshoot operations and he became a trusted auxiliary in these concerns.

Not long after *Pacific Fisherman* was starting to make its way Miller's partner, Max Bogle, pulled out to go into another venture, thus leaving Miller the sole owner and publisher of the journal.

In 1903, Miller inaugurated a unique new service to the people of the fishing industry. Previously it would have been unthinkable for a fish canning company to release its official catch and pack figures to any outsider, for these were jealously guarded secrets among the men in the industry. It was therefore a surprising accomplishment when Miller was able to persuade the people in each company voluntarily to submit intimate details of their businesses to a printed record of benefit to everyone in the industry. Thus, Miller's *Pacific Fisherman Yearbook* (originally called the *Annual Number* and *Annual Review*) took its place to become an unusual and valuable data-collecting publication which was to serve the industry in this capacity for more than fifty years. True, these companies reported their production, as required by law, to governmental sources, but months after the details were given to *Pacific Fisherman* and under the strict obligation that the figures were not to be revealed individually by the government. *Pacific Fisherman Yearbook* became a sort of bible for the fisheries people, as well as a pioneer venture of its kind.

Miller attributed the success of the *Yearbook* to the fact that he kept faith with the industry people, strictly abiding by the rules of confidence

52

he PACIFIC FISHERMAN

1903

PRICE 35¢

as originally laid down. In turn, he was afforded unusual insight into the innermost workings of the fisheries industry, which enabled him to give better service in that field.

At the time the *Yearbook* was started, a paper called the *Trade Register* was published in Seattle. It was a pioneer business paper with departments devoted to fisheries, lumber, dairy, mining, and the grocery business. It is possible that the management of this publication resented a competitor for some of its business. At any rate, shortly after the appearance of the 1904 *Pacific Fisherman Yearbook,* Miller was astonished to find that the *Trade Register* had pirated the *Yearbook's* salmon pack figures as well as some of its illustrations. These statistics had been printed in a special annual number of the *Trade Register* about to be put in the mail. By chance, an advance copy had come into Miller's hands, and he took it to Judge Bogle, who immediately obtained an injunction forbidding issuance of the edition on grounds that it contained material reproduced from a copyrighted publication. To Miller's astonishment, the *Trade Register* folded shortly afterward. Its advertising manager applied to Miller for a job. Miller hired the man and sent him to San Francisco where a considerable volume of *Pacific Fisherman* advertising was originating. He stayed with Miller Freeman Publications until he retired.

Illustrative of the accepted authenticity of *Pacific Fisherman Yearbook* statistics is an incident that occurred many years later. A telegram was received by the *Pacific Fisherman* staff at a time when the issue was a week late in coming out. The Territorial Government of Alaska wired that the tax roll figures could not be made up until the *Yearbook* was received. Surprisingly, the *Yearbook* figures, which came out sometime in advance of the federal figures, were being used as official ones.

Coming into a fast-developing industry was mighty valuable to the young publisher, and Miller partook of these advantages with enthusiasm. He profited from the experience he had gained when he published his farm paper, but the same amount of effort netted him a better profit on his new journal.

CIFIC FISHERMAN

ANNUAL REVIEW

FEBY. 1907

7
FIRST DECISIVE ACTION

I N 1903, SOON AFTER the establishment of *Pacific Fisherman,* one of Miller's lifelong campaigns had its beginning. One day as he worked on *Pacific Fisherman* proofs he received two callers at his tiny waterfront office. Before him stood two bespectacled young Japanese, smiling and bowing. They pleased and flattered the young publisher by asking to subscribe to his new magazine. Next they presented a polite letter from the Japanese Consul in Vancouver, British Columbia, asking Miller Freeman's help in placing two earnest young students in a fish cannery where they could learn the business firsthand. Here was a chance to do his bit toward improving Japanese-American relations. He got the Japanese the jobs they sought.

These two young students, however, proved to be only the advance guard of a potential army of earnest young Japanese who came to his office seeking, through him, entree into the infant United States fish canning industry. Before long it became clear to Miller that he was being used as an unwary agent in a well-planned Japanese program of colonization which would threaten the very industry he was trying to serve.

Chance had put Miller in a position where he could scarcely fail to recognize a little-disguised and well-organized plan of aggression by the Japanese into the American canning industry and he quickly withdrew as an intermediary in this operation. At the same time he was deeply impressed by the determined ambitions of the people and increasingly conscious that this "invading army," unless checked, would seriously cut into job opportunities of American citizens.

The flood of Japanese pouring into the West Coast from 1903 on did nothing to allay his fears. All West Coast industry was then a ripe target for the able and ambitious Japanese. And while these facts were not secret, the United States government seemed unconcerned and did nothing to curtail the invasion.

It was then that Miller began sounding editorial warnings about the danger of unchecked immigration of Japanese, and specific criticism of his government for doing nothing to control it. Over the next two years, repeated warnings appeared in his magazine regarding the threat Japanese overt ambitions would inevitably impose on the United States fisheries industry. Because of these editorials and his firsthand experience with the Japanese students in 1903, Miller was becoming recognized as one to whom fisheries people could turn when problems arose within the industry.

When, in 1905, a group of fishermen came to his office in deep concern to report the sighting of two Japanese fishing vessels operating in United States' territorial waters in Funter Bay, Alaska, he took one of his first important steps in behalf of the industry he served. After getting details of the incident from the men, it was obvious to him that international law was being flagrantly defied by the Japanese. Without further delay Miller typed a wire to President Theodore Roosevelt, stating what had been reported. He had it signed by those present, and sent it immediately to Washington, D.C.

Action by Roosevelt was equally prompt and within a few days the President had dispatched the United States cutter *Perry* to Funter Bay, where the Japanese ships were quickly spotted, and captured. The crews were imprisoned and later deported to Japan.

The incident was fully reported in *Pacific Fisherman*. It instilled even greater confidence among members of the Pacific Coast fishing industry in the ability and dedication of *Pacific Fisherman*'s publisher.

It seems evident that Miller's concept of his position within the industry began to develop more surely with this important action. He saw himself as an industry middleman, yet as one closely involved and knowledgeable about its innermost workings. He was neither a fisherman nor an operator, but he was in a unique position to provide a sort of clearinghouse with his journal. He spoke, in effect, for the people of the industry through editorials and through his own decisive actions.

Illustrative of Miller's growing involvement in the fisheries business is the following incident. The canners' and packers' interests, and the necessary controls to protect the resource, were sometimes in conflict. This became sharply evident when, a few years after the Funter Bay incident, a collision course on the issue was set.

In 1907 increasing concern was being voiced within the industry and by thoughtful students of the Pacific Coast fishing resource about the size of any one canner's seasonal catch and pack. Salmon canning was a new industry in its buoyant infancy and a growing and booming source of wealth. Those men fortunate enough to be a part of it were profiting largely. Bigger and bigger packs were the goal and the pride of the packers. But reasoned voices were sounding warnings against indiscriminate cropping of the salmon runs. Many urged that a limit be imposed on the amount of seasonal pack for individual canners in order to assure perpetuation of this resource.

A suggestion for control of the amount of each packer's seasonal catch gained impetus. A proposal was made that control should be self-imposed by those in the industry for the permanent benefit of the resource. Miller duly reported these developments in *Pacific Fisherman* editorials. He was himself firmly convinced of the wisdom of the proposition and repeatedly enunciated his support of this position.

But storm clouds brewed over the proposal within the industry, for the salmon canners adamantly resisted the idea of any control on their individual initiative. It became apparent, too, that the salmon canners, whom Miller knew as good friends and poker pals, were on the other side of the fence from him on this matter. The situation suddenly put Miller in the jaws of a dangerous pincer movement, for clearly the lifeblood of his magazine depended on the business and the goodwill of these men. They *were* the industry, in effect. Having made his position clear to them, Miller was at once subjected to heavy pressure to make him change his stand.

The pot boiled hot on the issue and on one memorable day a confrontation took place in Miller's office when the salmon canners presented their ultimatum. It was a threatening delegation that came and the situation was particularly disagreeable in that these men were personal friends who had generously supported *Pacific Fisherman* since its beginning in 1903. But there was no friendliness in them now. They were mad and were threatening to withdraw all support from Miller's paper. In effect, they clearly said they would wreck him. This he knew was a distinct possibility inasmuch as they were a powerful group in the industry. Their words were blunt, their implications were clear, and there was no fooling. It was a mighty serious moment for a struggling young publisher, because he knew that these men meant what they said.

Miller reddened with suppressed anger as he grasped their implications, but in his mind there was no question as to his course. He had been speaking for the industry as a whole, and not for a few men. The long-term health of the fishing resource was vastly more important than the short-range profit of these friends. As he saw it, the advantage was to the *many* over the long haul, as against the *few* who gained quick profit. And, surely, it was to *Pacific Fisherman*'s best interests, as well, if it could serve a perpetual-yield industry.

The set of Miller's jaw was hard, otherwise he showed little emotion. He quietly faced his one-time friends and said, "Well, gentlemen, we've set our course on this issue and we'll keep to it. If you want to sink us, we'll go down with our flags flying, but we won't change our course."

Having made their position clear and heard Miller's response, a silent but still angry group turned and left his office.

Miller was recognized as an able and tough poker player by these men. While the stakes were modest in those days, his wins regularly exceeded his losses. But this was one game and one play vitally different from the usual ones. The outcome meant vastly more than a few dollars. It meant virtual life or death for his young business.

Miller sat a long time in tense dejection following this session. He had no second thoughts about his decision, but it could mean some pretty drastic reassessment on a business level if things went as threatened.

Maybe the young publisher was born under a lucky star or maybe the way he went about his business activities influenced others. The fact was that this episode ultimately strengthened his position as publisher of *Pacific Fisherman*. When tempers cooled and the situation was viewed in the light of reason and weighted by undeniable facts, these same men accepted the wisdom of voluntary control. In the end, they realized that Miller Freeman was not working against them, even though his solutions to their problems were not always the ones they would have preferred.

The Yakima Indian came very near to annihilation that time but the experience added another solid block on his pile of learning.

8
The STORY of the IRON CHINK

THE EARLY PART of the century was an exciting pioneering period in the canning industry which was then new to everyone. Experimentation in technical methods went on continually. Illustrative of one of these developments is the story of the Iron Chink, a machine designed to butcher and prepare raw salmon for canning.

One of the early problems for salmon canners in Alaska was the shortage of labor at times of periodic need. Most of the butchers were Chinese and many were employed at one short, intensive period during the canning season, then were laid off indefinitely, making a stable manpower supply hard to maintain.

In 1902 a man named Edmund A. Smith rented space in the same building with Miller. The young publisher's curiosity was aroused by the regular delivery of quantities of raw salmon which were left in Smith's room. This seemed a strange procedure in an office building—and made the place smell like a fish dock.

Miller dropped in on his neighbor one day to find out what was going on. He was rewarded by discovering a swarthy three-hundred-pound giant of a man working on a strange machine consisting of a metal wheel, about six feet in diameter, which butchered fish automatically. Miller learned that Smith was at that time trying to sell his invention to the fish canners who were skeptical about its performance.

Miller was intrigued and pressed for further details—in particular the reason for the roulette wheels and parts standing around the room. It developed that Smith was an expert mechanic specializing in gambling machines. Originally from Chicago, where he had made a business of repairing roulette wheels, he was following the same trade in Seattle. He had, however, met two King County employees—Ben Brierly and John Wallace—who were organizing a salmon canning company on the side. These two enterprising men had sold Smith $4,000 worth of stock in their plant, which was to operate in Alaska.

After the first year's operation, Smith found that the venture was

60

not coming up to expectations. The management reported at a stock-holder's meeting that profits were negligible because it was impossible to get enough salmon butchers. Smith asked if anyone had thought of building a machine to do the job. The answer was that several attempts had been made but it was the impression of the industry generally that such a machine was not feasible.

Miller got the rest of the story from Brierly and Wallace, who had a small office on Seattle's Cherry Street. They told him that after the stockholder's meeting, Smith had frequented their office, expressing concern over his $4,000. During one visit, a peddler came in to sell lead pencils with the company's name printed on the sides. He offered them for $100 per thousand. Smith said he could furnish them for less.

The scoffing peddler said he would pay Smith $100 if he could make good his boast. Smith went to a carpenter shop in the alley and returned in a short time with a device that printed the pencils efficiently and rapidly. It was a crude affair but Brierly and Wallace were impressed. Later they asked Smith if he thought he really could build a fish dressing machine.

Showing complete confidence, Smith replied: "Sure I can. You get me a place to work, a lathe, and some steel and brass and I'll show you." Convinced that it was worth a try, Brierly and Wallace rented the room for fifteen dollars a month and provided the tools and metal. A pilot model—the machine with the big wheel that Miller had seen on his first visit to Smith's room—was soon built. The salmon were gripped to the outside rim of the wheel and were carried past the knives, saws, and brushes which slit them, clipped their fins, and scrubbed out the poke. The model, however, did not dispel industry misgivings.

Miller took a lively interest in the project and controversy. He invited a mechanical engineer to look at the apparatus and give his opinion on its value. This man, too, was skeptical of the inventor's claims. "It just won't work," he said. "It defies all the sound principles of mechanics. There isn't a positive motion in it. Every part in the machine functions by the use of springs and big flexible cams. It won't stand up under the terrific strain of cleaning 3,000 fish an hour, as Smith claims it will do." Miller decided this opinion made sense and declined to take a financial interest in the machine.

The first issue of *Pacific Fisherman*, January 1903, reported that E.A. Smith's salmon butchering machine was about finished and would be in operation in the salmon fisheries of Puget Sound the coming summer. A story appearing in an early summer issue of the magazine stated that the Smith machine was one of four different makes of fish butchering machines being operated in the Puget Sound area that season. It was not called "Iron Chink" until sometime in the fall, when the name was first noted in *Pacific Fisherman*.

Despite all predictions to the contrary, Smith's machine soon proved to be the best one on the market—and its inventor became a wealthy man almost overnight.

E. B. Deming, president of Pacific American Fisheries Company at Fairhaven (now South Bellingham), Washington, bought the first machine for $3,000 cash. Although Deming was given a demonstration in his own plant before the purchase, it is believed that advertising and news stories in *Pacific Fisherman* played an important part in the sale.

Smith, Brierly, and Wallace were soon flooded with orders from salmon canneries all along the coast. In a short time they were able to build a fine plant on lower First Avenue in Seattle for the Smith Cannery Machines Company.

Although Miller held back financial support from Smith during the experimentation period, the two men became good friends. About six years after Smith's astounding success Miller met him on the street one day. The inventor was attired in a well-tailored suit and was proudly standing beside a brand new Stanley Steamer—the finest automobile of the day. He invited Miller to ride out to the University area with him.

Miller was pleased to be asked to ride with Smith and gladly accepted the offer. With considerable excitement he took the seat next to Smith. All went well until they reached the particularly bumpy plank road which ran around Lake Union, when suddenly flames burst through the floorboards of the car. Startled, Miller leaped to safety, while Smith, too large to move fast in any event, stayed aboard to extinguish the fire. While considerably shaken by this alarming experience, Miller reboarded and the trip continued to the Alaska-Yukon-Pacific Exposition grounds where Smith had a proposition to put to the exposition president, Ed Chilberg, then head of the Scandinavian-American Bank. Smith explained that he was operating a salmon trap down the sound which caught a good many seals. He proposed to train a number of young seals to haul canoes around Portage Bay during the Exposition, carrying passengers at so much per ride. He figured that the concession would not only make money but would be a sensational attraction for fair visitors.

Following Chilberg's promise to see a demonstration of this attraction, the return journey to downtown Seattle was started. Again the car was jostled, and flames flared through the floorboards. Miller again jumped out and ran to a safe distance, Smith remaining in the car. Finally the flames died down and, after some coaxing, Miller was persuaded to get aboard once more. They continued safely into the city.

Three weeks later Smith was driving up Pike Street with his sister. As had happened when Miller was with him, flames burst through the floorboards and this time quickly enveloped the passengers. Both were large people and not able to move fast. Smith had time to push his sister to safety but, unable to jump out fast enough, died in the flames himself. Miller was astounded. Smith, a mechanical genius, could not be bothered to fix a leaky fuel pipe in his car!

Smith Cannery Machines Company was an early advertiser in Pacific Fisherman, *and Smith's invention was mentioned in the first issue of the magazine. PF's Fiftieth Anniversary Number carried this advertisement.*

FIRST FISH CANNERY ON THE PACIFIC WAS A "FLOATER"

On this scow the Humes and Hapgood canned the first salmon on the Sacramento River in 1864. T[...] authentic sketch was made for Pacific Fisherman in 1903 under the personal supervision of G. W. Hu[...]

FOUNDATIONS FIRST

Fishing Industry Was Built
On Basic Blocks Laid Down
In Decade of 1903 to 1912

FOUNDATIONS of the fisheries were laid in the first decade of our 50 years—from 1903 through 1912.

This was a decade of changing days, days when great fisheries were born, when tuna and California sardine canning had their real beginnings;

When power came to the fisheries and engines swept oars and sails from the banks and drifts;

When mechanization came to the canneries and the soldering iron disappeared from the plants as the water-bath had before it.

Pacific Fisherman was born in 1903, the year when the first sardines were canned at Monterey, when the first experimental model of the "Iron Chink" was put together, when the first engine was put in a purse seiner.

In every phase of the fisheries there was growth—the stirring of birth in Sardines and Tuna, the stretching out

War in the Market Place

Where to begin?

With Salmon, surely; for Salmon already was a great industry, still growing, but great; and it was a day of giants in the business, when Guggenheims and Morgans tried their hands at fishing—and lost their shirts.

The decade opened with one of the most dramatic scenes in the whole history of Pacific fishing—the Salmon War, when the Alaska Packers Association and the Pacific Packing & Navigation Co. fought it out in the market place. The former, with a pack of 1,223,000 cases, of which 1,007,000 cases were Reds, carried the price of Chums down to *16c per dozen* 1-lb. cans, and four months later Pacific Packing & Navigation went into receivership.

Reviewing the incident a year later, the Alaska Packers in an official statement said:

"This is the whole history of the so-called 'Pink Salmon War,' and illustrated

maintain living prices:

"First, the supply of a [...] must not materially excee[...] mand;

"Second, *those interested* [...] *taining prices should not* [...] *cutting, lest they lose con*[...] *knife.*" (Emphasis [...] tor to what is surely one [...] delightful utterances in [...] history of canned fish mer[...]

Fishermen's Pay in 19[...]

After the "war" was [...] prices in 1903, per doze[...] stood at: Reds, 92½c; [...] Pinks, 50-52½c; Chums [...] broker wrote: "It is a m[...] prices too high, but $[...] *needed for Red tails*; [...] $1.25 is *needed for tails*[...] Dr. David Starr Jord[...] costs $2 to pack a ca[...] Pinks cannot be cann[...] except as a by-produc[...] devoted chiefly to Red [...] he was a disinterest[...]

Article from Pacific Fisherman's *Fiftieth Anniversary Number recalls the early days of the canning industry in the years between 1903 and 1912.*

9
BEGINNING ACTION
on FISHERIES TREATIES

I N LINE WITH HIS VIEWS on good publishing practice, Miller formed the habit of being where the action was in matters involving the fisheries industry. In 1905, a meeting of cannery operators of the Puget Sound and Fraser River areas was called at Vancouver, British Columbia, to discuss problems regularly arising between United States and Canadian canners. Nobody invited Miller but he showed up anyway and went about his job of reporting the proceedings—a logical part of his service to the industry, he believed. (Much later he learned that, because he was an outsider and a publisher, his presence displeased some of the canners, but by that time he was an accepted and a trusted spokesman for the industry.)

Among the younger members of the group at this particular meeting was Ed Sims, a cannery operator from Port Townsend, Washington. Sims was a hearty, boisterous, and highly able individual, well known to many of the canners attending the meeting and also a friend of Miller's. During the election of officers for the Puget Sound Salmon Canners Association, Sims suddenly spotted Miller, the outsider, in the audience and promptly proposed him as secretary. Though somewhat surprised, Miller lost no time in accepting the office, which he saw was to his advantage and in the interest of the magazine.

Miller served for ten years as secretary of the association without pay. Later, commenting on his service to this association and his participation in the formation and operation of a number of such associations, he wrote: "In time, and perhaps as a result of experience, I came to feel that, in our role as editors and publishers, we should never forget that this was our primary function and it was paramount that I and our journals should be independent in thought and in act. We could strike the wrong when we felt it wrong and could point out error when we found it. At the same time, when we chose to praise, our words were recognized as sound and objective and not as the product of subservience."

Later he was offered $15,000 a year if he would accept the position of permanent secretary-manager of the association. Although $15,000 was more than he was making out of *Pacific Fisherman* at the time, he refused, because he felt instinctively that it would be a mistake for him to surrender his independence as a publisher. "Wanting nothing and taking nothing, I could protect my independence," he said.

As an officer of the canners association, Miller was given an exceptional opportunity to keep a finger on the industry pulse—a fact of great value to him and of primary importance to the strength of *Pacific Fisherman*.

He was closely involved, therefore, when knotty problems arose over the relative rights of the Canadian and United States cannery operators in disposition of the Puget Sound and Fraser River salmon catch.

It became increasingly evident to him that the canners themselves could not develop agreements satisfactory to both factions. And after a stormy meeting when more than usual confusion and disagreement seemed to stall all progress, Tom Gorman, head of a large cannery business with a plant in Anacortes, Washington, and the chairman of the 1905 meeting in Vancouver, came forth with a suggestion. He told Miller that he thought the only effective means to settle disputes would be the adoption of an international treaty establishing guidelines for Canadian and United States operators. Conservation by international action had also been propounded by John Pease Babcock, British Columbia assistant commissioner of fisheries. The idea made exceptionally good sense to Miller and he actively pressured from within the association for establishment of such a treaty. Augmenting his efforts, strong editorials regularly ran in *Pacific Fisherman,* urging the adoption of such a course for the ultimate benefit of the industry. But while many favored the idea, no actual steps were taken to bring about a treaty.

Miller waited impatiently for beginning action and at last, when none seemed imminent, he took a first step. In 1907 he went to California to call on Dr. David Starr Jordan, president of Stanford University, and a leading marine biologist. Miller thought it a good move to put the proposition to Dr. Jordan who was a recognized authority in his scientific field. Miller gave Dr. Jordan the background of the fishery disputes between the Canadian and United States canners, stressing that these disagreements were endangering the sockeye salmon resource and damaging the effectiveness of the industry itself. He told him of the failure of attempts in 1905 to deal with the situation through negotiations between the state of Washington and the Canadian government and of his own conviction that an international treaty was essential.

Dr. Jordan was greatly interested in what Miller had to say and in hearty accord with the idea of the establishment of treaty regulations. Shortly after this meeting, Dr. Jordan interceded with his good friend President Theodore Roosevelt, urging that he take action toward such a proposition with federal legislation. Following Dr. Jordan's suggestion, Theodore Roosevelt, in his message to Congress in December 1907, declared that the government of the United States should take a position in the conservation of its fisheries where national action was necessary. This seemed at least a good start.

It was in fact the start of a 30-year struggle for enactment of the sockeye salmon treaty—a treaty which was successful in saving the threatened Fraser River fishery, one of the richest and most highly concentrated salmon fisheries in the world.

The fight to save a rich regional resource will also run through much of this book. The details illustrate a number of principles that Miller pioneered with *Pacific Fisherman* and that guided his publishing enterprise in many of its aspects. Miller's campaign for a fisheries treaty was a gradually accumulating strategic method in shaping public opinion and action. It was carried on in three phases: by Miller Freeman personally; by *Pacific Fisherman* speaking for itself; and by Miller Freeman and his journal working together. Describing the campaign strategy later, he wrote:

> At times it seemed expedient for me to act alone and as an individual in the matter. At those times, months may have passed in which I was very busy on the project myself but in which *Pacific Fisherman* made no mention of it. There were times when it seemed best to work quietly. Again, and this was usually when the matter was rising to the crisis, the journal and I personally were actively and energetically engaged. On still other occasions, it seemed advantageous for *Pacific Fisherman* to wage an editorial campaign on its own, while I kept discreetly in the background. These shifts of emphasis were dictated by what seemed to be the wise strategy of the moment.

In 1907, however, Miller was just beginning his first and longest campaign in behalf of the fishing industry. He knew that Dr. Jordan would talk to President Roosevelt and, therefore, in the fall of 1907 he advocated editorially that the national government undertake international treaty negotiations.

In view of the federal ennunciation in December 1907, those in the industry were encouraged to take positive action, and in April 1908, a treaty between Canada and the United States was signed. It was admittedly an immature step but a first positive one toward an international treaty, and enormously satisfying to its supporters.

The treaty, which covered more ground than had been anticipated, involved an examination of all the boundary waters of the United States and Canada, together with the fishery problems arising out of their joint use. It set up a commission of two men, one from each country, to make the required study. Dr. Jordan and Professor E. E. Prince of Canada were appointed to this commission. After a year of diligent work, the two men completed the very difficult task of drawing up a set of regulations that would apply to the fisheries of Lake Erie, Lake Champlain, and the Bay of Fundy, as well as to the Fraser River and Puget Sound. The proposals then had to be acted upon by the United States and Canadian governments.

The Jordan-Prince Recommendations with respect to control of the Fraser River fishery (a major spawning ground for sockeye salmon) were innocuous enough but, while Canada immediately acted favorably on them, the United States interests viewed the proposals with a great deal of unwarranted suspicion. A "stall" ensued with respect to ratification of the treaty in the United States Senate with the disappointing result that the issue was finally shelved.

While this part of Miller's story encompasses his activities between 1897 and 1910, the long-term efforts to establish United States-Canadian fishing treaties run through the 1920s and most of the 1930s. In the interests of clarification, it seems advisable to mention here high points in these continuing campaigns. They will be told in greater detail in later chapters.

After the Jordan-Prince Recommendations were shelved in 1908, action on the salmon treaty was virtually suspended for several years. The issue drifted along in the United States Congress during the administration of President William H. Taft, who was lukewarm in his support. Revived when Woodrow Wilson became President, the treaty seemed close to passage in 1914, but failed following last-minute pressure from the opposition. In 1918, with the end of World War I in sight, fishery problems in boundary waters again claimed the attention of Canada and the United States. It was July 1937, however, before the salmon treaty was ratified.

Fortunately progress in effecting a treaty to control the halibut resource was less difficult, although a great deal of work and a number of years were required before the treaty was ratified in October 1924.

10
TIME OUT for a SUCCESSFUL CAMPAIGN– MARRIAGE 1906

USY AS MILLER WAS in these early days with the multiple activities of a young businessman, he was keeping an alert eye open for the right girl. He had been too busy for much dating, but he had been observing his friends' amorous adventures and his own ideas were forming. His bachelor activities brought him into contact with a good cross section of Seattle's younger people and he had looked over the field pretty well. He did not know much about going after a girl, but, he reasoned, he was thirty years old and it was admittedly time to look into this important phase of his life.

About 1905 he began to look very seriously at a young lady named Bessie Lea Bogle. She was the daughter of Judge William H. Bogle and sister of Max, Miller's partner in starting *Pacific Fisherman*.

Miller came across Miss Bogle frequently at social gatherings and it did not take him long to make up his mind to launch a campaign for her hand. He was a fast and direct worker by nature and he went about this new and untried business with vigor. Things did not go badly, but they did not go as fast as he wanted. There were some unexpected setbacks in his planned strategy.

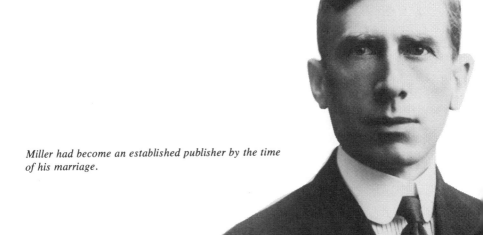

Miller had become an established publisher by the time of his marriage.

MILLER FREEMAN WEDS MISS BOGLE

Ceremony Performed at Home of the Bride's Parents Last Evening

Mr. Miller Freeman and Miss Bess Bogle were married last evening at the residence of the bride's parents, Mr. and Mrs. W. H. Bogle, of 749 Seventeenth avenue north. The ceremony was performed by Rev. James Wilson. Miss Carrie Atkinson was the maid of honor and Mr. Frank Case the best man. The young ladies who held the ribbons to make an aisle for the wedding procession were Miss Inez Calhoun, Miss Alice Taggart, Miss Lily Bogle and Miss Clara Whitson, of Spokane.

The bride wore a wedding gown of white satin, with bridal veil caught up with orange blossoms, and carried a shower boquet of white roses. Miss Atkinson wore white lace and carried a floral muff. The ceremony was performed under an arch of white and green.

Mr. Wendall Simonds played the wedding march.

The bride's table was arranged with a large centerpiece of yellow roses and wedding bells were suspended from the chandelier. Yellow roses and lighted yellow candles completed the decorations of the room.

The girls who served in the dining room were the Misses Mabel Allan, Mayme Allan, Rena Amos, Gertrude Simonds and Jane W. Dowd. About fifty guests were present.

Mr. Freeman is editor of the Pacific Fisherman and The Ranch, and his bride, the oldest daughter of Mr. and Mrs. W. H. Bogle, is a member of the Gamma Phi Beta sorority of the Washington. Mr. and Mrs. ... ately for an extend- ... and their

Marriage of Miller Freeman and Bessie Bogle was reported by the Seattle P-I

Bessie Bogle had gone two years to the University of Washington and, in the fall of 1905, was teaching kindergarten. She was not contemplating marriage as she enthusiastically started her career. However, during this period, it seemed that Miller Freeman was seen more frequently around the Bogle home on one pretext or another, and the two were becoming better acquainted. Being seven years her senior, Miller was a little out of the young lady's age category, and it was a surprise to her when he suddenly proposed marriage.

Shortly after Miller's proposal, which was left an unanswered question, Bessie and her sister left for a three months' steamship trip to the Orient—properly chaperoned by a family friend. Miller was at the dock to bid Bessie goodbye, feeling pretty well frustrated to be left hanging in mid-air. Issues left in limbo were unfamiliar to him, and girls were, in fact, pretty puzzling. Nevertheless, as the ship moved slowly away from the dock that cold January day, his determination grew

*Miller and Bessie Freeman with older sons
Bill and Kemper in about 1914.*

stronger. It was, he decided, just a matter of biding his time.

In May 1906, a few weeks after the great San Francisco earthquake, Bessie Bogle's ship docked in that devastated city on its first homeward-bound stop. Miller was standing determinedly at the gangplank ready to greet the shy, gracious, young lady as she stepped off the ship. She seemed properly happy to see him, he thought, and he was given courage to repeat his question.

Three months of travel, ending with the long sea voyage, had given Bessie time to carefully assess her suitor, and her mind had been made up. The answer this time was "yes." Suddenly, Miller had won his life's most successful campaign which would give meaning and purpose to all the coming campaigns.

Bessie Lea Bogle and Miller Freeman were married October 15, 1906. His wife's quiet strength was to provide the peace and the anchor for the Yakima boy who had come so far already.

11

PACIFIC MOTOR BOAT and the FARM GROUP

MILLER'S INTEREST IN SAILING began early in his bachelor years. Learning proficiency in the handling of small boats became an absorbing recreation for him and a group of congenial friends. As he became a seasoned salt and more affluent with his small business prospering, he decided he wanted to try a larger boat. In 1904, therefore, he joined with two other young men about town—George Vandeveer, prosecuting attorney of King County, and Frank Case—in the construction of a forty-foot fin keel sloop. She was built in the Ed Heath yard at Tacoma. The hull cost $1,200 and an additional amount was spent for sails.

Describing the sail boat later, Miller said, ". . . she carried a total spread of 1,100 square feet, considerably more than necessary, but it made George Vandeveer very happy, particularly when she heeled over and ran her gunwale under. George, being the originator of the idea, had the naming of the vessel and called her the *Imp*.

For several years the three young men raced the *Imp* in Northwest and Canadian waters, unfortunately never winning a race. That did not seem to matter for the sport provided endless enjoyment and fine opportunity for easy sociability with groups of other young people.

A few years later, largely due to the development of the compact internal combustion engine, the motorboat began to be popular and Miller's interest in sailing waned. Abandoning his interest in the *Imp*, he purchased the *Philistina*, a 28-foot powerboat.

With some of the finest cruising waters in the world at the Northwest's doorstep, Miller felt that motorboating was destined for increasing popularity and he began to think in terms of a boating journal. He knew that the East Coast had long supported a publication devoted to pleasure and commercial crafts. The eastern and western fields were too far separated for competition, he reasoned. Why couldn't a journal for the West Coast prove successful?

The Imp, *forty-foot fin keel sloop, stimulated Miller's interest in boating.*

Pacific Motor Boat, *established in 1908 when gasoline engines were being installed in work and pleasure boats at a lively rate.*

As he looked in depth into the field, he became convinced of its good potential. This was a time when gas engines were being installed in work boats and pleasure crafts at a lively rate. With his analytical mind and peculiar ability to sense the latent potentialities in new technological developments, Miller had already recognized that the internal combustion engine would open up further opportunities in the boating field. The powering of the Pacific fishing fleet had been a spectacular success and he had foreseen that this new motive source would soon spread to other work boats and to pleasure craft.

It became Miller's habit to walk into any machinery shop and tell them he wanted to see their experimental gas engine. In most cases, the owner would lead him to the back of the building and show him the engine he was getting ready to market. It appeared that he was seeing the initial activity of an industry which would inevitably grow.

In August 1908, Miller sent out a notice to all manufacturers of commercial boats, of yachting equipment and engines that he would begin publication of a new journal to be called *Pacific Motor Boat*. Thus, Miller began his second journal to serve a commercial field

The Philistina, *acquired in 1906, was later traded for an automobile.*

closely related to *Pacific Fisherman*. Within the course of a few years, it became a leading motorboat journal nationally as well as on the Pacific Coast. Its success and Miller's awareness of the potential of the diesel engine led to the establishment of *Motorship* in 1916.

With expansion into the fisheries field, Miller found that *The Ranch* was of secondary importance to him. He continued to publish it until 1907, however, then sold it to Leonard Fowler of Wenatchee, Washington. Fowler subsequently sold it to a man named Dean, who operated it from Kent, Washington. Apparently neither owner managed to make it a profitable venture.

While operating *The Ranch,* Miller had a New York agent, Sam Leith, to whom he paid a monthly retainer of twenty-five dollars to secure national advertising for him. In the East on business in 1910, Miller talked to Leith about the opportunities in farm publications. Although Leith was convinced that there was a real future in the farming field, he said that it would be necessary to have a circulation of

75

around 50,000 to sell a regional farm paper to the big national accounts. On learning that there were only about 50,000 farmers in the state of Washington, Leith said, "Why not take in the whole Northwest?"

That proposition interested Miller and he decided to take another whirl at farm publishing. Accordingly, he returned to Seattle, repurchased *The Ranch,* and changed its name to the *Washington Farmer.* It is interesting to speculate on Miller's adoption of the name of his father's publication, which he himself had worked on as a boy. Since Miller made neither oral nor written explanation, it is necessary to depend on a brief mention of the episode by a Seattle newspaper in reporting Legh's career. Apparently father and son worked out an arrangement whereby Miller took the name *Washington Farmer,* giving Legh, in return, a share in the profits from the larger venture. Quite predictably, however, father and son could not work together, and they soon terminated their business partnership, with renewed hard feelings on both sides. The result was a court case, which Miller won.

Going ahead with his attempt to reach the 50,000 circulation figure, Miller added two farm publications within the next two years. First he went to Portland and bought the *Oregon Agriculturalist* from C. D. Minton. Next he acquired the *Gem State Rural* from A. E. Jipson of Caldwell, Idaho. These journals became the *Oregon Farmer* and the *Idaho Farmer,* respectively.

As a result of this activity, by 1912 Miller was back in the farm publishing field with three journals. In addition, he had *Pacific Fisherman* and *Pacific Motor Boat.*

The three farm papers were printed in Portland, Oregon, by Binford Brothers. Writing about this venture in his *Memoirs,* more than forty years later, Miller said: "We went to work hard and finally built up the 50,000 circulation for the three books which Leith said was essential. Then when I told him we had it, and for him to go out and get the business he had promised, he said that times had changed and that a circulation of 100,000 now would be necessary for real results. With that I began 'looking around.' The cost of getting and maintaining the 50,000 circulation had proven to be very high and a difficult thing to do. Moreover, I had found the industrial publishing field, as distinct from agricultural, a simpler and more compact business. It just held a lot more attraction for me."

It was not Miller's policy to delay action once a decision was made regarding his publications. Throughout his career, if a journal did not prove profitable within a reasonable length of time, he got rid of it and moved on to other ventures.

Accordingly, in 1915, Miller sold the farm group to W. H. Cowles of Spokane, publisher of the *Spokesman Review.* The newspaper published a semiweekly rural edition that could be shifted advantageously to the tri-state farm group. Cowles had abundant resources and did not stint in spending them for the development of the three "Farmers." He built the group into a very valuable property.

12
AROUND TOWN ACTIVITIES

T HE ESTABLISHMENT OF his new magazine, *Pacific Motor Boat,* in 1908 further tied Miller's publishing interests to commercial and pleasure boating. He had owned a sailing sloop and a motorboat and had taken a lively part in the establishment, in 1906, of the first Yacht Club at Elliott Bay. The Elliott Bay Yacht Club catered to young men of moderate means.

As the time for the celebration of the Alaska-Yukon-Pacific Exposition neared, Seattle readied itself for a great regatta. The Elliott Bay Yacht Club, in cooperation with the members of the older and more affluent Seattle Yacht Club, took a leading part in the arrangements. It was decided at this time to merge the two clubs and to plan the building of a larger facility at another location to serve the needs of the larger group. The goal was to have the building completed before exposition time in 1909.

Miller, along with Mayor Hiram Gill, attorney Scott Calhoun, and many interested citizens, was active in seeking waterfront land to house the enlarged Seattle Yacht Club. A suitable piece of city property at the foot of Charles Street in West Seattle was found and a lease was arranged. Everyone was anxious to start the building so that it would be ready for occupancy by regatta time.

Only one major problem remained before clubhouse construction could begin. The operators of the small sawmill, which had long been located on this particular piece of city land, refused to move. Frustrated, Miller and the Yacht Club boys decided to pull a surprise takeover and move in over all protests of the mill owners. A tug and pile driver were hired and, as the mill hands left work on a Saturday afternoon, the yachtsmen moved in. They directed the placement of a solid barricade of piles across the front of the mill, entirely shutting it off from deep water and its supply of logs. When this maneuver was discovered, angry mill owners threatened an injunction. Unfortunately for them, no injunction action was possible before the following Monday morning. By that time the mill was completely surrounded by piles.

On Monday the irate mill owners filed an injunction but, without legal status, they were powerless and soon were forced to move to a new location.

A fine clubhouse was built in West Seattle where it remained until 1920, when the Seattle Yacht Club was relocated at the foot of Montlake Avenue. By exposition time in 1909 the new clubhouse was ready to honor the visiting dignitaries, one of whom was the renowned Sir Thomas Lipton.

After he had owned the *Philistina* for two years, Miller started looking at automobiles. He had had his fun with sailing and motorboating and, being a family man now, he saw far more practical use for a car than a boat.

He was standing at the curb in front of the Puget Sound National Bank one day when Roger Sands, a young partner in the hardwood firm of Ehrlich-Harrison Company, drove up in a Lozier automobile. Miller complimented him on his very "tony" car.

"Want to buy it?" Sands asked with a gleam in his eye.

Miller took some time to inspect the car, which looked all right to him. Among its other novelties was an extra seat suspended over the fender on the port side, and Miller thought this accommodation would be just right for his firstborn son.

"How about trading it for my cruiser?" Miller suggested.

"Let's go see it," Sands replied.

As finance committee chairman, Miller Freeman helped raise the funds for the Seattle Yacht Club's $10,000 clubhouse in West Seattle.

Miller piled in the car and the two young men set off for the Seattle Yacht Club where Miller's boat was moored. Together they boarded the craft and Sands looked her over carefully, obviously impressed by her appearance. But the next hurdle was to demonstrate the proficiency of the *Philistina*. Here Miller tensed, for her engine was temperamental and often coughed uncontrollably before coming to life. Luck was with Miller, however, and to his surprise and relief, the motor turned over immediately. Sands was pleased, and an even trade took place on the spot. Ownership papers were exchanged and Roger went for a run in the *Philistina* while Miller proudly drove his first car down the street.

The following day, Miller took the Lozier out to drive to his office. He was learning to handle it with ease and a good deal of real pleasure. Exhilarated by the experience, he was making a good twenty miles an hour as he neared the intersection of Westlake and Pine streets. Seeing a sprinkling wagon ahead wetting down the wood pavement where a downgrade began, he pulled hard on the hand brake. To his amazement, this action produced the most surprising results. The car at once started to slither sidewise. Out of control, it hit the concrete curb with a violent swing, neatly stripping off all four wheels, wooden spokes and

On November 19, 1912, San Francisco's Bulletin *carried this picture and story of preparations for an international regatta to be held during the Panama Pacific Exposition in 1915. Miller had suggested the race and led a delegation of nearly 100 from the northwest to take part in planning it. He is shown fourth from right clasping the hand of Sir Thomas Lipton.*

The Bulletin

SAN FRANCISCO, TUESDAY EVENING, NOVEMBER 19, 1912.

LIPTON HOLDS HANDS ACROSS SEA
MEETS LOCAL SALTS IN CONFERENCE

Reading from left to right: H. E. Picker, vice-commodore Corinthian Yacht Club, San Francisco; Captain John Barneson; J. R. Hanify, San Francisco Yacht Club; Sir Thomas Lipton; Exposition President C. C. Moore; M. Freeman, Seattle Yacht Club; George S. Shepherd, Motorboat Club of Portland.

all. After an earsplitting crash and a sudden shattering bump, Miller, in stunned amazement, was left sitting on ground level, still holding tight to the steering wheel. Four wheels lay strewn at random along the street.

A quiet street at once became a bedlam of hooting and jeering— from friends and strangers alike. Over and over again he heard, "Ha ha, why don't you get a horse? Look at that fine car, will you!"

Red faced, Miller climbed out, viewed his wreck in disgust, pushed through the crowd into the nearest building and phoned the automobile agency to come and get the car. A man soon arrived from the Lozier company and dismally viewed the car and its owner. He asked Mr. Freeman what he wanted done with the car to which Miller replied in disgust that, as far as he was concerned, it could be thrown in the bay.

Life looked pretty dark as Miller walked down to his office following the disaster. Arriving there somewhat late, he suddenly recalled the papers he had filed in his desk the night before after he had taken possession of the Lozier. Looking them over carefully he discovered an accident insurance policy. And suddenly things looked considerably brighter. He called the Lozier agency and directed the man to replace the wheels. In due course repairs were made and the Lozier did family duty for several years thereafter.

"I never again made the mistake of clamping on the brakes when striking wet pavement," Miller said in recounting the story some time after the accident. "And that's a pretty good rule in life and business generally."

Roger Sands also had his problems. When he next set out to take a cruise around Lake Washington aboard the *Philistina,* to his dismay he found her reposing on the lake bottom and nearly submerged. This initial calamity, however, proved only a temporary setback to his eventual enjoyment of the cruiser.

The Freeman family in Miller's first automobile, a Lozier. Bill rides in the seat over the wheel, while Kemper sits in his mother's lap.

13
Into POLITICAL HIGH GEAR
with the TOWN CRIER

MILLER'S CASUAL BEGINNING in a Republican political organization for young men did not in any way indicate the extent to which he would be involved. But, again, Miller had a way of being where the action was and getting into the thick of things.

Despite his Democratic heritage, Miller became a Republican. About 1905 he joined a small group of friends and acquaintances who were dedicated to upsetting the entrenched older Republican politicians in order to infuse new blood and new ideas into the machinery of the party. The cry was, "Down with the Old Guard! Give the young men a chance!"

The first meeting ground for this small nucleus was in Holcomb's livery stable on Western Avenue, and a friend urged Miller to attend the gathering. Enthusiastic young men arrived in sufficient numbers, and early enough, to pack the house; so the waterfront boys, who had heretofore run things, could only wedge in a scant, though vocal, minority.

The meeting which ensued turned out to be a general melee and, at its noisy conclusion, Miller found that he had been appointed chairman of the committeemen from five city precincts. He was unsure how this had happened and was not acquainted with what the job entailed—but he was willing to learn.

So, inadvertently, began Miller's political involvement which was to weave itself recurrently into his lifelong activities. Sometimes his political connections were the result of efforts to benefit the fields which his journals served. His later involvements were further removed from such direct interests, but all had the same roots. And all efforts along political lines went back to his firm conviction that one of the marks and obligations of a good citizen was an intelligent interest in honest politics.

While Miller, the Republican, and his father, Legh, the Democrat, went their politically opposed ways, their basic convictions as to the

The Town Crier *was established in 1910 to promote the Lake Washington Canal. Miller published it for several years to support other causes vital to him.*

importance of their own involvement in politics were remarkably similar. Each in his own manner remained committed to the value of the two-party system.

Miller committed himself deeply to causes he felt important. He never claimed to know what his course of action would be from start to finish of a campaign, but he was convinced a beginning was most vital. His credo was that *any* action is better than none.

The subject of the building of a canal to link Puget Sound with Lake Washington had long been under discussion in the Northwest. By 1910, it was a hot issue and Miller felt strongly that the construction of such a waterway, providing fresh water access to commercial and pleasure boats, was of the utmost importance to the growth and development of the area. Controversy had long seethed over the issue in the community—the pros and cons speaking out loudly.

To blow off steam on this issue, Miller began publication of his fourth paper, the *Town Crier,* in September 1910. The first issue was financed with $1,000 given him by supporters of the Lake Washington Canal project. The paper was started specifically to give strong backing to the proposition of a canal with locks. Miller employed the *Town Crier* at that time and for the following six years, to strongly support that cause and other political issues which appeared vital to him. He fought word battles using it as his tool, sometimes vigorously propounding propositions in which he believed, sometimes battling against those people with whom he disagreed on important issues.

Like his father, Miller took strong stands and fought hard for his convictions. But unlike Legh, Miller kept clearly in mind his concept of the rightful place for political propounding. He had been critical of his father for inserting outworn partisan stands into the columns of the *Washington Farmer,* a paper he thought should be a nonpartisan voice for the farmer and rancher. Thus, the establishment of the *Town Crier*

A ten-point program for Seattle's advancement presented in the Town Crier.

THE TOWN CRIER

A Program For the People of Seattle

Ten Lines of Public Endeavor in Which Every Loyal Citizen Can Earnestly and Actively Unite

THE next thing for Seattle to do is to get busy.

Not that the town is dull, nor that business conditions are indifferent. Few cities of the United States enjoy greater prosperity, and few indeed are there whose prosperity rests upon more solid foundations.

Still there is much that may be done; much that must be done. We look confidently into the future; why not bring the future a little closer to us? We safely predict continued and greater prosperity; then, should we not desire the early fulfillment of our prediction? Why not abandon the complacent self-assurance that "what is to be, will be," and get busy making the good things come true, and come soon?

Concentration is the keynote of successful endeavor. Business undertakings are carried forward on well-defined lines, guided....

HERE THEY ARE!

1: For the opening up and development of Alaska.
2: For the completion of the Pacific Highway.
3: For the reclamation of logged-off lands.
4: For the development of the Olympic Peninsula.
5: For the further improvement of Mount Rainier National Park.
6: For continuous work on good roads.
7: For the upbuilding of a great commercial harbor.
8: For immediate and continued increase in aids to navigation along the Alaskan and Northwestern coast.
9: For the success of the Golden Potlatch.
10: For publicity.

lected area of Western Washington to the instant benefit of Seattle and all other cities.

Fourth: The potential possibilities of the Olympic Peninsula are scarcely understood, even by the people of Seattle. Not until within the past few months has this great section received more than passing attention. The peninsula must be relieved of some of the burdens imposed upon it by governmental bureaucracy. With the better opportunity that such relief will give to the agriculturalist, the prospector, the timberman and the fisherman, railroad construction will quickly begin on routes already determined by extensive surveys.

Fifth: The further development of Mount Rainier National Park....

provided Miller with the means of expressing his political opinions while he continued to maintain a policy of impartiality for his business magazines.

On the canal issue, the *Town Crier* and its publisher were fighting the *Seattle Post-Intelligencer* and its owner and publisher, John L. Wilson. The railroads were also against the canal, believing that it threatened their interests. Repeated blasts from the guns of the *Town Crier* tore at Wilson as a "selfish" and "kowtowing" politician, at the railroads for attempting to block progress, and at all who opposed the proposition on whatever grounds. On the positive side the paper gave strong support to the politicians who were in favor of construction of the canal.

Miller's editorials bore strong resemblance to those of Legh Freeman's as they had long before appeared in his historic *Frontier Index*. On page one of its first issue, the *Town Crier* referred to "the pestiferous, perennial, pettifogging politician, the happily extinguished Senator John L. Wilson who loafs and lingers about from year to year, scheming and plotting to live in the Nation's Capital as one of the pawns of the American House of Lords . . . ." Thus, father and son alike rose in indignation to battle the forces which sought to block justified progress. But where Legh fought with heavy hand and unremitting pressure, Miller tempered his stands with practical tactics.

At the time of the fight for the building of the Lake Washington Canal, an issue came into the picture which today takes on particular meaning. Some who opposed the canal did so on grounds that it would deface the natural beauty of the environment. It was then that Miller crystallized and organized his ideas on what he considered to be the rightful role of conservation. "Conservation is use which does not destroy, use at the maximum level consistent with sustained yield," he decided. His stand, voiced then, was reiterated by him on many issues involving conservation of natural resources.

It made sense to him that a *wise use of a natural resource was essential to progress.* He would hold to this position whether it pertained to the protection of natural beauty or to the preservation of a valued natural resource. This theme would become one repeatedly propounded by him throughout his publishing career and would include all issues pertaining to the preservation and protection of basic resources connected with the industries his journals served.

Although Miller's active interest in the Lake Washington Canal did not begin until 1907, the desire to build such a link between the lake and Puget Sound went back to the early days of Seattle. On the discovery of coal at Renton, a plan was projected, resulting in the construction of a narrow gravity canal connecting Lake Washington with Lake Union. This canal carried coal barges from the mines into Lake Union and was also used for floating logs to the sawmills.

In the early 1890s, Captain A. B. Wyckoff, USN, championed

construction of a canal from Puget Sound into Lake Washington, where he wanted to establish the main naval base for the Puget Sound area. The proposal was discussed with considerable heat by politicians throughout the state.

John H. McGraw conducted his campaign for governor with a popular slogan: "Build the Lake Washington Canal, and build it in 1895." He was elected but by that time strong opposition had been developed by the waterfront interests of the Seattle harbor area and the railroads, who objected to the expense of bridging the canal.

In 1907, J. S. Brace organized the Lake Washington Canal Association, with himself as president and Miller Freeman as secretary. By

Lake Washington Ship Canal and locks under construction in 1914. Today, it requires about forty-five minutes to move a large log tow through the locks. (Courtesy U.S. Army Corps of Engineers, Seattle District.)

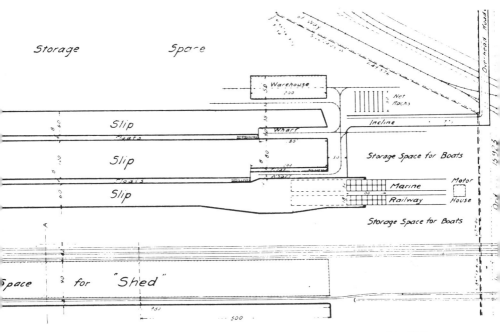

Detailed plan of the Salmon Bay fisheries fleet base opened in 1912.

this time another group had started a movement for dredging the Duwamish River and the two were at odds. Deciding that the two forces would destroy each other if the impasse continued, Miller proposed that they unite in attacking the opposition to both projects. He suggested a campaign for a $1,750,000 bond issue to be used to dredge the Duwamish and dig the canal.

Commenting on Miller's efforts, the *Coast,* "a magazine of Town and Country Life," said:

> Miller Freeman has sent out a vigorously written circular showing the urgent necessity for the completion of the harbor improvements, including the Duwamish waterway and the Lake Washington canal. His arguments are well presented and unanswerable. . . . In the past year or two all Pacific ports have been vigorously at work making ready for the increased traffic that will follow the opening of the Panama Canal; but Seattle has done practically nothing. . . . Mr. Freeman's warning is timely and should be thoughtfully considered by every patriotic Seattle citizen who desires to see our city hold its own in the commercial race.

After a bitter fight, the bond issue was passed on November 8, 1910. Early in 1910, Federal Rivers and Harbor funds had been provided for

Aerial view of the Ship Canal and Hiram M. Chittenden Locks today. (Courtesy U.S. Army Corps of Engineers, Seattle District.)

construction of the locks, contingent upon local funds being provided for digging the canal.

Passage of the bond issue did not end the fight, however. Although the War Department had the funds available, lobbyists for opposing interests succeeded in blocking the approval necessary for their expenditure until Henry L. Stimson became secretary of war. Even then approval could not be secured until state courts disposed of the last of several suits brought to block the project.

Finally, on June 29, 1911, Secretary Stimson directed the U.S. Corps of Engineers to call for bids on construction of the locks for the Lake Washington Canal. Construction was started in September 1911 and the locks were opened to traffic in 1916.

With the canal assured, Miller quickly shifted to a drive to make use of the canal for the fishing fleet. Through *Pacific Fisherman,* he undertook a campaign for a Port of Seattle project to develop Salmon Bay as a Fishermen's Terminal. This facility, opened in 1912, was said by the *Seattle Times* to be "the direct result of *Pacific Fisherman* and Miller Freeman." In recognition of his efforts in behalf of the fleet, Miller was made an honorary member of the Puget Sound Purse Seine Fishermens Protective Association.

Expanded and developed over the years, the terminal is now one of the largest and finest fishing vessel bases in the United States.

Fishermen's terminal at Salmon Bay allowed the fishing fleet to make use of the Washington Canal. (Courtesy Seattle Historical Society.)

For his help in securing Salmon Bay fisheries dock, Miller Freeman was made an honorary member of the Purse Seine Fishermens Protective Association.

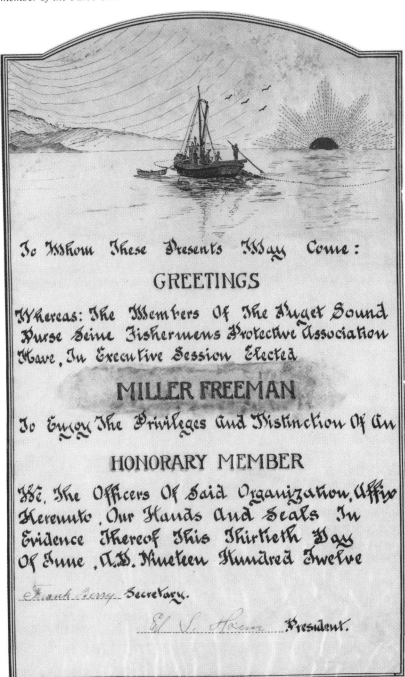

To Whom These Presents May Come:

GREETINGS

Whereas: The Members Of The Puget Sound Purse Seine Fishermens Protective Association Have, In Executive Session Elected

MILLER FREEMAN

To Enjoy The Privileges And Distinction Of An

HONORARY MEMBER

We, The Officers Of Said Organization, Affix Hereunto, Our Hands And Seals In Evidence Thereof This Thirtieth Day Of June, A.D. Nineteen Hundred Twelve

Frank Berry Secretary.

El S. Hoeen President.

14
At SEA with the NAVAL MILITIA

I N 1909 MILLER READ with deep interest an article entitled "The Coast Defense of the Northwest" published in *Harper's Weekly*. It was written by Colonel Garland V. Whistler, USA, commanding the Coast Artillery at Fort Worden, Washington. At that time Japan possessed the world's most powerful army and had, moreover, recently destroyed the Russian Navy at Port Arthur in a surprise attack (which in Miller's words, spoken many years later, gave a "perfect preview of Pearl Harbor"). She had then proceeded to rout the Russian army in Siberia and, flushed with victory, was a particularly truculent Pacific neighbor. The import of Colonel Whistler's article was to urge additional coast defense for the Pacific Northwest and particularly for Puget Sound. He specifically recommended the organization of a Naval Reserve.

Some time prior to this Miller had met George von Lengerke Meyer, United States Secretary of Navy, at an affair at the Seattle Yacht Club and he promptly wrote to him suggesting that authorization be granted for the organization of a small fleet of boats similar to the British Royal Naval Reserves. Secretary Meyer responded, saying that he did not believe the British pattern could be followed but that an organization of Naval Militia along these lines was already operating in several United States seaports. He added that he would welcome, and actively support, the establishment of such a unit on Puget Sound.

With this assurance, Miller arranged a special meeting of the members of the Seattle Yacht Club. Invited to speak on the nature and need of the Navy Militia were Colonel Whistler, Brigadier General George Lamping of the Washington State National Guard, and the commander of the Bremerton Navy Yard. At the conclusion of the meeting, Miller passed around a muster roll, which said, in effect, "the undersigned agrees to join the Naval Militia, if and when organized." All of those present signed. Miller then forwarded the muster roll to Secretary Meyer. Directives went to the right places and the upshot was that, when the state legislature of Washington next met, it submitted enabling legislation—subsequently passed—to support such an activity.

Thus, the formation of the first Naval Militia unit in the state of Washington took place in the winter of 1910. Having taken the lead in the movement to bring this about, Miller seemed the natural leader. Therefore, he suddenly found himself in command of the brand new unit, heading an enthusiastic group of friends, able yachtsmen, and entirely green deep-sea sailors.

Miller had no knowledge of naval protocol or military procedures of any kind. He, like the others, was a yachtsman. He had made these facts clear to all concerned. The nation and the world at large were at peace, however, and war was only a remote possibility to most Americans in 1910. An untrained but willing civilian seemed the right choice for the job of activating the unit. He was given a commission with the rank of commander.

Well aware that he was actually leading a project for which he had almost no training, Miller was willing to learn. Since his peers and the authorities had put faith in his ability, he would give the organization his best effort, he decided. And this he proceeded to do with energy and enthusiasm. He procured white uniforms for the enlisted men. He obtained the use of the armory at Western Avenue and Virginia Street and soon had a company vigorously drilling. Periodic trips were made around the sound for the purpose of practice landings. He even intimated that his men might undertake the capture of Fort Worden, but neither Colonel Whistler nor others in authority approved.

While the boys of the militia were still getting used to their new status and their commander was groping for the right answers to entirely new questions, Miller received one of his first official communiques. It startled him. The order informed him that the new Washington Naval Militia unit had been assigned the cruiser USS *Cheyenne*. Suddenly, and still quite unprepared, these men were to be officers and crew of a ship of the United States Navy. The *Cheyenne* was then anchored in San Francisco Bay, and Miller's unit of sixty men was ordered to leave forthwith for San Francisco to escort the vessel northward to its new berth in Puget Sound.

The commander had not had time to acquire a uniform with stripes suited to his rank, nor had the yachtsmen readied themselves for sea duty. Adding to the general problems confronting the young men was the question of money. No one was able to put out the necessary cash to get to San Francisco. The commander was sweating out his first real problem when he learned that the cruiser USS *Washington,* the largest of the United States fleet at that time and then at Bremerton Navy Yard, was due to leave within hours for San Francisco. With admirable dispatch, born of some desperation, Miller wired the secretary of the navy in Washington, D.C., for permission to gain transport for his unit to California on board the USS *Washington.* And, to his surprise, he received the desired orders immediately.

One of the next problems was to obtain a uniform so that he could *look* like a naval officer; *feeling* like one would have to come later, he guessed. Because of Miller's short stature and unusually broad shoulders, his uniform needed considerable fitting. The speed with which the unit had been called to action left little time for outfitting its commanding officer. The supplier worked frantically to alter the suit, and Miller proceeded direct from the tailor's shop to the ship, which was due to weigh anchor shortly after he arrived.

Being immediately propelled into a military situation was more than frightening. His insecurity grew as he approached the USS *Washington* and received his first snappy salute from a young seaman. His attempt at response was faltering and clumsy, and he walked self-consciously up the gangplank.

With sixty untrained militiamen and a green commander, the situation on board ship was fully appreciated by the cruiser's salty crew. Although the jibes flew freely over the decks, each new man was taken under the surveillance of a seaman and given a thorough indoctrination in procedure. A tribute to the cooperation shown on both sides is illustrated in the portion of a clipping from the *Seattle Times* of July 31, 1910, which read:

> On the trip to San Francisco the officers of the Washington Naval Militia were guests of the officers of the cruiser USS *Washington* and were comfortably quartered and well entertained. The men of the Naval Militia were assigned quarters and messes with the regular crew, according to their rating, and did duty along with their partners. The commanding officer of the *Washington* sent to Commander Miller Freeman, after the Washington Naval Militia had gone aboard its own ship the *Cheyenne,* a letter of commendation which stated that the reports he had received from his officers who were charged with the duty of reporting to him as to the efficiency of the organization, were in all respects favorable both as to officers and men . . . .

On arrival in San Francisco, the first glimpse of the *Cheyenne* was anything but reassuring to the newly indoctrinated commander. Formerly, the USS *Wyoming,* built in 1901, the *Cheyenne* had recently been rebuilt and recommissioned. While she was well appointed, she

was of a peculiar design for her main deck, even in the calm waters of San Francisco Bay, was scarcely more than four feet above waterline, while her vital works were below decks.

But like parents with a first child, the boys of Seattle thought she looked beautiful. They eagerly joined the seasoned crew on board their new baby for, with admirable foresight, the Navy Department had assigned a nucleus of competent men to protect the interests of the vessel, as well as the lives and safety of the green crew during the trip north.

In high spirits, the crew boarded the *Cheyenne* and enthusiastically headed out the Golden Gate. It was not long before the Pacific began to show a particularly nasty mood with a stiff northwester hitting the ship a steady quartering blow. The *Cheyenne* rose and plunged and the sea washed over her decks as, harried by violent seasickness, the men of the militia carried out newly learned orders. For four days the wind howled and the vessel galloped through mountainous seas as the green crew and its commander headed her northward.

Seven days later a considerably subdued but more experienced crew guided the ship proudly down the calm waters of Puget Sound. As the vessel reached Point-No-Point, she was greeted by steam whistle salutes from shore while several tugs and launches buzzed around her prow. One particularly insistent tug actually pointed its nose into the Cheyenne's path. Startled and angered by the crust of the fellow who first jumped from the tug to the low deck of the *Cheyenne*, the commander swore. The young man turned out to be a reporter from the *Seattle Times,* anxious to get a story of the historic trip. He was quickly followed by others of the press. Commander Freeman greeted the men

The USS Cheyenne, *floating home of the Washington Naval Militia.*

The Seattle Sunday Times

SEATTLE. WASHINGTON. JULY 31. 1910.

FIVE CENTS

EIGHTY-TWO PAGES.

CHEYENNE

—Photo by Times Staff Photographer.   Cheyenne steaming towards Seattle just before dark last night.

curtly, barking, "No orders were given you gentlemen to come aboard." Nevertheless, being a reporter at heart, his attitude quickly mellowed and he surprised and pleased the group by saying in a subdued voice, "But if there is any dope you boys want, seek and ye shall find." Russell Palmer, the young fellow who had first boarded the *Cheyenne,* was treated with the others to a full inspection of the ship.

While Palmer had momentarily angered Miller, the young man's initiative interested him. During the tour of inspection, Palmer displayed particular alertness. He stood out from the rest of the crowd and increasingly impressed the commander. As the gentlemen of the press prepared to leave, Miller turned to Palmer and quietly said, "If you're interested come down and see me at my office tomorrow."

Russell Palmer was receptive to Miller's invitation and the next morning went to his office. Convinced of Palmer's interest in business paper publishing, Miller hired the young man. A valued addition to the staff, Palmer remained with the publishing house until 1928.

Upon completion of the assignment and the activation of a smooth-functioning militia unit, Miller was ready to take inactive status. The publishing business was his major occupation, always holding priority with him. After about a year as commanding officer of the unit, therefore, Miller asked to be relieved from active duty and was retired to civilian life. On his recommendation, command of the Washington State Militia was assumed by W. B. Allison, a veteran of the Spanish American War. Miller knew Allison to be a man of ability.

As Miller closed this chapter of his naval career, he took some satisfaction in the favorable comment by Captain Richard N. Hughes, commander of the USS *Washington.* Hughes said, "I observed the officers and men of the Washington Naval Militia most carefully on the cruise. I want to compliment you on the personnel, [and on the] competence and efficiency of them all. I will report their splendid showing to the Navy Department."

Giving full coverage to the voyage, the *Seattle Times* of July 31, 1910, quoted Commander Miller Freeman's tributes to the militia and to the U.S. Navy officers who gave them the opportunity to learn through experience. "Rich and poor, young and old, the men from the officers down to the lowest common seamen, took their doses of discipline without a murmur. There was not a breach of discipline throughout the trip . . . . " he said of the militia.

Lieutenant Commander Henry La Motte, Lieutenant W. F. Andrews, the official navigator, and Captain Charles K. Owens who was in command of the *Cheyenne* on the return trip, all endorsed Commander Freeman's laudatory remarks, according to the *Times.* "There may be a war with Japan some day or there may not be," was the general trend of their remarks, the *Times* continued, "but after such a cruise as this, the Pacific Coast can look upon the prospect of war with complacency. When the other divisions of the militia are mustered in and drilled and have gained the training possible on these week-end cruises

Photos taken during organization of the Naval Militia made an interesting page in the pamphlet promoting Miller's election to the state legislature.

in the Sound, Washington will begin to assume a place of equal rank with the leading naval states in the country, not even excepting California.''

This was in 1910, and Miller was becoming recognized for his repeated warnings about the danger of the Japanese on two counts: first, their proven aggressiveness in invading United States and Canadian fishing waters, and second, their steady immigration to the West Coast where increasing numbers were inserting themselves into western business. Because of the Japanese dual citizenship concept, these people were enjoying all the rights of citizenship in Japan and in the United States as well.

Also, it was increasingly apparent to Miller that the Japanese were fast becoming a strong military force to be reckoned with. He was one of the few whose warnings about Japan were regularly repeated. And, in an era of peace, he was considered by many to be an alarmist.

In talking to the Naval Militiamen about the time of the *Cheyenne* episode, he was quoted in the *Seattle Times* as saying:

> I do not go to the extreme end of saying that war is inevitable, but I want you all to feel as I do, that a conflict with Japan is highly probable. You young men may expect at any time to be called upon by the government for actual service. I am not saying this to frighten you. I am not an alarmist, but I am not going to blindfold your eyes and let you go into this important branch of the coast defense with the idea that your term of enlistment will be an unbroken line of pleasure and jollity. We have serious work to do in preparing to aid in the protection of your home and your land.

These words predated Pearl Harbor by thirty-one years.

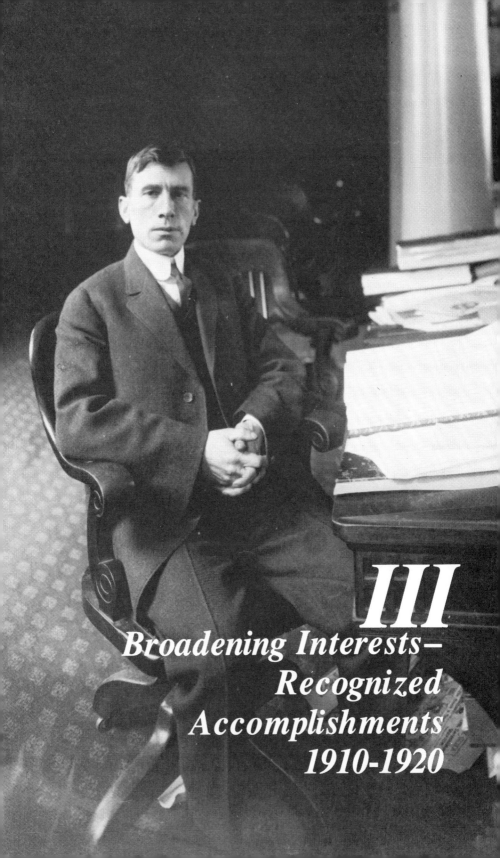

III
Broadening Interests–
Recognized
Accomplishments
1910-1920

15
BOUT with TUBERCULOSIS
and a POLITICAL COUP

I N 1912 MILLER'S CAREER came to a sudden halt when a protract-
ed bronchial condition was diagnosed as tuberculosis. Control
and cure for the illness were in a pioneering stage at that time,
and the name itself still struck terror to those who contracted it.
On his doctor's orders Miller moved with his wife and two small
sons to the town of Monrovia in southern California where he entered a
sanatorium. When he left Seattle he was not told how long it would be
before he could be cured, nor was he assured that a cure was certain.
However, it was thought that the lung problem had been detected early
and that a period of rest in a dry climate would arrest the illness.

To drop the reins of his business, leave his many activities, and
isolate himself from a normal life was a crushing blow and, at first, life
looked dark. Miller moved south a very depressed husband and father.

Russell Palmer, the young man whom Miller had hired two years
before, was proving a very valuable auxiliary to the publishing business. Miller and Russell, in fact, operated in much the same manner.
Therefore, as Miller left for an indefinite time in California he was able
to turn over the management of the business to Russell Palmer with
confidence that it was in good hands. Miller's trust in the young man's
competency freed his mind of some of the worry he might otherwise
have felt on deserting his office.

Good things often reveal themselves during emergencies. So it was
with Miller when his father-in-law, Judge Bogle, offered to underwrite
his medical and family expenses for the duration of his illness. This act
of generosity touched Miller deeply at the time, and he was to remain
forever grateful for it. While the Judge's financial help was not needed,
this offer served to free Miller's mind of financial worries when the
future of his health was in question. Without doubt, this freedom from
worry played an important part in his complete and speedy recovery.

Within a period of something over six months, during which time
the family lived near the sanatorium in Monrovia, his health steadily

MILLER FREEMAN

Campaign booklet used during Miller Freeman's candidacy for the Washington State Legislature told of his activities during 15 years in Seattle.

Candidate for Representative, State Legislature, on the Republican Ticket
FORTY-SEVENTH DISTRICT

improved and he was soon able to resume the regular activities of his Seattle life. In 1913 he was back at his desk, undoubtedly more willing to watch his health and to control his boundless energy.

After his initial experience with political activity as a precinct committeeman in 1906, Miller's interest in politics wove itself recurrently around his business career. Accordingly, in 1913, he ran for and was elected to serve one term in the Washington State House of Representatives. His special interest was in Seattle's waterfront growth and this concern, plus his knowledge of those particular facilities, resulted in his appointment as chairman of the House Harbor and Waterways Committee.

Seattle's harbor was confined exclusively to Elliot Bay, with only a portion of that shore developed. There was no room for the rapidly increasing fleet of commercial fishing vessels, motor vessels, and yachts. The 1913 legislative session, largely due to Miller's work, saw passage of the enabling act needed to effectuate previous legislation creating the Seattle Harbor Commission. Eventually this commission was to provide fine harbor facilities for the city.

At the same session of the legislature, Miller took up his role in the development of the cross-state highway over Snoqualmie Pass. As a member of the Highways Committee and the voice for the Seattle area interests on highway matters, he was given the task of pressing for the first pavement across Snoqualmie Pass. With the increasing use of the automobile, this link between eastern and western Washington—areas divided by the high and rugged Cascade mountain range—was becoming critically important.

Strong support was given the Snoqualmie Pass paving bill by many important and influential sources throughout the state, and it was with

To the Voters of the Forty-Seventh District

I have filed as a candidate for the legislature and beg to solicit your vote and support.

If elected I will specialize on legislative measures which are of vital importance to Seattle, King County and the State.

I am for a comprehensive good roads bill, which will enable trunk highways to be built throughout the state, including the Pacific Highway which is planned to extend from Mexico boundary to Alaska.

I will support a bill giving the state or counties power to clear logged-off lands and sell same to bona-fide settlers on long terms—thus opening up large areas of productive land in Western Washington.

Several important amendments to the port district law will be necessary. Inasmuch as I have been actively identified for a number of years with Seattle harbor development work, I am desirous that such changes as are made be not retroactive but for the betterment of the bill and enabling the present plans for creating here one of the greatest harbors in the world to be carried out without interruption or delay.

I present on the following pages a number of fac-simile letters and other data, showing that while during my fifteen years' residence in Seattle I have been engaged primarily in conducting my business as a publisher of technical journals I have rendered such services as are within my power for the promotion and the upbuilding of the interests of Seattle and the State. The showing made herewith will perhaps demonstrate that I have sufficient ability to make a good legislator—and what is most important, get results.

MILLER FREEMAN.

---

a feeling of triumph that its supporters saw it passed. But, to the amazement and bitter disappointment of many—for political reasons which are obscure—Governor Lister vetoed it. The enthusiastic mentors of the measure were stunned. The problem facing the Seattle backers of the bill was how they could generate sufficient strength to obtain the two-thirds majority vote needed to override the governor's veto. No trouble was expected in the Senate, but it was known to be touch and go in the House.

At the same session of the House, a group from Spokane was pushing for a different bill—one providing for the enlargement of the Cheney Normal School in eastern Washington. Some heavy jockeying and caucusing were carried on by these two forces, as each group energetically supported its own bill. Neither faction had sufficient backing on its own and, after considerable heated discussion, it became obvious that support of the two bills by both groups was the only means of assuring their passage. Mutual cooperation was pledged and it was assumed that, when the bills were called up for vote, the Seattle and Spokane blocs would support both measures.

The Cheney Normal School bill came up first and, with the support of the Seattle bloc, received the necessary majority. Next the Snoqualmie paving bill came up—and was voted *down,* to the frustration and anger of its supporters.

Having got their measure through, supporters of the Cheney Normal School bill broke their political pledge. Double-crossing the Seattle bloc, they voted against the motion to override the governor's veto.

Speaker of the House Sims—the same Ed Sims who had been influential in putting Miller in as secretary of the Salmon Canners Association in 1905—had become a powerful figure in Washington State politics. He was not the sort to take a beating without putting up a good fight in the process.

Sims asked Miller and several supporters of the Snoqualmie bill to caucus after the disappointing defeat. The situation looked pretty dark but, suddenly, Sims said in considerable excitement, "I've *got* it!" And he proceeded to outline a tactic which he thought might yet lead to a victory for the Snoqualmie bill.

Promptly the following morning, as the session convened, a motion was introduced by a member of Sims' team to "expunge the record" of the previous day. This, in effect, wiped out the record of the passage of the Cheney bill. Now, in their turn, the Cheney bill people were taken by surprise.

Political history boasts few such innovative procedures. The maneuver worked effectively and the astounded Cheney bill backers quickly saw the light. They threw their support to the Snoqualmie bill, and both bills were promptly passed over the governor's veto. If this particular play had not taken place, the first paved road over the Snoqualmie would not have been built at that time.

The experience was a valuable bit of political education for Miller. Perhaps the photograph of Miller Freeman, legislator, wearing a suit several times in excess of his needs, was taken shortly after this astounding success. It may have mirrored a measure of his political enthusiasm.

As an interesting follow-up to this episode, in 1914 Governor Lister was the principal speaker at the dedication of the first pavement across

Seattle waterfront in the early 1900s.
SS Cottage City *is in foreground.*
(Courtesy Seattle Historical Society.)

Snoqualmie Pass. Miller, and a good many others who had worked hard to secure the roadway over the governor's veto, listened with considerable amusement to his ringing oratory in praise of the accomplishment. But that was the way things went in politics and, so far as Miller was concerned, the political battle was history. The outcome made past considerations unimportant.

Miller toyed with the idea of remaining in politics. Following his brief session in the House he ran for the Washington State Senate from his district. He lost the election largely because he was not willing to devote the necessary time or money for an effective campaign. After this venture into politics, he settled back to concentrate on the business of publishing and never again seriously considered running for public office.

During his career, however, he showed great respect for the legislative process and repeatedly sought the support of political figures, both state and national, in bringing about legislation or applying pressure for the realization of specific goals. His brief experience with the actual working of politics served him double values: it gave him knowledge of where leverage could be applied at a political level and how best to go about using it to advantage. It also made him a friend of many men in politics to whom he could turn when he needed help.

16
FISH CONSERVATION:
A CONTINUING CONCERN

THE FIRST DECADE of the 1900s saw the beginning of Miller's active concern with conservation of Pacific Northwest fishing resources. After he had established *Pacific Fisherman*, he made it his business to meet as many members of the industry as possible and to study their problems. As a result, he became convinced of the importance of controlling the catch through voluntary action and international treaties. His initial efforts to help save a rich regional resource from destruction (related in an earlier chapter) had met with disappointment and opposition. The Jordan-Prince Recommendations to control the Fraser River fishery had been shelved in the United States Congress. Because of his convictions, Miller had been forced to oppose his friends in the canning industry on the issue of voluntary control. He had been made aware of an additional drain on the fishing resource through the activities of Japanese interests.

In the second decade of the century he continued his efforts toward conservation. He worked as he had before—sometimes as an individual and sometimes through *Pacific Fisherman*.

Once again, in 1914, the sockeye salmon treaty seemed close to passage. At the request of the Puget Sound Canners Association, Miller went to Washington, D.C., to nurse along the legislation. President Woodrow Wilson favored passage of the Jordan-Prince Recommendations and Elihu Root, Senate Foreign Relations Committee chairman, indicated to Miller that he was willing to act favorably on the recommendations. As he sat in the Senate gallery shortly after this brief encounter with Senator Root, Miller was gratified to see the recommendations passed. Since this action meant acceptance of the treaty, the way ahead looked encouraging and smooth.

The only remaining block to enacting the treaty into law was action in the House. President Wilson's signature was necessary, of course, but he had asked for the treaty's passage. Miller could foresee no problems and, anxious to return to the West Coast, he boarded the

A group of salmon canners at a 1912 meeting attended by Miller, front row, second from right, and his father-in-law, Judge W. H. Bogle, back row, third from right.

train for home. By his own admission, he made one of the major mistakes of his life. When he arrived in Seattle he learned that forces opposing the Jordan-Prince Recommendations had brought last-minute pressure to bear. The house had reconsidered and, instead of its expected favorable action, had shelved the bill. That summer war broke out and, in the fall, Canada killed the treaty by withdrawing from it.

Although it was to take another twenty-three years of slow progress to secure a salmon treaty, early in 1918 Canada and the United States made further efforts to solve some of their boundary problems. An international commission composed of federal officials of the two countries was appointed to inquire into the matter and, if it seemed advisable, to prepare treaties for action.

Previous to the international commission's hearings on the Pacific Coast, the salmon industry decided to appoint a local committee to prepare a suggested program that would be acceptable to fishing interests of British Columbia and the Puget Sound area. Miller was a member of this committee, and the plan drawn up seemed to him to have real merit. It had faults, he knew, but it was a start and to him that was the essential part of any campaign.

In the late spring, just before the full commission was to meet on the Pacific Coast, Miller was asked to be a member of an advisory committee to discuss the treaty with two men from the international body— Dr. W. A. Found, Canadian deputy commissioner of fisheries, and H. M. Smith, United States commissioner of fisheries.

Then on active duty in the navy, Miller secured the necessary authorization to attend the meeting in Victoria, British Columbia. The joint program worked out for presentation to the full international commission was not altogether agreeable to either side but it presented a workable foundation for a salmon treaty. Apparently it was accepted on that basis by the commission.

Something happened to change the commission's thinking, however, because the treaty draft that emerged the following spring was unacceptable to the industry. It confined the purse seiners to a portion of the American waters where sockeye salmon were almost never found and weighed against the fishermen in other provisions. The treaty died under purse seiner fire.

Meanwhile, editorials in *Pacific Fisherman* warned of an alarming decrease in the sockeye salmon runs. Several factors triggered particular concern over the issue. First, there was excessive fishing by both United States and Canadian fishermen, running over a three-year period between 1915 and 1918. Additionally, Japanese fishermen were continuing to invade the North American fishing grounds and were further threatening the resource.

A blockage in the river in 1913 had added greatly to the problem. During the building of the Canadian National Railways lines, the Fraser River, which is the spawning ground for the majority of sockeye salmon, had been blocked by a tremendous landslide. Earlier, when the Canadian Pacific lines were being built on the opposite side of the river, slides partially blocked the channel. The slides on these steep mountainsides were actually opposite each other at Hells Gate, where the 1913 blockage occurred. Although efforts were made to clear the river for passage of the largest salmon run witnessed up to that time, the attempt largely failed and the resource suffered enormous damage.

Keeping abreast of and publicizing details about the fishing industry of the entire Pacific Coast, *Pacific Fisherman* sounded warnings about this situation and on all potential dangers to the industry and its resource. Illustrative was an editorial in 1919 headed, "Japanese Invade the Codfish Industry." While these periodic alarms meant little to the average citizen, they were of vital interest to men in the fishing business and served as soundings indicating trouble for the industry.

Japanese intrusion into the Pacific Coast fisheries of North American territories also provided side advantages for the Japanese crews who gained detailed knowledge of the coastline. Now, with war foremost in the minds of everyone because of the European conflict, there were those who could not disregard the significance of a well-armed Pacific neighbor privileged to unlimited knowledge of every mile of North America's western coastline.

Miller often rather quizzically recalled an incident which he felt had something to do with shaping and sharpening his own objectives in regard to fish conservation and with encouraging him to pursue campaigns along those lines.

In the 1913 session of the Washington State Legislature one of the controversial fish bills was being discussed before the Legislative

A 1913 meeting of halibut vessel owners. At about this time Miller Freeman, front row, center, began to campaign for an international halibut treaty. E. A. Sims, mentioned elsewhere in this book, is second from left in back row.

Fisheries Committee, of which Miller was a member. One man after another pompously introduced himself and named the organization which he represented, stating why he either favored or opposed the bill. Each man was speaking strictly from his own or his group's viewpoint.

Finally, a slender, grizzled little man with his hair growing right down into his collar got up to speak. In a quiet voice, he announced he was Trevor Kincaid, professor of zoology at the University of Washington.

"Oh yes, Dr. Kincaid," said the chairman, "and whom do you represent?"

There was general laughter when Dr. Kincaid said, "I think I represent the fish."

Despite the laughter, Dr. Kincaid's remark had serious significance for some members of the group—perhaps for Miller particularly because of his publishing activities. He often thought of himself in later years, during the long campaigns for fisheries treaties, as the "spokesman for the fish."

In 1914 Miller was keenly interested in the problem and the effects of what he termed "the growing incursions of the Japanese, and particularly of their fisherman, in the economy of the Pacific Coast." He was convinced that one of the major reasons the Japanese were exceedingly good fishermen was because Tokyo had, at the University level, the only school of fisheries in the world which provided advanced technical and scientific knowledge to the fishing industry.

While it was true that the United States had a nucleus of excellent scientists at Stanford and Yale universities doing studies in ichthyology, their findings were of little help to the industry as a whole. Miller felt strongly that there should be an institution on the Pacific Coast

109

devoted to the biological and technical aspects of the subject—knowledge that would benefit those in the fisheries industry.

Pacific Fisherman editorials vigorously projected this view. Largely because of this pressure, positive action was taken and, by June 1914, it was announced that the regents of the University of Washington had authorized the organization of a School of Fisheries—the first such institution in the United States.

Europe was plunged into war soon after this announcement, and the United States followed suit nearly three years later. The plan to open a School of Fisheries at the university was temporarily pushed into the background as issues of more immediate importance took precedence. When the armistice was signed in November 1918, however, Miller again urged action. As a result, Dr. Suzzallo lost no time in activating the University of Washington School of Fisheries, which finally came into being on April 2, 1919.

In 1953, fifty years after the first issue of *Pacific Fisherman* was published, Miller took pride and satisfaction in presenting to the library of the University of Washington School of Fisheries the only complete file of these journals and of *Pacific Fisherman Yearbook*. The occasion was the dedication ceremonies for the school's new building. The present College of Fisheries still stands at the top of its field, having supplied men to serve throughout the world in administrative positions and in scientific study.

As he received honors at the 1953 ceremony, Miller once more took a long and somewhat humorous look at the day in 1913 when, impressed by Dr. Kincaid's remark, he had joined the professor as a "spokesman for the fish."

In 1953, the only complete file of Pacific Fisherman, *including the* Yearbook, *was presented to the University of Washington School of Fisheries. Dr. Henry Schmidt, university president, Miller Freeman, and Dr. Richard Von Cleve, school director, at the ceremony in the school library.*

17
WORLD WAR I and the NAVAL TRAINING CAMP

WHEN WAR ERUPTED in August 1914, the United States was determined to remain uninvolved in the conflict on another continent. However, as war dragged on and accelerated, the situation became more critical. Many in the United States were convinced that the country would soon enter the combat. By late 1916 Miller was among those who felt that it would not be long before the United States declared war on Germany.

Because of this conviction, in the fall of 1916, Miller offered his services to the Navy Department. He was called up for active duty two months before the United States entered the war. Miller's unit was, in fact, called out on April 7, 1917, the day after war was declared on Germany.

As the frantic war effort began, Miller was assigned to command a naval training unit preparing raw recruits for sea duty. His immediate problem was to find adequate space for such a facility. Eyeing the spacious grounds of the University of Washington, he decided that a portion of the campus would be ideal for the purpose. Miller made the suggestion to the proper authorities, and a committee from the University, headed by President Suzzallo, soon met with Commander Freeman to offer University facilities to the navy for whatever uses they could best serve. With satisfaction Miller reported this offer to Captain Robert Coontz (later rear admiral), commandant, Thirteenth Naval District at Bremerton, and was immediately ordered to establish a Naval Training Station on the campus of the University of Washington.

Plans for the establishment of the training camp quickly got under way on campus land which lay along the Lake Washington canal in the section between the Montlake bridge and Portage Bay. Besides military barracks and office facilities, a house for the commanding officer and his family was included. (After the war, this house was to become the clubhouse for the University Golf Course.)

Establishment of the camp was a big assignment requiring prompt

111

yours for the U.S.A!
Mill Freeman
april 4th 1917

organization. Miller went into fast action to set up a training center for navy personnel, the purpose of which was to assure a speedy supply of trained manpower for U.S. ships. As a businessman, Miller had had little experience in military procedures except those to which he was exposed during his very brief Naval Militia duty in 1910. He felt confident that he was able to handle men, however, and that this job needed what he could offer.

The training station soon mushroomed to include several thousand men. Organization and administration required endless and lengthy procedures involving navy red tape and much paper work to which Miller was unaccustomed and generally unsympathetic. Getting the necessary jobs done took infinitely more time than would have been required in the business world, and the endless stalling was irritating and frustrating to him.

However, he quickly gathered around him efficient navy personnel

Commander Miller Freeman of the Naval Training Station in 1917.

Air view of the Naval Training Station on the University of Washington campus during World War I. The picture looks from Portage Bay, foreground, through the Montlake section of the canal, toward Union Bay and Lake Washington.

During the war the Freeman family lived in this house, assigned to the commandant. It later became the clubhouse for the University Golf Course.

with knowledge and experience in military methods and these men were able to speed up routine activities. One particular young man, Lieutenant Stetson, was at his elbow as an invaluable help, expediting and writing requisitions with a know-how and talent that brought materials faster than normal through navy channels.

In World War I, women were for the first time taken into military service as secretarial and clerical assistants. These young women, called yeomanettes, proved to be invaluable auxiliaries in the execution of much office work. As a yeomanette, Miller's private secretary, Ann Bathurst, played an efficient and necessary part in his wartime assignment.

Despite the well-trained personnel who worked with him, endless delays brought countless irritations. Miller found that one of the hardest jobs was to proceed fast with the work at hand and, at the same time, stay within the bounds of navy regulations. He seemed to be

constantly running afoul of time-wasting details. Annoyed as he was with these roadblocks, he knew he in turn was causing headaches for navy brass hats.

Miller soon formed the habit of taking his troubles to Captain Coontz, who proved an invaluable friend and expediter. On numerous occasions the two men, by talking across the table could, in a few minutes, "reduce a mountain of headaches to the dimensions of a molehill," Miller said.

While without question Miller shattered regulations and annoyed some military personnel, it was generally conceded he was accomplishing a job that needed doing, and it was hard for the navy to argue that fact. And despite the growing pains of getting under way, the training camp was soon operating as a highly efficient and valuable auxiliary to the war effort.

Under Miller's guidance, the camp undertook training of seven thousand men in a year and a half. His leadership was needed in bringing together many forces in the community to work in close

cooperation with the overall war effort. In the desperate struggle of the nation at war, barriers were broken, lengthy procedures were shortened, and people were bound together in a swell of patriotic emotion.

While the early months of war were tense and hectic as the nation fought to bolster its allies with men and material, there was no time for relaxation. Patriotism rose to tremendous heights with rallies, war bond drives, parades, and military bands becoming a way of life. Shifting from a quiet civilian life, Miller now found himself at the epicenter of one of the nation's most vital war services. He lived at the naval base and was involved day and night with matters having to do with the camp and the training of the several thousand men who were under supervision at one time.

Often during these tense days Miller relieved tensions with humor. Always the first to laugh at his own weaknesses, he liked to tell the story that he had no ear for music and could not recognize the United States national anthem when it was played. He said that he kept Lieutenant Stetson close by his side at patriotic events to alert him

when the band played the "Star-Spangled Banner." Otherwise he might have failed to salute at the proper time.

Miller's part at the Navy Training Camp during the war period brought him to the forefront of public attention. Aside from the feverish activity of life at the training station, Miller found himself involved in many outside activities in the Northwest community. Captain Coontz gave Miller varied duties in addition to those pertaining to the camp. The commandant took Commander Freeman to all official gatherings and directed him to stand near in order to tell him the names

of local people. Coontz, a meticulous man, found Miller an important liaison to provide knowledge of the community which made his assignment easier and more effective.

One of the most bizarre experiences of the war occurred when Commandant Coontz, after himself receiving orders from Washington, D.C., telephoned Miller and directed him to put under guard the Russian merchant ship, *Shilka,* which was then tied up in Seattle's harbor.

Miller took a squad of bluejackets down to the pier, boarded the vessel, and asked to see the captain. After he had explained his mission, the captain replied that a committee of the Soviet, consisting of members of his crew, had taken possession of the ship and, therefore, Commander Freeman should do business with them. To this statement Commander Freeman promptly replied that he would not do business with the crew. He recognized the captain as the ship's senior officer, he said, and the *only* one with whom he would deal.

When the *Shilka's* captain realized that his authority was, in effect,

---

Commander Freeman with Admiral Robert Coontz, commandant, Thirteenth Naval District at Bremerton, who gave him special assignments during the war.

The camp commandant takes part in ceremony.

being reinstated by Miller's orders, thus wresting control from the Proletarian Committee, he was markedly pleased. There was a Russian guitar-like instrument (probably a balalaika) hanging on the wall of the cabin and Miller later said he fully expected the captain to "grab it and break into song."

The *Shilka*'s captain was allowed shore liberty, "on his honor," by Commander Freeman, but the members of the crew were kept on board. A bluejacket guard was placed on the gangplank to prevent anyone from looting the ship or having contact with the vessel or the members of its crew.

The *Shilka*, it turned out, was loaded with rice and other products from the Orient—plus quantities of Communist literature printed in English. On the run to Seattle the crew had mutinied on receiving a radio message broadcast to all Russian ships when the Kerensky government fell and power was seized by Lenin and Trotsky.

Four more ships of the Russian Naval Reserve were seized in this manner by Commander Freeman and placed under guard. While there was considerable debate by authorities in Washington, D.C., as to what to do with these vessels, they were ultimately released and returned to their country.

Another equally strange experience occurred when the commandant at Bremerton phoned Miller and said that a group of Japanese aviators were arriving in Seattle. He requested Miller to entertain them at dinner because he specifically did not want them to visit the Bremerton Navy Yard.

Miller engaged a private dining room in the New Washington Hotel where he entertained the group. He learned that this entourage was being guided around the United States by a Japanese named Emo Takaki, whom Miller had met before the war. Takaki spoke flawless English, but was the only one of the group who did.

Able to communicate only with Takaki, Miller asked him the reason for the presence of the Japanese aviators in the United States. Takaki replied that the Mitsubishi Company had two aircraft manufacturing plants in New Jersey and a large chemical plant in the South which these aviators had visited. Furthermore, he said, the funds to pay for the visit were being provided by American sources. Miller raised his eyebrows in surprise at this intelligence.

Takaki remarked that he had recently visited with Thomas Edison and had asked to see plans of a new torpedo the U.S. Navy had just perfected. To his disappointment, Takaki continued, Mr. Edison replied that he could not do such a thing. Emo Takaki then reported his response to Edison: "Well, you know, everybody says that one day the United States and Japan are going to war. As yours is a great sporting nation, you certainly would want us to be as well equipped with up-to-date weapons as you are." Miller listened in amazement. This was an immensely interesting philosophy for Commander Freeman to contemplate inasmuch as the United States was at that time locked in a deadly battle with a European adversary. The possible implications could scarcely be missed.

A little later Takaki said to Miller, "I know, of course, that you are the publisher of a journal devoted to the commercial fisheries. A company in which my family has an interest is preparing to build a fleet of vessels, equipped with gasoline engines, to catch halibut and salmon in the open ocean. We are thinking of making the base for this fleet in Seattle. What would you think about that?"

"This is not the time or place to discuss that point," Miller replied. "However, I would be very glad to talk to you later about it. My advice at this moment is: Don't do it, as public opinion in this country would be definitely adverse."

Not long after this episode, Miller noted with particular interest a dispatch from New York which stated that Emo Takaki had been run down and killed by a street car. A suspicion long haunted him that

Takaki may have been done away with by Japanese undercover agents for talking too much.

Colonel Clarance (sic) Blethen, well-known publisher of the *Seattle Times,* was an acquaintance of Miller's. Their paths crossed with increasing frequency as Miller became a widely recognized wartime figure in Seattle. Active in the Coast Guard Artillery of the National Guard, Blethen was made brigadier general, U.S. Army Reserve, in 1924.

During the war, Miller and Blethen often conferred on community issues dealing with the national emergency and occasionally on military matters. The two men were in all ways diametrically opposed. Miller took satisfaction in humility while Clarance became increasingly pompous under the pressures of his wartime civic responsibilities.

Miller waggishly enjoyed Clarance's vanity. Because their wartime meetings sometimes touched on military matters, it was not surprising that a personal call for Commander Freeman came through from Colonel Blethen to the Naval Training Station one day. It would be a routine matter, Miller thought, but the repercussions from the call reached unexpected proportions. Commander Freeman listened attentively as Blethen's indignant voice boomed over the wire. He was incensed about a bothersome airplane which was flying low over the city, annoying him and many others. Angrily he told Miller he had

better see that the plane stopped flying from his camp or he would order the Coast Guard to "shoot it down."

Although Miller understood him well, in sudden anger at Clarance's bluntness, he asked him to repeat the charge, which the former did with growing irritation. Promptly, and without explanation, Miller said, "That's all right with me, Clarance. So far as I'm concerned you can shoot it down." A stunned silence followed and the receiver at the other end of the line clicked down.

To his amazement, two months later a telegram arrived for Miller from Admiral Coontz, having to do with a military court martial against Commander Miller Freeman. He was, in fact, ordered to appear before the admiral the following morning.

Miller ferried to Bremerton feeling an increasing degree of concern. Arriving at the naval base he was met and promptly transported to the admiral's office and into his stern presence. After a curt acknowledgement of Miller's presence, Admiral Coontz sat silently eyeing a thick sheaf of papers which lay on his desk. Presently he picked up the pile and passed it across his desk to Miller. As Miller scanned the top papers, the truth of what had happened began to dawn on him and his face reddened.

It appeared that Clarance Blethen had raised the point of Miller's "insolence" with his own army superiors, who, according to protocol, had passed the protest up the line of army brass and hence from desk to

Comfortable quarters were provided for navy personnel at the training center.

desk across the country. Reaching the top, the complaint had then been passed to equal ranking navy brass and down the line until it reached Miller's superior, Admiral Coontz.

Miller's anger flared as he considered Clarance's pettiness. There seemed no justification for such action on a trivial matter. Nevertheless, his tension quickly began to dissolve as he saw the humor of the situation. Primarily, he realized he owed his superior an explanation. He had just heard a story which seemed applicable.

"Admiral," Miller said, "this situation reminds me of the fellow who got on a crowded passenger train in which all the seats were occupied. Finally, he found a seat occupied by a man who had two suitcases alongside him and said,

"Take those suitcases out of here, I want to sit down."

"I'll do nothing of the sort," said the man in the seat, turning back to his newspaper.

"If you don't, I'll throw them out the window."

"Go ahead, I dare you."

The irate passenger tossed them out of the train. The man in the seat said: "It's all right with me. The suitcases didn't belong to me."

Miller concluded: "That airplane Clarance was complaining about did not come from the camp; it belonged to Bill Boeing."

The admiral relaxed visibly and a twinkle hovered around his usually solemn eyes. With a gesture of resignation mixed with humor he looked steadily at the younger man before him. Suddenly, with a laugh he said, "Watch out, Miller. Don't try that kind of thing again with someone like Blethen."

And with that the case was summarily dismissed. The batch of letters pertaining to it were filed in the wastebasket. Robert Coontz had far more pressing matters before him than a stack of unfounded court martial papers.

Many years later Miller thought back on this incident. The plane that flew so disturbingly low over the city of Seattle, and Colonel Blethen's domain, had taken off from the small Boeing field. It was the forerunner of the Boeing bomber—the aircraft that played so vital a part in the winning of World War II.

While the plane in question had not come from the Naval Training Station, the base under Miller's command had also played its part in the development of United States air strength. The camp boasted one of the first air cadet schools in the country. Quartered in separate barracks, these carefully chosen trainees were given basic instruction in the assembly, operation, and maintenance of airplanes.

Considered an elite group by their peers, they became pioneers in aviation. Along with the relatively small number of other servicemen throughout the country who received early aviation training during World War I, they formed the nucleus of the group that later played an important part in the building of the first United States Air Force.

Statistics tell a clear story of the part the U.S. air force played in

World War I. With a fleet of only 55 planes as she entered the war in 1917, the United States lagged far behind her European neighbors in air strength. And most of the U.S. planes were outdated, as well.

Necessity had earlier spurred the European countries involved in the hostilities to pioneer in the field of aviation. Consequently, Germany began the war with a fleet of 300 planes, ending up in 1918 with 15,000. Great Britain's air force, likewise, grew from 300 to 22,650 by war's end.

In comparison, when the Armistice was signed, the United States Air Force could claim but 740 planes, only 196 of which were of American manufacture.

The busy aviation operation of W. E. Boeing, situated not far from the Naval Training Station, was already contributing its valuable part in the growth of the infant United States' aircraft industry.

While Miller's part in a vitally important naval war effort brought him considerable public attention, when the war ended he looked forward to returning to civilian life, and to again devoting full time to publishing. The press of those days, however, mirrored the attitude of many people in regard to the kind of job he had done.

Wing of a biplane, possibly a Boeing, above the training station.

An article in the *Seattle Post-Intelligencer* of December 8, 1918, said in part:

> Whatever the future of the Naval Training Camp on the campus of the University of Washington may be, nothing can rob Commander Miller Freeman and his faithful associates and subordinates of the confidence and satisfaction in knowing that individually and collectively they performed a difficult task in a manner which won deserved approval from superior officers in the naval department and unanimous commendation from those civilians who are familiar with what has been accomplished. Commander Freeman will not venture to forecast the future of the camp. He is pleased with the accomplishments so far and zealous in insisting upon due credit being given associates and subordinates. . . . To quote him, he said 'Don't get the impression that we have done something extraordinary out here, for we haven't. We have just moved along, meeting the problems as they were presented. . . . These men who made this camp are American citizens like you and me and the real personnel of this camp has been the spirit of the men. What success has been attained is due to the fundamental characteristics of the American boys.'

In 1919, following Miller's retirement from active service in the navy, the *Seattle Post-Intelligencer* commended him editorially. The following is extracted from the editorial, entitled "Work Well Done."

> Commander Miller Freeman, of the naval training station at the University of Washington, can most assuredly retire to private life with the consciousness of a great war work well done. It would indeed be difficult in this day of complimentary approval to do accurate justice to Commander Freeman's services, as modestly given as they were effective in their results. The results, however, speak for themselves; they can be put into statistical tables and are beyond the need of any conventional encomiums. Commander Freeman, as far as we know, is unique in that he was the only man to go from civil life to a position of such importance in the navy. . . .
> Seattle has much of which to be proud in the way of war work. But in all its many activities of a patriotic character there is none for which it can feel a greater satisfaction than the university naval training station, conceived and brought to its full development by Commander Freeman.

The plaudits were heartwarming to a man who looked back on humble beginnings. His confidence was nurtured by the accolade and he took tremendous pride in the job that had been accomplished. But without much wasted time he immediately turned his energies to postwar activities and became deeply involved in publishing once more.

After his return to civilian life, Miller was given the rank of captain, United States Navy. For the rest of his life he was frequently addressed as Captain Freeman. Miller was proud to have had this rank bestowed on him and readily accepted the use of the title.

18
POSTWAR PROBLEMS

I N 1919, IMMEDIATELY FOLLOWING the end of the war, Miller was appointed to serve on the Washington State Veteran's Welfare Commission, a body charged with the responsibility of finding jobs for returning veterans in the Northwest. At this time, when servicemen were returning to their homes in great numbers, it is significant to review some of Miller's thinking on the subject of the problems posed by the large influx of Japanese into coastal areas.

The *Spokesman Review* of June 23, 1919, quoted Miller Freeman at length following his discussion of the problem during a visit to Spokane. Pointing to the increased numbers of Japanese on the West Coast, he said that their spread in every line of business and industry had been most amazing and had brought about the closing of many job opportunities to returning veterans. He stated that the Japanese frequently operated under dummy corporations to bypass state laws; that they were leasing property on a large scale; taking over hotels; preempting much of the agricultural business; and becoming a particularly powerful business force in the Northwest.

Miller restated the essence of the Gentleman's Agreement, made in 1905 between Theodore Roosevelt and the Japanese government, when it was agreed that Japan would prohibit all immigration of the laboring classes from Japan to the United States. Miller stated that, while this agreement had in all probability been applied technically, passports had been issued in wholesale quantities to alleged Japanese businessmen, representatives of commercial houses, and students. And quite recently, he said, this immigration had taken renewed life.

He pointed out in his discussion that this colonization movement by Japan was being aided greatly by the "picture brides" whose arrival he termed a subterfuge providing technical violation of the immigration laws whereby Japanese women were brought to America to raise families. Since any children born here were U.S. citizens, the Japanese were securing a foothold for the next generation.

He continued:

> Nothing I have said is intended as a reflection on the Japanese as a race. They are not in any sense an inferior people. In fact, quite the contrary, I will readily admit of their greater industry and their wonderful powers and methods of organization. They are willing to labor hard for 15 to 18 hours a day. But Americans can not compete with them unless we are ready to meet their standards of working and living. If as Americans we choose to set as our working day only six or eight hours it is our own affair, and it is unreasonable to expect us to change our standards of work and living. . . .

At that time Miller had sent a personal communication to the Washington State attorney general in Olympia, calling to the attention of his office the numerous long-term leases on property in the state which were being executed in favor of the Japanese. He said he believed these leases were in violation of the alien property law and specifically asked that they be withdrawn.

Repeated reminders of Japanese intrusion into areas of historic American rights seemed apparent to Miller. He resented the overcrowding of public schools because of the influx of Japanese into the Northwest. As a concerned parent, he visited the Seattle School Board to protest the fact that grown Japanese, 18 to 30 years of age, were overcrowding the city schools. He cited the case of his ten-year-old son who had been forced out of Stevens School because his classroom was crowded with these Japanese "children."

With dogged determination, he pursued his campaign against the inequities resulting from lax U.S. immigration laws. He pressured to make the United States adopt a realistic law to control the flood of Japanese. Repeatedly accused of being anti-Japanese, Miller ignored the attacks and kept his guns trained on a goal: specifically, a proper immigration law. It seems clear that this quarrel was not with the Japanese people but with his own country for the laxity it had shown in facing up to this problem.

Keeping up the pressure, he sent a specific request to the House Immigration Committee to visit the Pacific Coast and to make a thorough investigation of the problem. This the committee did in 1920 and their findings contributed much toward the development of a proper immigration policy, adopted by the government in 1924.

Soon after World War I ended, the United States was plagued by labor strikes instigated by the communist elements which were infiltrating the labor unions. The International Workers of the World (a group known as the IWW) were extremists within the unions, avowedly out to sabotage industry and to weaken the country in every possible way.

Shortly after Miller was out of uniform, Seattle was threatened by a paralyzing general strike. Labor leaders announced a strike deadline and panic gripped the citizens of Seattle. It was threatened that banks and utilities would be shut down and many food stores closed, with deliveries of all commodities choked off. Union leaders further terrorized the city by using blackmail methods with promises of immunity to merchants who were willing to pay high fees to the unions in return for being allowed to operate. Fear reached near hysteria as people frantically sought to obtain basic foods and vital necessities to stow away against threatened shortages.

In the midst of the crisis the governor suffered a serious heart attack which added to the general terror and confusion throughout the state. Immediately following his attack, Governor Ernest Lister was able to function sufficiently to realize the dire necessity of action at this critical time. He called Dr. Henry Suzzallo, president of the University of Washington, and his close friend, to come to his bedside. Dr. Suzzallo asked Miller to accompany him and Miller was thus witness to a strange political happening. Governor Lister, perhaps befuddled by his illness, turned to Dr. Suzzallo and said, "As long as I live, you are to be acting governor." This designation bypassed Lister's lieutenant governor who should rightfully have stepped into the governor's place in his incapacity. It was apparent that the governor lacked confidence in the lieutenant governor, who would, of course, succeed him in the event of his death.

Assuming leadership according to the governor's orders, Dr. Suzzallo, accompanied by Miller, called on General Leitch, the commanding officer at Fort Lewis and acquainted him with the facts about the strike emergency. Leitch at once wired Washington, D.C., asking for and receiving immediate authorization to move troops into Seattle. The naval commandant at Bremerton took action to insure that ships would be moved into Seattle's harbor and wartime naval procedures would be put into effect in the city. The night before the midnight strike deadline Seattle was well armed. A state of emergency existed—with Miller again recalled for active duty and in uniform. At 11 p.m., one hour before the strike was to take effect, the ringleaders entered Mayor Ole Hanson's office to declare the strike's beginning at midnight. As the door of the mayor's office swung open the strikers were met, not by the mayor, but by General Leitch and his staff and Captain Gay and his staff, which included Captain Freeman.

The strikers, suddenly faced with a totally unexpected situation, were thrown off guard. General Leitch made it clear to the ringleaders that he conceded the unions the right to strike, but if the strikers attempted to shut down utilities, prevent deliveries of food, or in any way interfere with the rights of the citizen, he would take necessary military action. In view of the military assemblage standing with him, it was obvious that he was prepared to do so. The Communist-controlled union committee was caught completely unawares and speedily withdrew.

While this effective action had hit at the heart of the strike, general disorder reigned the following day. Instructions issued by the unions to effect the city's disruption could not be rescinded before dawn. Thus, the morning of the scheduled strike saw a milling crowd of union fanatics surrounding the steps of the City-County building and the mayor's office. Many of the strikers were known to be carrying arms, and the situation appeared dangerously explosive.

Standing on the steps of the municipal building, side by side, the county sheriff and Mayor Hanson assessed the situation and came up with an unusual idea. It is not clear which man actually hatched the plan, but it was decided to enlist the aid of professional pickpockets temporarily impounded in the county jail. These men were taken from the jail by the sheriff and were directed to infiltrate the crowd, lifting all guns and weapons carried by the strikers. They proceeded to carry out this order effectively and, understandably, with a great deal of personal enthusiasm and pleasure.

The story of the pickpockets' part in the affair circulated widely in town. With the strike threat dissolved and the citizens beginning to relax, the sheriff's act became particularly heroic and a great source of fun. While the sheriff became a hero due to his innovative procedure, Mayor Ole Hanson gained the real spotlight for the whole strike-breaking affair and, overnight, emerged as a national hero. He was soon to tour the country to receive nationwide plaudits. Arthur Brisbane, chief editorial writer for the Hearst papers, gave Seattle's mayor a banquet and actually proposed that he be nominated for president of the United States. It was a boom which, according to Miller, "soon flattened out."

IV
Business and Pleasure in the Roaring Twenties
1920-1930

19
BRANCHING OUT

W HEN THE DECADE of the twenties began, the western world still rocked from the violent dislocations brought on by World War I. American business, profiting from the tremendous technological boost which had been generated by wartime necessity, was suddenly forced, in 1918, to come to a lurching halt and to rechannel its efforts toward peacetime production. The economy seethed and writhed into peacetime roles.

The early twenties were dark days for American business. Additionally, the war had unleashed forces that fostered social change and shook society to its roots. Restlessness was in the air. The public did not settle back into its prewar pace. Vestiges of the Victorian age were laid aside, with shocking substitutes put forward in their stead. Women felt emancipated, raised their skirts above their knees, lowered their sashes to their hips, bobbed their hair, smoked, drank illicit whiskey along with their men. The waltz died and jazz took center stage.

In a move to expand his business base that preceded U.S. involvement in World War I, Miller had started publication of his third industrial magazine, *Motorship*, in 1916. Now at the beginning of the twenties, his papers, *Pacific Fisherman, Pacific Motor Boat,* and *Motorship*, were serving closely related fields.

With the sale of his agricultural triumverate, the *Washington Farmer,* the *Oregon Farmer,* and the *Idaho Farmer* in 1913, as well as the demise of the *Town Crier,* Miller had narrowed his publishing fields to those of fisheries and boating.

Motorship had been established to serve the field created by the large diesel-powered, ocean-going craft. Miller had watched the acceptance of the internal combustion engine by the fishing fleet and, realizing that commercial boats of other types and pleasure boats would soon adopt the new gasoline engines, he had established *Pacific Motor Boat*. When he saw the first diesel engines come into use on the Pacific in the fisheries field, he knew that the diesel carried a potential that would take it above the size class of vessels covered in *Pacific Motor Boat*. Accordingly he established *Motorship* and, after publishing it successfully on the Pacific Coast for a time, took it to New York.

Profit levels were spare as the decade of the 1920s began, and Miller pruned and tailored his operations to fit the times and his balance sheet. Thus, as he expanded to take advantage of a favorable business climate, conversely, in slack periods he quickly retracted in order to remain in sound financial position. However, cautious and hardheaded as his policies were, he and "Doc" Palmer were always willing to survey new fields in which the potential looked good. Accordingly, in 1920, despite a period of business depression that followed the end of the war in Europe, Miller again broadened his publishing base with *Canning Age*. Miller's contacts through *Pacific Fisherman* with fish canning people, plus his closeness to the agricultural field in earlier years, seemed to pave the way naturally for the establishment of a magazine devoted to the canning industry.

In 1922, a young man destined to play an important part in the publishing house joined the Miller Freeman organization. Lawrence K. Smith was in the School of Engineering at the University of Washington when war broke out. He left college, served for twenty months in the balloon corps in Europe, and returned in 1918 prepared to continue his education. However, getting back into engineering school looked pretty tough after two years away and he therefore considered other possibilities. Having spent several summers working in an Alaska cannery as a boy, he had developed an interest in the fisheries business. So, as an alternative to engineering, he decided to enter the newly opened School of Fisheries at the University of Washington.

Two years later Lawrence Smith was graduated in the first class of the new school and, armed with a diploma, a fine war record, and considerable fame as a Huskie football hero, he procured a job with the United States Bureau of Fisheries. His first assignment was in a Fisheries Bureau at Cook Inlet, Alaska. Although he approached his job with enthusiasm and idealism, he soon developed strong reservations about the effectiveness of the bureau's operations and, more specifically, about some of the men who headed it in Washington, D.C.

About this time he saw an editorial in the October 1921 issue of *Pacific Fisherman* entitled, "A Question of Fitness." He read it carefully and was struck by the fact that it voiced some of his own critical feelings about the men working in the Fisheries Bureau in Washington, D.C. Also, he admired its tone because it minced no words. It would without question antagonize some people in top positions, he felt.

The editorial said in hard-hitting words that the men of the United States Bureau of Fisheries had not provided vitally needed leadership for the Pacific Coast fishing industry. Accusing the bureau chief of eight years of inaction, blundering, and failure, it went on to say that, although long treatises were published on fish of the South Pacific, one would look in vain for definite information on the habits and life history of the salmon. Vital facts, essential as a basis for the regulation so urgently needed, were still a matter of opinion and argument, the editorial pointed out. There had been no manifestation of definite or consistent conservation policy toward the Alaska salmon fishery, and similar negligence was apparent in the bureau's attitude toward salmon propagation, it continued. Noting that an effort had been made of late to give an appearance of activity, the editorial found it doubtful that the constructive attitude required by his position could be consistently maintained by a man of the commissioner's temperament.

Lawrence decided that these words well expressed his own feelings and that he would like to work on *Pacific Fisherman* magazine for Miller Freeman. Because of his association with John Cobb, dean of the School of Fisheries at the University of Washington, he felt that he had entree to Mr. Freeman. Cobb, who earlier was the editor of *Pacific Fisherman*, had subsequently gone to work for the Alaska Packers Association and, when the new Fisheries school opened, had become its head on Miller's recommendation.

Lawrence returned to Seattle in December 1921, and visited with Miller Freeman in his office. Miller often recalled the stocky, smiling young man with a bearing of self-confidence, who in a straightforward manner gave his background and said without further hedging that he would like to go to work on *Pacific Fisherman*. Miller was immediately impressed with Lawrence's forceful, determined attitude, but told him regretfully that at the time there was no opening in his business.

Lawrence's reply was one that the publisher had not before heard from an applicant. It impressed him deeply. Smith said he had made up his mind he wanted to work for Miller Freeman and his publishing company, he would like to go to work at once, and he was willing to do so without a salary to begin with. He concluded with an assured attitude that he knew he could make good if he were given a chance.

While startled by the forthright proposition, Miller was increasingly well-impressed with Lawrence Smith and was inclined to believe he would prove an asset to the business. He was immediately given a desk and put to work on special assignment with a small salary. Smith was thrown on his own resources to accomplish his first job—compiling a list of all the salmon packers on the Pacific Coast. Whatever problems he may have had with this assignment, the list was published as the *Salmon Packers Register*. The success of this first directory of people in the salmon industry ensured its continuation for many years.

As Miller talked to the young man, he was struck by his likeness to Dr. George Smith of Anacortes, whom Miller had known as a boy when he lived there with his own father in the mid-1890s. Questioning young Smith, he discovered that he was, in fact, Dr. Smith's son. Miller mused further that his father, Legh R. Freeman, and Dr. Smith had

Rate card for Motorship, *started in 1916.*

been involved in an unsuccessful Alaska mining venture. Thus, when Lawrence came aboard the staff of *Pacific Fisherman*, Miller experienced a feeling of gratification over the historic continuity which this new contact brought.

Not long after Lawrence's arrival, a major decision was made by Miller and Russell Palmer. Possibilities for expansion of the business were uppermost in the minds of both men. Up to this time their operations had been limited to the West Coast, and primarily to the Northwest. However, it was becoming apparent that publishing trends would increasingly tend to include wider national industrial fields which would therefore offer good opportunity for a publishing base on the East Coast. With these thoughts in mind, they surveyed a broader field and, convinced of good business potential, Palmer moved to New York City to open and head an eastern publishing venture owned jointly by the two men.

Four journals subsequently became the foundation for the New York operation. *Canning Age* and *Motorship* were moved from Seattle to New York. The *Fishing Gazette* of Boston was acquired. *Oil Engine Power* was established as a new publication to serve the field of stationary power plants. And so the eastern venture got under way.

By 1923 a settling process in business trends was discernible. Moderate profits began to show after the lean years following the war's end. As the year 1924 started, signs of a real business boom were evident. The expansion and move to New York came in time to catch the start of the economic acceleration of late 1924. Palmer proved himself an aggressive executive, thoroughly at home in the "big time" atmosphere and fully capable of taking advantage of the tide of national business prosperity. The New York publishing branch was in running order and ready to ride the wave of prosperity of the mid-1920s—a period of astounding business affluence, now remembered as an historic period of wild, unchecked stock market speculation.

Meanwhile on the West Coast, Miller too launched on a course of expansion. He looked primarily to California for acquisitions and spent considerable time searching out and purchasing existing publications. These he established in a San Francisco office, with a manager to act as his deputy.

Miller's shopping for likely acquisitions at this time produced a group of journals in generally unrelated fields. The following were published in the San Francisco office: *Western Plumbing and Heating Journal, Service Station News, Western Canner and Packer, Western Beauty Shop, Western Baker, Furniture Reporter,* and *Pacific Laundry and Cleaning Journal.*

Apropos of his ownership of *Pacific Laundry Journal,* Miller enjoyed telling the story of his call on the president of American Laundry Machinery Company of Cincinnati, one of the leading U.S. laundry equipment manufacturing outfits. After opening pleasantries, Miller came to the point of the visit. He asked if the company would sign an advertising contract for the magazine's front cover position. The president, after some discussion, agreed to the proposition. As the interview was ending, however, Miller sensed that there was something bothering the man for he was eyeing him critically. Finally, in closing the discussion he said, "Mr. Freeman, there's something I think I should tell you. As the publisher of a laundry publication, to be wearing a detachable collar [which obviously saved on laundry] would not be considered appropriate." Conceding there was wisdom in the president's observation, Miller laughed and thanked him—and continued to wear detachable collars.

Miller's surveying for acquisitions proved a stimulating experience which produced some good laughs for him. He often boisterously recalled one approach he made to the owner of an undertaking magazine, who said, in response to Miller's interest in purchasing his book that, "he believed in riding on top of the hearse himself."

The West Coast operations moved into high gear along with all business, for when Miller's customers profited, so also did his publications. He believed in vigorous publishing, with no overspending and no money wasted on unnecessary frills. His balance sheets looked good, for in no spot is the health of the economy reflected more quickly or clearly than in the advertising market. Like a weather vane, the publishing house is often the most sensitive to variable business trends. The winds were blowing hard and advantageously all over the United States in those days, and the eastern and western publishing offices were doing well.

In an era of almost unprecedented profit-making, the stock market soared. Easy credit allowed margin buying which, for the lucky ones, made fortunes overnight. On paper, at least, many people found themselves suddenly wealthy beyond their wildest expectations. For many investors it was a business utopia with no predictable end in sight— and, in any event, very few cared to look for one.

Miller enjoyed the phenomenon along with the rest of the business community, but not without a degree of healthy skepticism, tempered with reserve. An economy so obviously overheated—a situation in which concrete values were greatly inflated and almost completely disregarded in an unreasoned mood of optimism—seemed to him subject to suspicion. The opportunities were obviously great but, in Miller's view, to be partaken of within the bounds of caution. Thus, in an era of stock market plunging, Miller remained a conservative.

Miller was conservative in other ways, too. The 1920s saw a breakaway from much business tradition. One facet of this trend was evidenced by changes in the familiar business office with its frosted glass door, bare floor, plain working desk, and metal filing cabinets. The "bare bones" look was gradually being replaced by more luxurious surroundings. And while it was still a rarity, the carpeted, tastefully appointed office caused much favorable comment and became popular with companies that could afford these luxuries.

From the outset of its popularity—and quite predictably—Miller had no interest in such ostentation. Perhaps the new rage for extravagantly appointed offices served to firm Miller's philosophy that his was basically a hard-working operation. He believed his customers would feel more natural with him and respect his adherence to a plain business office without the frills—and he continued to maintain this attitude for the duration of his publishing career.

20
CONTINUING BUSINESS EXPANSION

W HILE EXPANSION OF Miller's publishing operations in the twenties had moved with considerable energy and momentum, east to New York and south to California, he continued to call the Seattle office his major publishing headquarters and the heart and home of his business. In 1926, a vital infusion of new energy took place in the Seattle office when its base was enlarged by the founding of *Pacific Pulp and Paper Industry*—a magazine later to become *Pulp and Paper* on the national scene. Two years after this move, Miller acquired *West Coast Lumberman*. With these moves he launched his publishing house in the forest industry.

The story of Miller's beginning interest in the pulp and paper field is perhaps typical of the way his activities developed along publishing lines. On a cruise in the Puget Sound waters with his three sons—William, Kemper, and Miller Junior—in 1926, their sailing craft was coming down the Strait of Georgia, when across the water and through the rising mists were seen the tall stacks of the Powell River Pulp and Paper mill. Miller was struck by the magnitude of this display and the obvious indication of a burgeoning new industry.

Upon his return to Seattle, he and Lawrence Smith pursued some in-depth studies of the pulp and paper business. Smith did a particularly careful analysis and put together some figures which he laid on Miller's desk a few weeks later. These events and the facts uncovered set the course for the establishment of the new magazine.

In its first issue, February 1927, *Pacific Pulp and Paper Industry* ran an editorial entitled "This Journal—It's Purpose and Policy." The first paragraph stated the journal's intent "to promote the sound development of the pulp and paper industry in the West in a manner that will result in the maximum benefit to this region and the greatest prosperity to its people."

Acquisition of the *West Coast Lumberman* was timed to take advantage of a radical change about to take place in logging methods. In

PACIFIC PULP and PAPER INDUSTRY

FEBRUARY, 1927

Volume 1
Number 1

$4.00 P
Single C

EDITORIAL

This Journal—Its Purpose and Policy

To promote the sound development of the pulp and paper industry in the West in a manner that will result in the maximum benefit to this region and the greatest prosperity to its people.

This journal will chronicle the news of the industry and act as a medium of exchange of technical and practical information. Its columns will be open to all who have constructive ideas to present for the advancement of the industry's best interests.

The products of the pulp and paper industry are basic commodities in universal and steadily increasing demand. While this region is peculiarly favored in all the requisites for the development of this industry to first magnitude, it must be recognized that its products must go into the markets with those of other countries of the world, and be prepared to meet that competition on the basis of merit and price.

We have no intention of booming the industry or in any way exaggerating its possibilities. The fact is that some serious problems confront its development in this section. Those who rush blindly into it will court disaster. Large capital, and exact technical and operating knowledge are required.

We are for the promoter of legitimate enterprise. We are against the mere exploiter.

The policy of this journal will be independent, with no preconceived theories to advance.

While we will publish all matter we can obtain, designed to bring out the facts that will be of assistance to those engaged in the industry, publication of contributions does not mean endorsement by this journal of statements therein.

THE ST. HELENS PULP AND PAPER COMPANY
Opened at St. Helens, Oregon, December 18, 1926

West Coast Lumberman *was acquired by MFP in 1929. Later it became a national journal, and the company purchased its chief competitor, the* Timberman. *Changing industry patterns resulted in consolidation of the two magazines into* Forest Industries *in 1962.*

1928 logging railways were still used in the woods, and steam donkeys moved the logs from the stump to the rails. Use of diesel engines in the woods was practically unknown. Miller sensed, however, that the diesel which powered tugs and towed log rafts could be made to tug logs in the woods and the diesel which could raise anchors and haul nets on fishing vessels could also yard a log in the woods. He knew that trucks could be made big enough and tires tough enough to carry the largest log. And he realized that all these changes would mean substantial cost savings for the operator and increased opportunity for the industry journal.

At this time with the two new and closely related publications, *Pacific Pulp and Paper Industry* and *West Coast Lumberman,* Miller's interests turned toward stepped-up activities in matters of timber conservation and, with dedication, he entered this new arena. Through his papers he emphasized the possibilities of modernized production

The first issue of Pacific Pulp and Paper Industry, *February 1927.* PP&PI's *first editorial clearly stated its purpose and policy.*

which opened the way to better and fuller utilization of the forests. The policy of the journal strongly supported the sustained yield theory of forest utilization. His editorial policies urged truck and tractor logging as the most effective means of selective harvesting of the timber crop in such a way that the mature trees could be removed without destroying the immature undergrowth. Thus the younger trees, suffering less competition from the towering older growth, would increase in size and strength more rapidly.

During the business boom of the 1920s Miller decided to move his family from Seattle to the suburbs. He wanted his boys to have space around them and the opportunity of seeing nature and beauty and life beyond the city streets. The city would continue to be the place to work, but the country was the place to live, he said.

The exact location for the site of a new home had not been determined, but he was making forays into surrounding areas seeking the ideal spot on which to build.

Aboard a small cruiser on a summer day in 1927, he passed close to the shore of a wooded point of land on Lake Washington's east shore at the entrance to Meydenbauer Bay, near the town of Bellevue. As the cruiser chugged lazily along the shoreline, Miller looked long at this particular point and its wild tangle of undergrowth beneath the towering firs. As the boat slowly rounded the point, his excitement mounted for this land appeared to have all the features for which he and his family had searched. It sloped gently upward from the water, offering a broad outlook from three sides.

One could look eastward to the snowcapped Cascades; southward and across the lake to majestic Mount Rainier, and westward to the city of Seattle and the Olympic Mountains beyond.

Miller turned homeward that evening determined to seek out the owner of the property. Memorable was the hurdle of dealing with M. F. Wight, the Yankee who cherished his pristine acres on the shores of the lake and guarded them with an eagle eye from his own home on a nearby hill. When Miller approached him it was more than a simple matter of offering a price and procuring the land. Meeting Wight's price was the first step but qualifying for ownership meant that he must show proper appreciation for the prize land he would be getting.

Miller proved equal to the challenge on both counts and success-fully met all of "old man" Wight's stipulations. But upon becoming the proud possessor of the property, he was dismayed to find that a small square of land in the heart of the acreage was owned by a man on the East Coast who, when found and contacted, despite all lures, refused to sell.

Admirably disregarding what proved to be a disturbing irritant, Miller decided, after discussion with the architect, to build around the bit of foreign soil. He hoped that continued bait held out to the stub-born owner would be taken. In due course it was.

Into the house went the finest materials to make a place of gracious beauty—an English manor. Completed in 1928, the home became for Miller a symbol of all he had worked to accomplish and a perfect setting for the family he loved.

The Freeman home at Medina Point in Bellevue, Washington, completed in 1928.

21
The IMMIGRATION BILL and the HALIBUT TREATY

BUSINESS CONSUMED A MAJOR PORTION of Miller's attention in the 1920s, but momentum on his campaigns was never long relaxed. For many years he had watched with concern and increasing criticism of the United States government, as fast rising numbers of Japanese steadily infiltrated key business positions on the Pacific Coast. To quote him: "This was done, moreover, with the backing, encouragement, financing, direction, and the very real intelligence of the Japanese government." On the other hand, the United States was almost entirely indifferent to the matter, partly, Miller felt, because this infiltration was almost exclusively a West Coast problem.

Miller was particularly critical of the fact that the United States not only recognized but sanctioned dual citizenship for American-born Japanese. He believed, as did many, that these people could not claim true loyalty to Japan and to the United States as well. On the basis of these convictions and acting as a spokesman for the United States fishing industry, he launched renewed efforts to bring these facts to national attention.

In a move led by Miller, a positive step was taken when the three Pacific Coast States—Washington, Oregon, and California—undertook a campaign which was to bring about state laws limiting fishing licenses to citizens, or to those Japanese who had undertaken to become citizens. It seemed a good move, but at that time California fisheries operators were benefiting largely from "cheap" Japanese labor and bitterly resisted the proposition.

Not long after these moves on the West Coast, however, sufficient national interest was aroused to get action in Washington, D.C. To Miller's deep satisfaction, Congress undertook a measure that would forbid the entry into the United States of any alien not eligible to become a citizen. This, in effect, would constitute a bar to further immigration as our laws already prevented foreign-born Orientals from acquiring citizenship.

Following this step, Congress formulated a Japanese Immigration

Bill and, in 1924, such legislation was put before Congress. However, a particularly significant and far-reaching event then occurred. Because there had been a disproportionate influx of Japanese to the United States between 1905 and 1924, it was decided when the Immigration Bill was written, to "hold for absolute exclusion," which meant that the doors were closed to all Japanese immigration.

This decision sounded like a particularly tough and discriminating position to many people in the United States—and especially to the Japanese. Because of the strong public sympathy for the Japanese, the wording and intent might well have been softened but for an event that took place immediately prior to the passage of the bill.

In considerable anger, the Japanese ambassador, upon learning of the "absolute exclusion" clause, sent a note to the U.S. secretary of state threatening that very grave consequences would result if it were appended to the bill. When his irate communication was read in Congress, the implied threat so angered the legislators that the bill was immediately called up and passed overwhelmingly.

On May 26, 1924, President Calvin Coolidge signed the Immigration Law containing the final key clause. This action successfully laid to rest a vital concern of Miller's on the issue of the Japanese and of their unchecked immigration to this country.

It was not, however, to be the end of his deep concern over the other problems pertaining to the Japanese. The import of his further activities will fall into the context of his story in proper sequence at a later time. However, as a finale to this particular campaign, he said:

> The signing of the Immigration Bill marks the culmination of a long fight and defines definitely a policy, a proper policy, on the part of this country. The charges that it discriminates against the Japanese are untrue, in that the law affects approximately one half of the world—all Orientals . . . .
> The Japanese now legally residing here are entitled by treaty and law not only to protection for themselves, but also to engage in any occupation not in conflict with the laws of the federal and state governments. The Japanese and other aliens should be treated with scrupulous regard for their rights, and with courtesy as well. Persons who commit overt acts against such aliens should be apprehended and punished by the government.

The year 1924 also brought ratification to the halibut treaty, providing for a closed season and a research program which were to result in rehabilitation of the threatened northern Pacific halibut fishery.

Although concern for depletion of the older halibut grounds was expressed in *Pacific Fisherman* as early as 1910, the first mention of a closed season appeared in the May 1914 issue. The Pacific halibut fleet had increased steadily following adoption of the internal combustion engine. Because of this growth and other factors, the fisheries were overworked. The industry generally accepted the closed season as a necessary measure to prevent depletion of the resource. During 1915 and 1916, therefore, approval of the fishermen was secured and the governments of Canada and the United States were petitioned for international action. A bill, contingent on concurrent action by Canada, was introduced in the United States Congress in 1916. It provided for a closed season and, to protect very young fish, closure of a nursery ground in southeastern Alaska. This bill passed in the Senate but failed in the House.

An International Joint Commission was instrumental in obtaining a wartime reciprocal fishing agreement in 1918, but little was done to further the passage of a halibut treaty while the United States was engaged in World War I. Following the armistice, however, Canada and the United States resumed their endeavors to bring about ratification of both salmon and halibut treaties. The case for a closed season in the halibut fishery was presented at hearings of the joint United States-Canadian Commission, and a halibut treaty was submitted to the two countries in the fall of 1919. This proposal included a provision for reciprocal port privileges and was opposed in the United States.

The pressure for winter closure increased, however, and in 1922 a treaty draft, simplified in wording and principles according to Miller's suggestions, won support from the fishing industry in both countries.

A. L. Hager, Canadian leader and head of the large New England Fish Company, expressed some of the jubilation felt by the men in the industry—and perhaps most keenly by the publisher of *Pacific Fisherman*, who had been influencial in molding a proposition that was palatable to all. Speaking in Vancouver, Hager said, "Here we have an unprecedented situation of everyone being unanimously in favor of a conservation measure."

The U.S. halibut industry, in approving the treaty of 1922, had recommended the establishment of an International Commission to conduct scientific investigations of the resource. Always insistent that resources be studied before they were regulated, Miller was instrumental in securing the recommendation for research. Before the vote was taken, he added to the motion: "Such investigation shall be undertaken as soon as practicable." This phrase, he felt, would be of great importance to the success of the treaty because it sounded a note of urgency to override any delaying tactics that might arise.

The simplified treaty, dealing solely with the closed season and the International Fisheries Commission for investigation of the halibut fishery, was signed in March 1923. Canada accepted promptly but the U.S. Senate, in approving the treaty, added a proviso that its terms should apply to all British nationals. The Canadian government, which had signed the treaty without the Senate amendment, then passed a halibut enforcement act containing a provision unacceptable to the United States. In May 1924 the controversial matters were resolved and the way was cleared for ratification of the treaty.

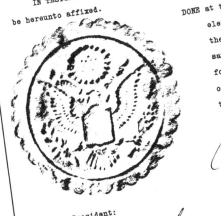

CALVIN COOLIDGE,
President of the United States of America.

To all who shall see these Presents, Greeting:

KNOW YE, That reposing special trust and confidence in the Integrity and Ability of Miller Freeman, of Washington, I do appoint him a Member on the part of the United States of the International Fisheries Commission as provided for in Article III of the Convention between the United States and Great Britain for the Preservation of the Halibut Fishery of the Northern Pacific Ocean, Including Bering Sea, signed at Washington March 2, 1923, and do authorize and empower him to execute and fulfil the duties of this commission, with all the powers, privileges and emoluments thereunto of right appertaining, during the pleasure of the President of the United States for the time being.

IN TESTIMONY WHEREOF, I have caused the Seal of the United States to be hereunto affixed.

DONE at the City of Washington, this eleventh day of November, in the year of our Lord one thousand nine hundred and twenty-four, and of the Independence of the United States of America the one hundred and forty-ninth.

By the President:

President Calvin Coolidge appointed Miller Freeman to the Halibut Commission.

The treaty between Canada and the United States for the preservation of the halibut fishery of the northern Pacific Ocean, including the Bering Sea, was ratified on October 21, 1924. It provided a three-month closed season each year and called for a joint investigation of the life history of the halibut. The commission was charged with the investigation and, following it, with "recommendations as to the regulation of the fishery that may be deemed desirable for its preservation and development."

The International Fisheries Commission set up to guide policies included John Pease Babcock, assistant commissioner of fisheries for British Columbia, chairman; William A. Found, Canadian minister of fisheries; Miller Freeman; and Henry O'Malley, United States commissioner of fisheries. W. F. Thompson was appointed director of investigations, bringing to this work the experience and knowledge gained from investigations in Pacific halibut fishery on behalf of the British Columbia provincial government.

The signing of the Northern Pacific Halibut Treaty was regarded as an historic event. It was the first independently negotiated treaty entered into by Canada and the first effective treaty ever signed with the objective of conserving a threatened high seas fishery. The document was to become a pattern for treaties dealing in these matters.

The scientific investigation of the halibut fishery covered a coast line of about 1,800 miles. It included complete records of landings and of operations at sea, with extensive information on individual catches covering every season for years back to 1906. Biological studies determined rates of growth according to locality, migrations, "races," and spawning habits.

Characterizing the Pacific halibut fishery as the greatest in the world, representing about 60 percent of the total catch, the 1931 report of the International Fisheries Commission nevertheless pointed to a steady decline in yield and size affecting both the older and more recently exploited banks. The level of production had been maintained by extending fishing operations to new areas, as the catch on older grounds decreased, and by increasing the intensity of the fishing effort. "Under the stress of this great intensification of fishing effort the abundance [amount in pounds as landed] of fish on the older banks has fallen enormously, to 16 percent of the abundance in 1906," the commission report stated.

By 1954, however, the situation had changed. The *Seattle Post-Intelligencer*, reporting a record halibut catch that year, editorialized in its August 31 issue: "Record catches are always welcome—but here is one made not at the expense of the future, but rather by accomplishments of the past. And the real accomplishments of the halibut commission can never be measured in pounds of fish alone, nor in dollars. Obviously, the attainment of this commission—over 30 years—has been this: a great resource, conserved and rebuilt. . . ."

22
A VITAL DECISION BEFORE
the STOCK MARKET CRASH

IN 1928, AT THE HEIGHT of business prosperity, an eastern investment house proposed the consolidation of several groups of
industrial publications into a large company. Miller was invited
to join and to head the group in what he said, "seemed like a very
attractive proposition." He was, by his own admission, "uneasy regarding the trend of affairs," but tempted and flattered by the proposal.
While Miller wrestled with his decision, he decided to seek the advice
of Henry W. Phelps, who was then president of the American Can
Company.

When Miller called on him at his New York office, Phelps was at the
peak of his power, influence, and affluence. As the head of one of the
greatest corporations of America, he was still a very human individual
and a firm friend. Miller told him about the decision he was facing.
Henry Phelps in Miller's words, "thought it over carefully and then,
exhaling a great cloud of blue cigar smoke, said, 'You know, Miller, I
often wish I was back on the Pacific Coast with a little business of my
own.' "

This observation helped Miller to crystallize the decision already
forming in his mind. He sold his interest in the eastern publications and
went back to the Pacific Coast. Explaining his decision, he said, "I'd
rather be a big fish in a small pond than a small fish in a big pond."

Russell Palmer also sold out his interest at this time and later
developed his own publications on national and international levels. In
the first weeks of the depression, which soon followed, the great
consolidation of national journals, of which Miller's and Russell's New
York magazines had become a part, collapsed in the first wave of
business disasters.

It is interesting to look more closely at what happened soon after
Miller sold his New York interests. In 1928, the United States
businessman was perched atop the pinnacle of the glorious economic
bubble. Many lost themselves and their true identity in an orgy of
moneymaking. The stock market gambler-plunger was proving that his

methods of borrowing and playing the market were profitable. He reveled in ticker tape wealth and his business prospered as well.

During this period, the national attitude suggested that a golden age had dawned for American society. Americans were saying, in effect, "Had not our country helped to win the war for her allies?" (And many left out the word "helped.") "Was not America the land of opportunity for all? Had it not been proven that the poor man, as well as the rich, could wave a wand and multiply his dollars by borrowing and balancing them on the stock market? Couldn't anyone? Had not America surged economically ahead of a depressed and groping Europe?"

Somehow, everyone felt, America had found the answers to the establishment of a permanently successful society. Only a few voices rose to warn of coming disaster, but those words of caution came from stodgy old men to whom no one paid much heed.

During this heyday Miller enjoyed the fruits of handsome profits without losing his general perspective. For him, it was possible to feel pride in his earning power without allowing it to sway him from a base of honest humility. In this period of the twenties while he happily rode the tiger with the rest of the United States businessmen, he applied nevertheless a good measure of healthy caution in all of his operations.

In October 1929, like a gyroscope gone off balance, the business world was flung into unprecedented chaos almost overnight. The monetary house of cards tumbled and the stock market plunged abysmally in one appalling day to presage repeated drops. The floor of the New York Stock Exchange was buried under a deluge of ticker tape as every man sought frantically to sell his stock in order to save his fortune—or what part of it was left. Everyone who owned a share of stock within hours found himself poorer by one half of the market value, and with little assurance that the bottom had been reached. Those who had bought on margin and had indulged in large investments were not only wiped out but were in debt in sums beyond their ability to repay. The bigger the "fortune," based on margin loan, the harder the victims fell. Only those who had exercised caution were left with a vastly shrunken kernel of assets.

This was the beginning of the slide which gained momentum to become one of America's worst depressions. The nation would long remember the years of economic agony which followed the first shock wave of October 1929 when America was plunged into the depths of a sick economy which affected all people and touched every facet of American life.

During the desperate period which followed the first dark hours of 1929, the national mood underwent drastic changes. People developed strong hatred for those whom they felt bore some of the responsibility for the collapse. Conversely, they flung themselves emotionally toward new figures who promised hope for relief of the national distress.

Pacific Fisherman was in its third decade when the stock market crash of 1929 brought an end to a period of business prosperity. In its digest of the years 1923-1932, the magazine's Fiftieth Anniversary Number recorded the developments of the middle years. Excerpts include what was happening in the industry when the market crashed.

Decade of Drama And Development

THE Middle Ten of *Pacific Fisherman's* First Fifty Years was a Decade of Drama—1923-1932. Starting with resurgence from the swift Shake-Out of 'Twenty-One, the business boomed through the Golden Age of the Big Bull Market, only to crash into the Great Depression as the decade closed.

Every phase of the fisheries underwent development in those days—development which in some cases was only the forerunner of decline—but the Middle Decade left growth rings on the Pacific fisheries as plain and as indelible as the annuli on a salmon scale.

Into these years was packed more of advance in fishery technology than into any other 10. The conservation based on sound scientific research had its real beginnings. International cooperation in scientific research and basic biology was initiated.

Tuna fishing shook off its shorebound shackles, launched the first clippers, and set-out upon oceanic enterprises whose ultimate horizons even today cannot faintly be perceived.

Three aspects of the Middle Decade's development stand-out:

1. *Technology*
General adoption of diesels; quick freezing; mechanical innovations, vacuum seamers, collapsed cans, high-speed fillers, casing and handling machines, sardine cutters, steam precooks for sardines.

2. *Research and Conservation*
Halibut treaty and its sequel of applied scientific research.

3. *Commercial Exploration*
Extension of tuna production; oil and meal manufacture; vitamins; ~~production~~; crab canning;

Control of Fishing Intensity Prime Problem Then as Now

The decade opened in January, 1923, with *Pacific Fisherman* sounding a note familiar through the years —familiar today: "The outstanding fact of the situation is: *It will cost considerably more to pack a can of salmon this year.*"

Things were on the move in Alaska that year. The Bureau of Fisheries announced a new program by which each cannery would be given a *permit to pack a certain quantity of salmon, using a fixed amount of gear.* This permit system developed a lot of support in the established industry, but Congress wouldn't swallow it. For all its faults, the Permit Plan recognized that *authority and courage to control the intensity of fishing* is as essential to conservation as authority to dictate *where* and *when* and *how* fishing shall be done.

The early 'Twenties were times of small beginnings. The name of Nick Bezmalinovich, "a fisherman of Gig Harbor," first appeared in the pages of *Pacific Fisherman,* where it was noted that he was building a boat to operate as a cannery tender for A. & P. Products Co., afterwards Nakat. Jack Salmon showed up as a salmon salesman, and A. W. Wittig first made the news columns as he bought into International Packing.

Term "Clipper" Was Born As the "Market" Crashed

The fall of 1929 was full of drama. A "huge merger" of most California fish canneries was projected in early September. No more was heard of it after The Crash as the month ended.

It was in this month of doom that Mexico inaugurated its bait-and-anchor licenses in an effort to replac~~e~~ the income from export tariffs lost a~~s~~ ~~fishing~~ moved off-shore.

During this period, Miller was not among those who panicked. He was, however, one of millions who saw his wealth shrink alarmingly, but who could console himself that he remained solvent due to the caution he had exercised. It was a period when those who were backed by financial security, however small, and had jobs, felt tremendous thankfulness for themselves and great pity for the millions who were jobless and hungry. Those around Miller were encouraged when he showed no signs of panic at this time. His attitude acknowledged a tough situation but clearly indicated his belief that the situation was temporary. He was certain that the country would survive. His perspective, as always, was long-ranged and generally optimistic.

Perhaps these years in the depths of the depression encouraged Miller to broaden the scope of his reading. While he had virtually educated himself through reading, at this time he chose books on history, biography, philosophy, and the classics. This activity seemed to bolster his ability to look philosophically at the dark events of the late twenties and the early thirties.

This too was the time when Miller "discovered" the Bible. He had not been a religious man but now it became evident to those around him that he was reading the Bible carefully, analytically, and critically. He seemed to discover the basic truths which it revealed. He studied it as would a scholar and his respect for the Christian tenets he found buried in the ancient wording seemed to strike a deep chord within him. He often talked about his findings in the old scriptures and marveled at the revelations that applied as well in his own day as they had two thousand years before. There were those of his family who enjoyed this late discovery and respected him more for his intellectual honesty.

As the door closed on the decade of the twenties the United States wallowed in a deep economic depression and many Americans looked with fear and dismay toward the frightening unknown of the thirties.

V

Campaigns, Controversies, and Victories
1930-1945

THE WHITE HOUSE
WASHINGTON

September 1, 1932.

My dear Mr. Freeman:

I wish to record the hearty appreciation that the whole country feels for the public service rendered by the conference in which you shared last Friday, and to express my own thanks for your personal contribution to its usefulness.

Yours faithfully,

Herbert Ho

23
DEPRESSION and the
COMING of the NEW DEAL

FATE DESTINED HERBERT HOOVER to be President of the United States when the stock market collapsed in October 1929. He had been in office less than a year, during which time the nation rode the crest of a wave of unprecedented prosperity. It is significant to look briefly at the man who became the symbol of the business collapse of the late 1920s and of the ensuing depression of the 1930s for his name would be permanently linked with these events.

Hoover was a successful mining engineer and an astute businessman. Rising gradually to national prominence he became widely recognized during World War I because of his chairmanship of relief commissions in Europe and subsequently for his work as United States Food commissioner when America entered the war. After the armistice he was appointed by President Woodrow Wilson to administer the United States relief program in Europe—one that fed and clothed many thousands of Europeans who neared starvation at the war's end. Hoover accomplished this task with speed and remarkable efficiency, thereby gaining worldwide recognition for himself and for the United States as a humanitarian nation.

In the 1920s Hoover served as secretary of commerce during the Harding and Coolidge administrations. His eight years in that cabinet post, added to his international recognition for his war work, brought him to the forefront in Republican political ranks.

When President Calvin Coolidge, toward the end of his first term of office, made his cryptic statement regarding a possible second term, saying, "I do not choose to run," Hoover appeared to be a man of sufficient stature to qualify for the office. At the Republican convention of 1928 he easily won the nomination and in November he defeated the colorful Democratic candidate, Governor Alfred E. Smith of New York.

When Hoover came to office he faced an already runaway economy. Whether he or another president could have applied the brakes in time to avoid so disastrous and continuing an economic slide is debatable. The facts are starkly true that Herbert Hoover, then, and for many years following, bore the brunt of blame in the minds of many of his countrymen for the stock market collapse of 1929 and America's agony of the 1930s.

The years 1930 through 1932 were desperate ones for increasing millions of people. The economy continued a steady, dismal, downward slide following the first sudden market jolt of October 1929. Business failures in every community across the country continued unabated and necessitated the laying off of competent men in every line of work. Young people faced the grim fact that, despite skilled training and college or university degrees, there was no work for them. Fathers and husbands who had every assurance of maintaining good earning power were suddenly faced with the bitter reality of hunger for their families and themselves.

Businessmen who were lucky enough to have stockpiled sufficient capital to carry them along, or those who clung thankfully to such jobs as there were, became universally depressed and frightened at the grim reality of a collapsed economy. A mood of hopeless and helpless fear gripped the nation.

Meanwhile in Washington, D.C., as the depression deepened, drastic measures were applied to pump lifeblood into the sick economy. The accumulation of all these efforts produced little change and the business climate grew steadily worse. As election year 1932 approached, the public image of the Republican party and President Hoover had sunk to an alarming low. As he fought to bring order out of chaos, the President was subjected to a campaign of bitter personal vilification. It seemed evident that, whoever his Democratic opponent might be, Hoover's campaign for reelection would have desperate undertones, and he had little chance to be elected for a second term.

Despite all of these facts, the hard-core Republicans and the business community clung to the belief that the President's programs, then being applied, would eventually bring the country out of the economic depression. Miller was one who believed this.

During Hoover's term as United States secretary of commerce, and on earlier occasions, Miller had frequent contact with him in regard to West Coast fisheries matters. As commerce secretary, Hoover headed the Bureau of Fisheries. Miller had specifically urged that the United States government regulate the volume of catch to permit sufficient escapement of salmon up the Alaska streams for natural spawning to perpetuate the supply. Subsequently, due to Hoover's initiative, such regulations were established.

In the fall of 1932, Hoover appointed Miller to a commission to advise him with regard to foreign depreciated currencies which were having an adverse effect on western business and agriculture. The worldwide depression, touched off by the depression in the United

States, had caused many countries to go off the gold standard and to depreciate their currencies, giving them material advantage over the United States and further damaging its economy.

Miller attended a White House conference which dealt with these and other problems facing the country at that time and was cognizant of the desperate measures the President was employing in an attempt to bolster the faltering economy. He knew Hoover to be a highly capable economist and supported him.

Unrecognized by most people, however, a curtain was already falling on a President, his administration, and a political era. A new and shining personality was already pointing the way to historic change. To many Americans, in 1932, Franklin D. Roosevelt's voice of hope in the blackness of economic tragedy seemed the only bright light on an otherwise bleak horizon.

Roosevelt, the Democrat candidate for president, offered a new approach to old problems. He promised an infusion of lifeblood into a sick economy with a set of new ideas, new social plans, the sum of which he called the New Deal. Most important of all, he seemed to dispel fear with a buoyant outlook which made people gravitate in desperate hope toward his optimism.

The hard-core Republican businessmen who had survived financially took small consolation from Franklin Roosevelt's assured declarations. In their estimation, the national ills could not be cured by

A note of appreciation from Herbert Hoover.

THE WHITE HOUSE
WASHINGTON

September 1, 1932.

My dear Mr. Freeman:

I wish to record the hearty appreciation that the whole country feels for the public service rendered by the conference in which you shared last Friday, and to express my own thanks for your personal contribution to its usefulness.

Yours faithfully,

Herbert Hoover

Mr. Miller Freeman,
Seattle, Washington.

fiscal irresponsibility and new programs which to them seemed to promise the impossible. These men listened to Roosevelt's magnetic radio voice and his hard-hitting campaign speeches. They tried to read practicality into his plans—and were chilled by his nonchalance. This man was a new breed of candidate whom they distrusted. Dark as were the days through which they were living, darker days, they said, were ahead if Franklin Roosevelt became president. As election day of November 1932 approached, the old-guard Republican could not accept the possibility that enough people would be convinced by this man's arguments to elect him.

They did elect him, however, and the morning after Franklin Roosevelt had resoundingly defeated Herbert Hoover the blow seemed more crushing to most Republicans than any that had gone before. It was, in fact, to be the final curtain for the Republican party as a major political power until General Dwight Eisenhower's election in 1952—twenty years later.

What was Miller's attitude in 1932? He was a realist with a good measure of optimism thrown into his forging. He had healthy doubts about many of Franklin Roosevelt's promises and more uncertainty about his financial responsibility. Also Roosevelt's debonair approach to the national emergency did not instill in Miller the feeling of confidence that it so obviously did in many Americans.

While Miller did not vote for Roosevelt, when Hoover was defeated he did not join with other hard-core Republicans in "crepé hanging." It was apparent that he maintained a more open-minded attitude toward FDR than most Republicans who had voted against him. It appeared he was willing to give the new President some benefit of the doubt.

An added factor contributing to Miller's acceptance of Franklin Roosevelt's presidency was the fact that he had corresponded with him during his presidential campaign, and while he was still governor of New York.

These circumstances brought the correspondence about: At the time of Roosevelt's acceptance speech following his nomination for president, he enunciated his desire to see a "federal program for the states in the conservation enterprises." Miller took particular note of this statement. He was looking for further support for conservation of all resources and specific support for the sockeye salmon treaty. He decided that the implications made in Roosevelt's speech were worth pursuing. And at this point before election it looked as if Roosevelt had a pretty good chance of winning. Things were looking increasingly dark for Hoover and the Republican party. Accordingly, Miller wrote to New York's Governor Roosevelt asking him to elaborate on his reference to conservation.

In his reply, written September 6, 1932, Roosevelt said that he believed the care and enlargement of the forests of the nation "offer a promising and profitable field for the employment of idle men." After commenting on the experience of short-term employment in forest tree

This letter from Franklin Roosevelt in reply to Miller Freeman's request for elaboration of his views on conservation led to creation of the Washington State Planning Council.

STATE OF NEW YORK
EXECUTIVE CHAMBER
ALBANY

FRANKLIN D. ROOSEVELT
GOVERNOR

September 6, 1932

Mr. Miller Freeman,
Miller Freeman Publications,
71 Columbia Street,
Seattle, Washington.

Dear Mr. Freeman:

This is the first opportunity I have had to answer your letter of July 13th asking me for a statement of my ideas with respect to reforestation for the benefit of the readers of your publications.

I have used the term "reforestation" to cover all aspects of the protection, conservation and enlargement of our forests, and it is in that sense I understand you make inquiry. As I indicated in my acceptance address, I believe that the care and enlargement of the forests of the Nation offer a promising and profitable field for the employment of idle men. In the State of New York we were able this year to give short-time employment to 10,000 men in our forest tree nurseries and in tree planting. They were recruited from the rolls of the needy unemployed. We have given work to several thousand more in forestry activities, such as trail and road building and similar improvements in the State Parks and State Forests. We have found that the work done in this way with emergency labor under competent direction is efficient and a sound expenditure of public funds. It is entirely out of the class of the ordinary "made jobs" devised to meet the unemployment emergency.

2.   Sept. 6, 1932

I think it will be sound economy for the Federal government to encourage similar activities in other States under a loan plan perhaps by the government coupled with direct assistance from the States.

In the vast national forests there is opportunity and need for a greatly increased program of improvement. This would give work to many thousands of men during the present emergency. One of the prime needs is for road and trail building for fire protection and funds for this purpose would, in my judgment, be a wise expenditure to be classed as dividend-paying capital investments. There is also in these forests the opportunity for tree planting and improvement cuttings. When we have emerged from the present depression, we will be able to do such work as cheaply and effectively as it can be done now.

Apart from the present emergency I think we need a more definite and comprehensive national plan for protecting, conserving and enlarging our forest resources. This plan should have among its objectives more effective stabilization of the forest products industry. The excellent program adopted this year by the Society of American Foresters needs to be translated into more effective co-ordinated action by individual forest owners, the several States and the Nation. We need also, as I have said on other occasions, a soil survey of the entire nation and a national land-use program. This has an important bearing on reforestation, which must be jointly a State and Federal concern, but with more effective encouragement from the Federal government than it has received in the past.

Sincerely,

[signature: Franklin D. Roosevelt]

nurseries and tree planting in New York State, he continued: "I think it will be sound economy for the Federal government to encourage similar activities in other states under a loan plan, perhaps by the government coupled with direct assistance from the States. . . . Apart from the present emergency, I think we need a more definite and comprehensive national plan for protecting, conserving and enlarging our forest resources. This plan should have among its objectives more effective stabilization of the forest products industry . . . . ''

Upon receipt of Roosevelt's letter, Miller took it to the University of Washington and showed it to Dean Hugo Winkenwerder of the School of Forestry, who was greatly interested in its implications. Miller suggested that the dean consult with other members of the faculty and that they prepare a program by which the state of Washington could take a lead in availing itself of the opportunities offered by Roosevelt, if he should be elected.

Dean Winkenwerder lost no time in acting on the suggestion. Soon after Roosevelt's election, the faculty committee drew up a proposal calling for the organization of a state planning council to study, recommend, and sponsor long-range projects dealing with conservation. Thus the state would be in a position to obtain federal help if and when offered.

Miller saw in these events encouragement in the areas of conservation, and viewed Roosevelt's stand as opening the way once more for efforts toward reactivation of the sockeye salmon treaty and hopes for its eventual ratification.

24
END of the THIRTY-YEAR WAR

DESPITE REMOTE SIGNS OF HOPE for an eventual salmon treaty, the 1930s began with a big disappointment for Miller. Sometime prior to 1930 supporters of the treaty had prepared a new agreement which Miller believed to be better than any of its predecessors. It was finally signed in May 1930, and there was further encouraging action when Canada ratified the treaty agreement and was ready and waiting for United States Senate ratification. Miller considered that, at last, the long push for this ultimate regulation and control of the mutually shared salmon resource was at hand.

Suddenly, however, events took an unexpected turn which immediately posed roadblocks to United States ratification. Trouble began when various groups within the large Washington State fisheries industry disagreed on specific wording in the treaty document. While the goals of all concerned were the same, shades of differing opinion developed over minor points. Wrangling ensued within the industry, the major issues were fogged with confusion, and the politicians, on whom success depended, alternately favored and disfavored its passage according to the variable winds of industry feeling. Finally the issue became a political ploy which no one trusted. To the bitter disappointment of its supporters, these circumstances brought about an indefinite stall on the issue.

During the political jockeying, however, Miller and other supporters of the treaty still held out hope that it would be brought up and passed in the Senate. But, on the eve of its closest point of passage, a final death blow was dealt the proposal by Governor Hartley of Washington who denounced the treaty in a radio broadcast. Senator Wesley Jones immediately took a stand against it. The treaty issues were then so confused in the public mind that hopes for its passage seemed increasingly dim.

In a last-minute effort to clarify the issues, Miller, as the recognized spokesman for the treaty, was asked to appear before the Seattle Bar

159

Spokane Chronicle *photo of State Planning Council at 1940 meeting.*

Association. While he was able to convince that group of the importance of ratification, it was too late to mend the breaks. In Miller's words, the treaty lay gasping and near death.

The political element delivered the final mortal blow by shelving the treaty in the Senate. There it lay to gather dust, with Canada deeply disappointed and periodically threatening that, if the treaty were ever brought up again and rewritten, they could not promise its passage. As had been necessary many times before, Miller and the supporters of the sockeye salmon treaty retreated to bide their time and to regroup their forces for a fresh assault.

It was two years before new momentum on the treaty was generated. In 1932, the defeat of Republican Governor Hartley and Senator Jones, also a Republican, put Democrats in these offices. Governor Clarence Martin and Senator Homer Bone were both in favor of a salmon treaty and receptive to Miller's urging for further action in this direction. Once again things started moving.

Governor Martin proved a valuable ally to Miller in his continuing fight for the treaty. Early in 1933, Miller went to Olympia to lay the proposal for a Washington State Planning Council before the governor. He was armed with the report of the University of Washington faculty group approving a planning council—the action taken following receipt of Roosevelt's letter of September 1932—and was accompanied by Dean Wickenwerder and Von Tanner, publisher of the *Seattle Post-Intelligencer*. Governor Martin subsequently supported legislation establishing the council, which was passed without opposition.

Miller was appointed to the council and later was made chairman of its Fisheries Committee. These were very satisfying assignments, for they gave him, in his words, "an opportunity once more to set in motion the machinery grinding toward ratification of the sockeye treaty." He wanted, he explained, to make progress slowly but very surely. The Fisheries Committee studied the entire matter carefully for

160

more than a year. In the late fall of 1934, they reported favorably on renewal of a project to bring about a treaty that would establish a commission for the scientific investigation of all species of salmon originating in the Fraser River system and passing through the boundary waters of the two countries. The commission would have no regulatory authority. It would be solely a body to sponsor and carry out scientific research designed to develop the facts as a basis for subsequent treaty action.

Considerable added impetus was given the issue when Governor Martin told Miller he would use the treaty as an issue in his campaign for reelection in 1936. He also asked Miller if he would personally undertake, in his behalf, a campaign for its ratification. Miller accepted his proposal, provided he were given authority "to speak for him and write for him" on this subject; to this Governor Martin readily agreed.

Miller set off the new campaign by using an interesting psychological device. He drew up a questionnaire which was sent to all organizations connected with the fisheries industry. The first question was, "Do you believe in conservation of the sockeye salmon resource of the Fraser River and the boundary waters of the United States and Canada?" The obvious answer was, "Yes." Obtaining this important answer in writing—and overwhelmingly in the affirmative—provided him with a clear declaration for the record that all who were most vitally concerned were unanimously in favor of conserving the resource. The other issues posed in the questionnaire—on which there was bound to be some disagreement—did not count. He had what he most wanted in the answer to the first question. The next step was to approach these organizations, one after another, and find out what each thought should be done about the sockeye question.

The following two years were devoted almost exclusively to efforts by Miller to bring pressure to bear in the right spots and to accelerate U.S. action on the salmon treaty. He had been given excellent leverage. He had sound political cooperation this time and the omens for its passage were good.

A move by Senator Bone gave Miller great satisfaction and touched off a final countdown for ratification of the treaty. The senator called together the United States fisheries people and he said, in effect, "Either you get together and accept the treaty as it stands—or revise it as you feel it should be to your satisfaction—and you do it *now*; otherwise, out it goes. It will be discarded and it's up to you boys when, and if, it ever gets a chance in the Senate again."

Senator Bone said that he had two hours to devote to the discussion and that treaty supporters and opponents could each have one hour. Some of the members of the group said that Miller Freeman was the only one present on his side of the matter and, therefore, should speak first.

Miller got up and said in essence: "You all know that I am here representing the governor. You all know where Governor Martin and I stand on this matter. You all know, and if you don't I am telling you now, that we are advocates of no particular treaty. We will take any treaty which, first, the Canadians will accept; second, which Congress will ratify. I do not need an hour to tell you that. So I will waive my hour and give it to the various groups here so they may have two hours in which to present their positions to the senator.''

Everyone had ample opportunity to get into the fight and a general free-for-all followed. Each representative had his own ideas and they clashed with those of everyone else on at least one point. At the end of two hours Senator Bone took the floor to point out three things made evident at the hearing: the interested people represented did not want the 1930 treaty; they had not consolidated their ideas on the kind of treaty they did want; they believed in the conservation and rebuilding of the sockeye salmon resource. He then asked the gentlemen present if they thought they could make a new treaty that would be satisfactory to the United States side and could be substituted in Congress for the present one.

The response was affirmative. The hearing was adjourned and a treaty-drafting committee was set up. This committee worked for several weeks and then decided to go up to Canada and talk the matter over with a representative group from various elements of the industry there. When the Canadians spoke their piece, the essence of it was that the treaty of 1930 had been ratified by the Canadian Parliament. It had been in the United States Senate for more than six years awaiting U.S. ratification. If it were thrown out and effort made to negotiate a new treaty, the Canadians would have a very different attitude. For one thing, they would not accept a fifty-fifty division of the run.

It had been made quite clear to the U.S. industry that the present treaty was the best they would get. When the delegation returned to Seattle, its members discussed the matter with Miller who in turn consulted a number of leaders in the purse seine fleet. Out of these industry talks emerged the main misgivings of the several groups. These points were discussed at a conference with Governor Martin, and it was agreed that the governor would request the Washington senators to bring up for ratification in the Senate the treaty of 1930, subject to the addition of an appendix providing certain restraints on the commission's authority. Under these provisions, the commission could not authorize the use of any type of fishing gear contrary to the laws of the state of Washington or the Dominion of Canada. It could not adopt regulations for the fishery until the scientific investigations provided by the treaty had been pursued for two full cycles of the sockeye run, or eight years. An advisory committee composed of five persons from each country, representative of the several branches of the fishery, would be set up by the commission.

In June 1936, within a few weeks after discussions with Canada and Canadian acceptance of the three items in the U.S. appendix, the treaty was ratified by the Senate. Final acceptance by Canada and exchange of ratification took place on July 28, 1937. The long, seemingly endless campaign for the sockeye treaty was ended. The thirty-year war was won.

Miller was to say later, "I have always felt that it was extremely interesting that the industry which so bitterly opposed and fought the treaty in 1930 should accept it with the simple reservations of 1936. Actually, the fishermen who opposed it never knew what was wrong with the treaty of 1930. Governor Hartley had put his curse on it and made it anathema. But the time was to come when they were unable to find any solid fault with it."

The International Pacific Salmon Fisheries Commission created by ratification of the treaty was charged with the protection, preservation and extension of the sockeye salmon fishery of the Fraser River system. It was responsible for investigating the natural history of the sockeye salmon, hatchery methods, spawning ground conditions and related matters.

The required eight years of scientific study were concluded in 1945. The commission report for the year 1948 pointed out that during this period a thorough study was made of the decline in the runs of sockeye salmon in the Fraser River—a decline that had resulted in economic loss to the fishermen of the two countries since 1913 of over $279,000,000 on one cycle alone based on United States Government prices for 1942.

Responsibility of obstructions at Hell's Gate and other points for the depletion of the runs was determined and corrective measures were instituted with the result that, by 1948, the Fraser River was relatively free from obstructions.

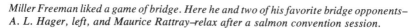

Miller Freeman liked a game of bridge. Here he and two of his favorite bridge opponents—A. L. Hager, left, and Maurice Rattray—relax after a salmon convention session.

25
In the INTERESTS of FISHING:
A LABORATORY and the BERING SEA INCIDENT

MILLER HAD LONG BEEN CONVINCED that the Pacific Coast fisheries industry would benefit from the establishment of a laboratory for the study of the resource. He had doggedly pushed for such a facility, personally interceding where he felt his urging would bring action and repeatedly voicing his sentiments in *Pacific Fisherman* editorials. No one in the Washington Bureau of Fisheries paid any attention to the request, nor could Washington's Senator Wesley Jones make any progress on his plea for its establishment. Miller was getting pretty disgusted.

On a visit to Washington, D.C., in 1928, Miller went to the Bureau of Fisheries quarters in the Smithsonian Institution. He met the official in charge and asked, "Why can't we get anywhere with this appropriation for a fisheries laboratory in Seattle?" The official answered, "That's easy, because you people out on the Pacific Coast don't draw any water in Congress."

Miller lost no time in going to visit Senator Jones in his office and taunting him with the fact that he had been told Seattle didn't get its fisheries lab because Washington people didn't bear sufficient weight in Congress. This stung the senator into action. Political pressure was soon brought to bear in the right places and, with the help of an added ally in the person of Henry O'Malley, then United States Commissioner of Fisheries, proper action was taken. Within two years, construction of the laboratory was begun on Portage Bay in Seattle.

Construction of the laboratory was a clear victory which gave Miller considerable satisfaction. He was exceedingly disappointed, however, with the manner in which it functioned when completed. It became a storm center and for years struggles for control between the biologists and technologists made the facility almost completely ineffectual in the role for which it was intended.

Finally, after 25 years of turmoil it became, in actual fact, the valuable facility and influential institution it was intended to be. Sometimes these petty internal battles were pretty disappointing to the fellow who beat his head against the wall to attain something of potential value. But Miller had proved before that he was able to wait long for encouraging developments on this and other fronts.

In the 1930s there was alarmingly stepped-up Japanese fishing activity in the Aleutian Islands, the Bering Sea and the Bristol Bay area off the Alaska coast. By 1932 there was real concern in the American fishing industry over the invasion of these waters by Japanese fishermen. Miller was approached by United States operators and asked to initiate a campaign of action against this encroachment.

He willingly consented to act as spokesman for the American industry. Worth emphasizing, however, is a fact typical of Miller's approach to his campaigns. While he felt strongly on issues and supported his opinions vigorously in his editorials, he did not thrust himself into leadership until he was specifically requested to head a movement. In this instance he had been asked to lead the fight and he mounted the campaign with energy for the protection of the West Coast fishing industry.

In 1936 the Association of Pacific Fisheries passed a resolution in which it declared that:

> The announced plans of the Japanese to exploit the salmon fisheries of Alaska on the high seas are a serious menace to the life of the American salmon canning industry in Alaska and to the 30,000 fishermen employed who are directly dependent upon it.
>
> Officers of the Association are instructed and authorized to cooperate in every way with Mr. Freeman, who has been active in investigating the Japanese situation and in organizing measures to beat it. A vote of thanks is given Mr. Freeman for the effective work he has already done in this matter, which is so vital to the future of the industry.

Miller found as he faced his new campaign that he had two major roadblocks to contend with. The first was the United States Bureau of Fisheries which refused to take any action against this encroachment with the result that its position amounted to giving the Japanese fishermen an advantage over American fishermen. The second was the Institute of Pacific Relations, an organization that advocated close ties between the United States and Japan and, as a result, favored the mutual sharing of resources. The philosophies of this group were, in fact, gaining disturbing national favor at that time.

Miller, thoroughly frightened by the aims of the IPR, became a member in order to better follow what went on in its inner circles. With its purposes clearly revealed, he was increasingly convinced that its attitudes amounted to dangerous complicity with Japan and were a distinct threat to the American fishing industry and to the United States as well.

While Miller believed that those who led and directed the activities of the institute were, for the most part, citizens of sincere goodwill, he considered that they were thoroughly misled and were dangerously misleading American thinking. He was convinced that their philosophies and pronouncements were opening the way for activity by forces dedicated to the undermining of United States strength. (It is fair to say that subsequent Federal Bureau of Investigation studies of this organization, and of others like it, proved his assessment to be correct.)

At that time Miller launched strong attacks against the IPR in an attempt to alert people to the dangers inherent in its policies. He was considered by many to be a reactionary because of his outspoken warnings against those in his country who would "give away all" for the sake of peace and thus, in his opinion, weaken the United States.

Despite his editorial attacks on the organization of which he was a part, Miller attended, in 1936, a memorable meeting of the Institute of Pacific Relations held in Yosemite National Park, California. Miller seethed as Japan's Seiji Konda called specifically for "international action to define the positions of the two countries with respect to division of the fisheries of the eastern Bering Sea." Miller was infuriated by the naivete of the institute leadership which countenanced such a proposition to share an American resource.

He often recalled a luncheon meeting during this session, which he attended as a reluctant and critical member of the institute. Sitting next to Konda, Miller expressed some of his feelings on the subject of these particular waters of Alaska, implying that he saw no reason for such international action on the matter of Japanese rights in an area clearly under United States jurisdiction. Konda turned to Miller and said, "Apparently you, Mr. Freeman, feel that each fish in these waters has the stars and stripes emblazoned on its tail." Miller, with a cold glint in his gray eyes, replied, "It is certain, Dr. Konda, that they do not bear the Rising Sun."

Now thoroughly alerted to Japan's intentions and alarmed by them, representatives of the American fishing industry—and particularly its Joint Committee for the Protection of Pacific Coast Fisheries, with Miller as its chairman—applied continued pressure on government officials to review the situation. The Joint Committee had been organized by representatives of the union, fishermen, vessel owners, and cannery operators in the Alaska salmon industry; and its effectiveness in the 1930s was in a measure responsible for development of the Pacific Fisheries Conference in the 1950s.

In November 1937, as a direct result of the Joint Committee's work, the United States Department of State released the Cordell Hull Doctrine, enunciated in a letter to the Imperial Government of Japan. This doctrine said, in effect, that after reviewing the facts of salmon biology, their relation to a home stream, their rearing in lakes within national jurisdiction, the huge sums which had been spent in Alaska for the protection and propagation of the salmon, and the importance of the resource to Alaskans and their economy, "the American government believes that the rights or obligation to protect the Alaska salmon fisheries is not only overwhelmingly sustained by the conditions of their development and perpetuation, but that it is a matter which must be regarded as important in the comity of the nations concerned."

It was regarded as a partial victory when, in March 1938, the government of Japan announced the suspension of its "survey" of Bristol Bay; further, that it would license no vessels to fish for salmon in those waters and was prepared to punish any vessel that might do so.

At this time Miller was also deeply concerned about Russia's aggressive activities. In the mid-1930s he saw both Japan and the USSR as very real threats to the United States. He sometimes saw—and more often carried on correspondence with—an old friend of the early days in Seattle. John Kingsbury was an intellectual who, in Miller's words, had "gone off the deep end and become starry-eyed over the great Russian experiment." The two grappled with their differences at their rare meetings, since Kingsbury had moved to New York, and their friendship had become strained.

In a letter to John Kingsbury a year and a half after the meeting of the IPR in Yosemite, Miller alluded to a significant substitution of words in the new USSR Constitution. He wrote:

> You highly endorsed the new constitution adopted by the USSR. A copy of this was given to me by Vladimir Romm, who attended the Institute of Pacific Relations session at Yosemite in 1936. Romm, by the way, has been exiled or shot—perhaps because he was seen talking to me.
>
> The constitution gives the right of free speech, freedom of the press, and freedom of assemblage, which does not seem to be working very well in that country. Why?
>
> When Karl Marx laid down his doctrine in 1848, he included the declaration as a fundamental principle of the totalitarian state that: "From each according to his capacity; to each according to his needs."
>
> In the new Russian constitution, this has been changed to read: "From each according to his ability: to each according to his work."
>
> This seems to me to be convincing evidence that after twenty years the effort to establish the idealistic social system has failed because of the human element. Substitution of the word "capacity" for "ability": also the word "work" for "need" means, in my opinion, that they are getting down to realities.
>
> I suggest you think about what would happen to the New Deal if it adopted this plank of the Russian constitution.

26
On the PUBLISHING FRONT

MIDST CONTINUED CAMPAIGNS, controversies and a few victories, the publishing house rode out the hard times of the 1930s with an able crew to carry on effectively during the publisher's many absences. However, while Miller was working on projects which did not pertain directly to the running of the business, he was not long away from his Seattle headquarters at 71 Columbia Street. He maintained as regular a schedule of office hours as he found possible. Affairs were always kept under his watchful eye during the rough years of the thirties.

Like a turtle under attack, Miller reacted to hard times by pulling in and presenting an invulnerable shell which the wages of economic misfortune could not penetrate. By reducing salaries and ruthlessly cutting all extraneous expenditures, he maintained the important nucleus of his business, for its benefit and for that of his customers and readers, as well. And, most important, he was free to use his editorials as projected arms, valuable in the pursuit of his campaigns.

By 1939, however, the climate for expansion began to appear more encouraging and the publishing house looked carefully at another basic resource industry. In recent years mining operations had mushroomed in the West. In-depth studies showed that there were as many as 8,000 mining operations throughout the eleven western states. And while there were national mining magazines and a regional published in Arizona, it appeared there was potential for another journal to serve the western field. The decision was soon made to establish *Mining World*. With its first issue in July 1939, the organization branched out to serve another industrial field.

In 1944 Miller became aware that regional publications were showing less favorable prospects. The war, he said, had "flattened the Rocky Mountains as an economic barrier dividing the country." He began to think in terms of strengthening some of his magazines by converting them to national journals. Accordingly, at that time *Marine Journal, Log, Pacific Pulp and Paper* (which became *Pulp and Paper*),

With establishment of Mining World *in 1939, MFP entered another industrial field. First published as a regional, then as a national journal, it was sold in 1963 and was renamed* Metal Mining & Processing *in January 1965.*

NOVEMBER, 1941

West Coast Lumberman (which became *Lumberman*), and *Mining World* went national. A New York office was opened to handle business for this group.

Those journals which served West Coast industries remained unchanged and included: *Pacific Fisherman, Pacific Motor Boat, Western Canner and Packer, Pacific Laundry and Cleaning Journal,* and *Service Station News* (later renamed *Western Automotive Service*).

As a member of the Washington State Planning Council, one of Miller's most spirited contacts with an agency of the federal government took place during the summer and fall of 1940. The controversy centered

Soon after Mining World *was launched in 1939, Miller Freeman and his sons study the cover design. Standing from left: William, Kemper and Miller Junior.*

around two divergent philosophies about the conservation of natural resources.

To reiterate, the Washington State Planning Council was first established as a direct result of Miller's correspondence with Franklin Roosevelt just prior to the latter's election in 1932. That body was established to study and to recommend in an impartial spirit those long-range steps designed to best protect and preserve the natural resources of the state of Washington. The men appointed to the council by Governor Martin represented citizens of high repute whose interests were above prejudice or sectionalism.

Largely because of Roosevelt's interest in conservation, there was pending in the late 1930s national legislation which would vastly enlarge the amount of timber land to be taken over and converted to National Parks. Roosevelt had appointed Harold L. Ickes as his secretary of the interior and, in this capacity, it was Ickes' job to recommend such action as he felt advisable along these lines.

Ickes had been an aggressive Chicago politician before this assignment and he had assumed the new job with eager determination. In the interest of conservation, he believed it was imperative for the federal government to insert its power into that of the states in order to preempt and set aside valuable forest lands to permanently protect them from commercial uses. The economics resulting from this policy as it applied to the states affected seemed of little importance to him.

Since timber is one of Washington's vital industries, there was general concern when it became apparent that two enormous sections of timberlands in the state were under scrutiny by Ickes and the Interior Department. And when area maps were made available showing the extent of the lands that might ultimately be locked away under Federal Park jurisdiction, public apprehension increased.

Most of the designated area was already federally owned land which allowed multiple use—notably different from land under Federal Park jurisdiction which allowed only recreational uses. Therefore, to declare these lands national parks meant that they would be unavailable for commercial uses. They could not be utilized for irrigation, power generation, grazing, or timber cutting—all vital resources of the state of Washington. Such a program, if put into effect, would clearly spell economic disaster.

The governor and many state authorities viewed the threatened federal land takeover with considerable alarm. Almost immediately the Washington State Planning Council was assigned the task of making a thorough study of the full implications of such legislation and to present recommendations on these matters.

After months of exhaustive study and with careful consideration of all aspects of the problem as it related to conservation and to the basic economic needs of the state, that body presented a lengthy report to the governor. The effect of the findings as relayed to the Interior Department, and to Ickes specifically, was to say "hands off."

The fireworks began when the essence of the findings of the Washington State Council were reported in the July 1940 issue of *Mining World* under an editorial entitled "Conservation—Should it Serve—or Only Save?" This was followed by an exchange of letters (all reproduced in subsequent issues of the magazine) between Miller Freeman and Interior Secretary Harold Ickes. *West Coast Lumberman* also reported the findings of the State Planning Council in August 1940. It followed up in November with "Ickes Olympic Dictator," commenting on the effect of federal policies on the Olympic National Forest.

On August 7, 1940, *Mining World* received an angry letter from Ickes, suggesting that, before printing its "obviously biased attack upon the Department of the Interior," the magazine "might have attempted to ascertain the facts" from any authorized representative of the Department. "You might have asked the Washington State Planning Council to let you read the material presented by the National Park Service, which the Council had buried in its files, while giving publicity to a theme to which it was already committed. . . ," Ickes continued.

The result of this communication was to insult and infuriate the members of the Washington State Planning Council as well as Miller Freeman, the publisher of *Mining World* and *West Coast Lumberman*

Reprint of a story run during Ickes-Freeman controversy on national parks.

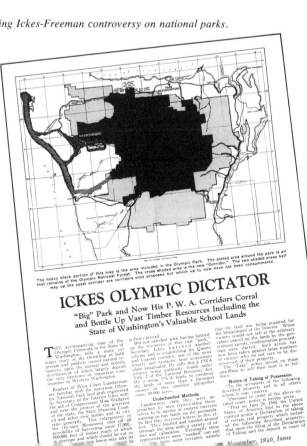

and a leading conservationist. In answering Ickes, Miller said, in part, "We shall not reply to, nor resent, the charge of 'Sectionalism, sensationalism and inaccuracy' which you lay against this journal, but we do resent and resist your castigation of the Washington State Planning Council and the special advisory committee for its Cascades Mountain Study. You typically attribute roguery to those who have the temerity honestly to disagree with you." (The *Mining World* editorial, the article, Ickes' letter, and Miller's answer are reproduced in whole or in part at the end of this chapter.)

Three final communications brought a truce. Miller sent copies of his correspondence with Ickes to President Roosevelt, asking for his "careful examination." The President, in his reply, said that he failed to see wherein enactment of H.R. 9351 to amend the Antiquities Act "would threaten forestry lands. The President has had the authority to remove lands from the national forests since 1897, and there are more national forests today than ever before."

In acknowledging the President's letter, Miller commented, "I am impressed by your statement that 'The bill to amend the Antiquities Act, if enacted into law, would provide that the public reservations established by the President, under that authority would be open to public water conservation projects, prospecting and mining, grazing, and hunting in accordance with State and Federal laws.' Your interpretation that such multiple use would be mandatory rather than permissive is most reassuring." Refusing to back down on the objectivity of the Washington State Planning Council study, however, Miller said, "In all honesty and sincerity, I maintain that the Cascade Mountains Study . . . conformed in fact with the highest standards of objective study. The Secretary of the Interior disagrees, evidently because the conclusions of the Council run counter to his personal policy." He concluded by suggesting that the time was ripe for re-enunciation of national policy touching conservation and the public domain, and by listing a four-point policy which he termed "sound" and "simply stated."

Miller Freeman with staff members attending a Seattle conference in 1944. From left: (seated) Nard Jones, Lawrence K. Smith, Miller Freeman, W. E. Crosby, Stedman H. Gray, (standing) Miller Freeman, Jr., Max Holsinger, Stuart F. Leete, David Pollock, John L. Parker, Arthur W. Ponsford, Albert W. Wilson, Carlton Hillyard, J. B. (Ole) Olson, Daniel L. Pratt, Charles L. Shaw, DeWitt Gilbert, Karel A. Wegekamp, Chester A. Fee, and J. R. H. Cruickshank.

Correspondence between Miller Freeman and Interior Secretary Ickes was reprinted in Mining World, *whose July 1940 editorial and report started it. Ickes' letter protesting the journal's position appeared in September. . .*

Mr. Ickes Would "Liberate" the Cascades By Bringing Them Under His Dictatorship

THE SECRETARY OF THE INTERIOR
WASHINGTON

Mining World,   Aug. 7, 1940.
71 Columbia Street,
Seattle, Washington

Gentlemen:

I have received a copy of the July issue of "Mining World." On page one of this issue I note that "Mining World" devotes itself to its field "without sectionalism, without sensationalism, and with scrupulous regard for accuracy." Thirty pages later I come to an article entitled "Conservation — Should it Serve — or Only Save?" which is composed chiefly of sectionalism, sensationalism, and inaccuracy.

I suggest that before you printed this obviously biased attack upon the Department of the Interior you might have attempted to ascertain the facts from any authorized representative of the Department. You might have asked the Washington State Planning Council to let you read the material presented by the National Park Service, which the Council buried in its files while giving publicity to a theme to which it was already committed. If you had made inquiry you would have found newsworthy facts.

You would have found that in the early stages of the study the Planning Council held seven public mass meetings to pass public judgement on a park proposal which had not been made, and in the light of facts which had not been ascertained. You would have found that after this park proposal had served its purpose in arousing public apprehension, the Council then broadened the scope of its study to include a general inventory of the resources and potentialities of five National Forests in the Cascade Range, and concluded that since those five national forests as a whole, had extensive resources and potentialities no area therein could be considered for national park status. The council now cites the sentiment of the seven mass meetings as evidence of the soundness of its position.

Had you made inquiry, you would have found that the Planning Council asked the National Park Service for policy statements, which statements were supplied by Superintendent Tomlinson of Mount Rainier National Park and by the Director of the Service. The Council ignored these official statements of policy and used instead its own statement of National Park Service policies, even after the Park Service had notified the Council that the Council's statement was inadequate. The Council included in its report a national forest policy statement which was largely prepared by the Forest Service.

Your readers would have been interested in knowing that I authorized the Park Service to state that if the study should result in recommending an area for park status that included important mineralized zones, I would be willing to recommend to the Congress that prospecting and mining be continued. That assurance was given in complete candor. How could it possibly be construed as a threat to mining? Yet, both the Council and your magazine played down my statement, and you informed your readers that this Department's "ambitions threaten to close important areas to prospecting and mining."

You also did your readers a disservice when you further elaborated the Planning Council's fantastic statements about H. R. 9351, a bill to amend the Antiquities Act. That bill contains no new authority for the President; it actually restricts existing authority. If the bill were passed, the reservations that the President would be authorized to establish under it would be less restrictive than the national monuments that he can now establish under the Antiquities Act. If the bill were passed, the President would no longer have authority to establish national monuments, which are closed to mining, closed to water conservation projects, and to hunting; under the amended act, he would have authority only to establish recreational areas, in which prospecting and mining, water conservation projects, hunting and grazing would be permitted. The purpose of the bill is to permit the recognition and to integrate the development of outstanding recreational resources with the development and use of certain other resources in the same areas. The bill rightly provides no authority for logging in such areas, because the management of timber producing lands is already the responsibility of established Federal agencies.

The authority that the President has to eliminate lands from national forests, and that you view with such alarm in connection with this bill, he has had for forty-three years. He has had, also, authority under the Antiquities Act to remove lands from national forests and to establish them as national monuments since 1906, or for thirty-four years. Those powers of the President exist whether this bill is enacted or not. The real question involved in the bill is a very simple one: do you want recreational reservations set up by Executive Order that are closed to prospecting and mining, water conservation projects, hunting, and grazing, or do you want them open to these activities?

There are undoubtedly areas in the High Cascades that are primarily recreational, and that cannot justifiably be classified as timber producing lands. Even the State Planning Council admits this in a modest statement tucked away on page fourteen of its report, where it says:

> "In addition to its national parks, comprising more than 1,140,000 acres, Washington has 1,207,-694 acres within the national forests of the Cascade Mountains dedicated by executive order primarily to recreational uses."

The purpose of the study, of course, was to determine how these and similar lands might best be used, but at no time could the Council bring itself to the collection and analysis of facts pertaining to the point because it was so captivated by its symphonic development of the multiple-use theme.

If you had taken the trouble to analyze for your readers the meaning of this term "multiple use," you would have found that it is a meaningless expression. It is definitive of nothing. Its conflicting promises are as subject to question as are the promises of any patent medicine that claims to cure all ills. What conflicts will be resolved by repeating multiple-use platitudes? Any land use may be said to be a multiple use or a single use, depending upon one's point of view, but whether land use is called multiple or single is of no consequence. The main problem in land planning is to determine the most profitable use or combination of uses to which an area may be put. If there is to be profitable management, the area must be devoted to its dominant use or uses, and the extent and kind of subordinate uses must be gauged accordingly.

How best can the great scenic areas of the Cascade Range be used? That is the problem that the Washington State Planning Council had before it when it undertook the Cascade Mountain Study, but its final report throws no light on the question. The broad generalities and fine-sounding assumptions between the report's imposing covers have very little to do with the case. We may as well face the unpleasant fact that the "study" was not a study at all. It was merely a smoke screen to cover a dilatory maneuver. It produced fifty-six pages of nothing new.

Mount Baker, Glacier Peak, Mount Adams, Mount Saint Helens, Mount Hood, and the scenic wilderness areas of the High Cascades are national recreational resources. They cannot profitably be considered as timber producing, or forestry, lands. They should in fact be established as National Recreational Areas, to be administered, like Boulder Dam National Recreational Area, by the one authorized recreational agency of the Federal Government. In this liberal type of recreational reservation prospecting and mining, water conservation projects, and grazing should be permitted, and hunting in accordance with State and Federal laws.

For years the scenic resources of the Cascade Mountains have been subordinated under a land management system that did not dare to recognize one resource above another. Establishment of National Areas will liberate these outstanding resources, to the benefit of both the State and the Nation.

Sincerely yours,

(Signed)   HAROLD L. ICKES
Secretary of the Interior.

Miller Freeman's reply to Harold Ickes also appeared in September . . . with a letter to FDR and reprint of the piece that started the exchange.

MINING WORLD
Miller Freeman Publications
71 Columbia Street

Seattle, Wash.
Aug. 20th, 1940

Mr. Harold L. Ickes
The Secretary of the Interior
Washington, D. C.

Dear Mr. Secretary:

We have your letter of August 7th in which you comment at some length upon the article headed "Conservation — Should it Serve, or Only Save?" in the July issue of MINING WORLD.

We shall not reply to, nor resent, the charge of "Sectionalism, sensationalism and inaccuracy" which you lay against this journal, but we do resent and resist your castigation of the Washington State Planning Council and the special advisory committee for its Cascade Mountains Study.

You typically attribute roguery to those who have the temerity honestly to disagree with you.

The writer of this letter has served as a member of the Washington State Planning Council from the time of its creation six years ago. It is a non-partisan, non-salaried body, composed of men of high character and intelligence — men far above the petty lack of principle which you imply.

You accuse the Council of having ignored an official statement of National Park Service policy which it requested. I wonder if you know this official statement of policy was received by the State Planning Council in exactly nine days less than six months after it had been formally requested. Moreover, the National Park Service statement omitted any reference to "national recreational areas", an element of its program to which you point in your letter.

For these reasons, the Council and its committee rejected the official statement of policy as inadequate and used its own well-considered statement.

People of the West know that National Park Service policies are better expressed by present evidence and the record of historic fact than by statements composed to conform to current expediency.

You point out in your letter that you had given a pledge, hedged by conditions, that you would recommend to Congress that prospecting and mining be permitted in Cascade lands given national park status.

Frankly, the people of the West have no faith in such pledges, whether they be made by yourself or the National Park Service.

Still fresh in memory is such a pledge, given at the time the Rainier National Park was created, only to be rescinded later by obscure and unheralded legislation.

You quibble about portions of the Cascade Mountains national forests which "cannot justifiably be classed as timber producing lands", and overlook the evident desire of the National Park Service to escheat to itself vast regions which cannot justifiably be classed as possessing the unique characteristics for which national park treatment is desirable.

The Western states prefer that the enormous areas of the public domain within their borders be administered by the Forest Service rather than the National Park Service because the former has shown willingness to permit true public use of the public domain; to permit people to work, as well as play on it; to permit men to earn, as well as spend on it.

You say the term "multiple use" is a "meaningless expression . . . . definitive of nothing". Perhaps that is true in Chicagoanese, but to us in the West, as applied to the public lands it means employment of those lands for the benefit of Americans just as fully as is consistent with sound conservation of their resources.

Conservation has been defined as meaning "wise use". We conceive wise use of the public lands to include logging of ripe timber on a sustained yield basis; prospecting and mining of mineral deposits; grazing in such manner as to preserve the pastures; utilization of water for power and irrigation; enjoyment of their recreational aspects in full measure.

To the West, wise use of the public domain does not mean its dedication solely to recreation, save for those rare portions whose character specially recommends such treatment.

We will stand on the conclusions of the Washington State Planning Council that the Cascade Mountains do not come within this category.

Mr. Ickes, we wonder if since becoming Secretary of the Interior you have read the Parable of the Talents and have considered Christ's view of hoarding, compared with utilization, expressed in this parable?

You may remember that the "wicked and slothful servant" only saved the talent with which he had been entrusted; but the "good and faithful servant" employed his talents and increased them — put them to "multiple use", if you will.

It seems to us that this parable applies to public servants and the public domain with singular directness.

Very truly yours,
MILLER FREEMAN
Publisher.

WASHINGTON STATE PLANNING COUNCIL
Aug. 22nd, 1940.
Hon. F. D. Roosevelt, President
Washington,
D. C.

Dear Sir:

Your careful examination is requested of the enclosed letter from Secretary Ickes and my reply.

As a publisher of industrial journals, I have been for many years actively interested in the conservation and wise utilization of the resources of this region.

I am enclosing copy of a letter you wrote me Sept. 6, 1932, outlining your ideas on a national conservation program in which you said:

"This must be jointly a State and Federal concern, but with more effective encouragement from the Federal Government than it has had in the past."

Shortly after receipt of this letter I initiated the movement to create the Washington State Planning Council, which has now been in existence for more than six years. No planning body in the union has a finer record of achievement in a like period of time.

We certainly haven't had any encouragement whatever from Secretary Ickes.

The irony of all this is that while the Council has devoted itself so largely toward coordination of efforts of the State and Federal Government, it is the subject of condemnation and vilification by Mr. Ickes in language unworthy of a member of the Cabinet.

After you have examined the matter, I would be glad to hear your present views in the light of these developments by which it seems plain that the Secretary of the Interior entirely ignores State interests, and is attempting to arbitrarily enforce Federal Dictatorship. Do you support his position? If so, you might as well abolish the State Planning Boards, as their further continuance would be futile.

Yours respectfully,
MILLER FREEMAN

Conservation—
Should it Serve—or Only Save?

THE ambition of the National Park Service, Department of the interior, and its long-standing feud with the Forest Service, Department of Agriculture, for decades have threatened Western states, their cities, their agriculture and their natural resource industries.

Under Secretary Ickes, the National Park Service has assumed a more trenchant attitude, has already completed two notable conquests, and today moves steadily toward still more ambitious projects.

The Olympic Peninsula of Washington and the Kings River Canyon of California have been made national parks. In each case active protest against at least some elements of the projects have been made by the states concerned, but ignored. These protests essentially have maintained that the parks created have embraced enormous areas which have not the unique natural characteristics for which national park treatment is desirable.

Regardless of these protests, the two parks have been created. Prospecting, mining, logging, grazing, irrigation diversions, power development, flood control works, municipal and industrial water systems are forever excluded from their confines.

The National Park Service has still more ambitious projects afoot, including the Snake River Canyon with its enormous power possibilities, its mineral probabilities, and its present importance for grazing.

Overshadowing and dwarfing all other National Park Service ambitions, however, is the proposal that the heart of the Cascade Range north and south through the entire State of Washington be constituted as a national park. The exact boundaries of this project have never been delineated, but recently the National Park Service Cascades Committee, consisting of five representatives of the National Park Service, issued a report recommending that six areas approximating 1,775,000 acres, and four additional areas of undetermined size be transferred from the Forest Service to the National Park Service.

The Washington State Planning Council has prepared a report of its Cascade Mountains Study. The council is headed by B. H. Kizer of Spokane as chairman, and includes eight other outstanding citizens of the state—men whose honesty, breadth of vision and public-mindedness is above criticism. In its study of the entire Cascade Ridge the council was assisted by an advisory committee headed by R. E. McConnell, president of the Central Washington College of Education at Ellensburg, and including four other citizens of high character representative of the regions most directly affected by the Cascade Park proposal.

Although the report deals strictly with the Cascade project and the State of Washington, the council's findings and recommendations apply in large degree to all Western states, and directly to those where National Park Service ambitions threaten to close important areas to prospecting and mining.

Inasmuch as these findings and conclusions are cogent and applicable to all mining states, they are here reproduced with very slight condensation.

Roosevelt's reply to Miller Freeman . . . and Miller's letter expressing gratification at the President's support of a multiple-use program.

THE WHITE HOUSE
Washington

September 19, 1940

Mr. Miller Freeman,
   Publisher, Mining World,
      71 Columbia Street,
         Seattle, Washington.

My dear Mr. Freeman:

    I have received your letter of August 22 with several enclosures concerning an article which you published, entitled, "Conservation—Should it Serve—or Only Save?"

    Your article is a warning to your readers and "to all mining States" that Secretary Ickes' "ambitions threaten to close important areas to prospecting and mining." Your article also states that if a bill (H.R. 9351) to amend the Antiquities Act is enacted into law "it would be possible for the President of the United States, 'in his discretion,' to transfer virtually any or all of the (national forests in the Western States) from National Forest to National Park status, removing them forever from prospecting, mining, or other use of their resources . . ." and that "the states concerned might never know of the contemplated action before it had been taken." Your article presents these warnings as the "findings and conclusions" of an unbiased study recently made by the Washington State Planning Council.

    Secretary Ickes pointed out in replying to you that the Council, as a part of its study, held public hearings to pass judgment on a park proposal before the facts had been ascertained; that the Council requested material from the Department of the Interior and then refused to publish it, whereas it published copiously from other sources; and that, during the study, members of the Council spoke at public meetings against park status for any additional area in the Cascades. The Secretary further pointed out that he had given assurances that if important mineralized areas were recommended for park status, he would support appropriate legislative measures to permit the continuation of prospecting and mining, if a national park were established.

    In replying to Secretary Ickes, you, as the founder and a charter member of the Washington State Planning Council, state that you ignored his pledges because, you state, the people of the West have no faith in his word, and, morever, that they prefer that the public lands be administered by some other agency.

    Perhaps the Secretary had these actions and expressions of attitude in mind when he called to your attention the fact that the study had not been objective.

    The bill to amend the Antiquities Act, if enacted into law, would provide that the public reservations established by the President, under that authority, would be open to public water conservation projects, prospecting and mining, grazing, and hunting in accordance with State and Federal laws. The national monuments now established under the Antiquities Act are closed to such forms of exploitation. The amended Act would apply to those public lands that are primarily and outstandingly of recreational value. The more liberal reservations that would be established under the authority of the new Act would be National Recreational Areas, and not national parks or national monuments.

    I fail to see wherein the enactment of this bill would threaten forestry lands. The President has had the authority to remove lands from the national forests since 1897, and there are more national forests today than ever before. From 1933 to 1939 the Forest Reservation Commission, of which Secretary Ickes is a member, has had net appropriations of more than $54,000,000 for the purchase of new national forest lands, or more than twice as much as had been allotted to the Commission in the 22 years of its existence prior to 1933. Since March 4, 1933, 12,540,223 acres of forest land have been approved for purchase by the Commission. From 1933 to 1936 alone, I allotted to the Commission for land acquisition $46,712,150 which has made possible the purchase of more than 11,000,000 acres of forest land.

    I believe that my forest conservation record measures up in every respect to the policy that I stated to you in my letter of September 6, 1932.

    In view of these facts I can see no reason why the findings and conclusions of the State Planning Council should be in the nature of a public warning against the Secretary of the Interior and against the President of the United States as enemies of sound public land administration.

    This administration has cooperated with and given more encouragement to resource-planning agencies than has ever been given in the history of this country. The Secretary of the Interior was giving such cooperation when he appointed a representative, at your request, to collaborate with you in the Cascade Mountains Study; he was cooperating when he submitted data to you, and when, in fact, he submitted the whole question of the Cascade recreational resources to a joint study. If resource-planning agencies are to retain the confidence that the people have placed in them, they must maintain the standard of objective study that the people have a right to expect.

                                                      Very sincerely yours,

                        (signed)   Franklin D. Roosevelt

MINING WORLD

A Miller Freeman Publication

Seattle, Washington

October 1, 1940.

Mr. Franklin D. Roosevelt,
The White House,
Washington, D. C.

My dear Mr. President:

Your letter discussing our article "Conservation—Should it Serve, or only Save?", the Cascade Mountains Study of the Washington State Planning Council and our controversy with the Secretary of the Interior is much appreciated and has been carefully studied.

I am impressed by your statement that "The bill to amend the Antiquities Act, if enacted into law, would provide that the public reservations established by the President, under that authority would be open to public water conservation projects, prospecting and mining, grazing, and hunting in accordance with State and Federal laws".

Your interpretation that such multiple use would be mandatory rather than permissive is most reassuring.

Your letter concludes with the sentence: "If resource-planning agencies are to retain the confidence that the people have placed in them, they must maintain the standard of objective study that the people have a right to expect".

This is perfectly true. In all honesty and sincerity, I maintain that the Cascade Mountains Study of the Washington State Planning Council conformed in fact with the highest standards of objective study. The Secretary of the Interior disagrees, evidently because the conclusions of the Council run counter to his personal policy.

I will not impose on your time and patience with further harrowing of the trivia raised by Mr. Ickes with respect to the facts and acts which preceded utterance of the Cascade Mountains Report by the Washington State Planning Council. This is no surrender of position, but merely an unwillingness to bother you with another of Mr. Ickes' personal quarrels. After all, what have these quibblings to do with the largest aspects of conservation and the proper use of the public domain?

As I conceive them, the essential facts are these:

The Washington State Planning Council, set up under a program encouraged by yourself, and composed with its special committee of thirteen qualified citizens of the State of Washington conducted a comprehensive study of Cascade Mountains region.

The Council, as result of its study, reached several conclusions, of which the essential are:

That the natural resources of this region should be developed on the multiple use principle as now applied by the United States Forest Service;

That no additional lands of the Cascade Mountains be converted into use as a national park.

We will stand or fall on this position. The region is now in the public domain. Its resources are now being conserved and saved from waste and destruction, but they are also being employed for the benefit of all the people—not merely reserved to those seeking commercialized recreation.

Such lands and resources should not be involved in a struggle for balance of power between departments of the Federal Government.

Mr. President, may we make so bold as to suggest that the time is ripe for a re-enunciation of national policy touching conservation and the public domain?

A sound policy could be very simply stated:

1. Conservation is the wise use, and the fullest use, of natural resources consistent with their protection from waste and destruction.

2. Multiple use of the public domain should be impaired only with respect to those features whose characteristics are unique, and which might truly suffer damage under the broader conservation policy. Reservations accorded restricted status should be limited strictly to the unique natural features involved.

3. Metallic resources are of no value, esthetically or economically, unless they are discovered and developed. Consequently, no strictures should be laid upon prospecting, and none upon development consistent with protection of the public domain and the national interest.

4. The national government has an obligation to the states with respect to the public domain within their boundaries, and should make no fundamental change in the status of such lands without approval of the states concerned.

Very truly yours,

MILLER FREEMAN

MF:L

27
The LAKE WASHINGTON FLOATING BRIDGE

WHEN MILLER MOVED HIS HOME to the east side of Lake Washington in 1928, he expressed the desire to take himself and his family away from the pressures of city life. He showed his lakeshore property, site of the new home, to Dr. Suzzallo soon after its purchase in 1927. As the two friends looked over the property, Miller explained his reasons for building there, implying that he would be less involved in that setting and would enjoy a kind of country gentleman's life in the beautiful area then developing around the Bellevue-Medina district.

Doctor Suzzallo's amusement was great when he said, "Don't kid me. You will soon be sparking ideas all over Medina. You will be involved in a water project. You will be building. You will be getting new roads and better roads built, you will be involved in community affairs and you can't help it. You won't even want to help it. You are coming over here to get away from something when, actually, you will be getting into something—a lot more than you realize. You will be into all kinds of projects. Why, I wouldn't be surprised if some day you were to get involved in a scheme to bridge the lake."

Although it might have sounded unrealistic to talk about bridging the lake in 1927, when there was little activity in real estate on the east side, it was not entirely unpredictable in view of the development already discernible. When, in the thirties, Miller heard rumors that various east-side groups were meeting to discuss the possibility and feasibility of a bridge between their community and Seattle, he may well have thought back on the words of his old friend, who had since died. Perhaps it was in a whimsical mood that he began to attend a few of the meetings to hear what was going on.

The interests of several groups representing diverse areas on the east side were at odds as to the best location for a crossing to Seattle if, and when, a bridge could be financed and built. Miller was favorable to the idea of a bridge that would provide better access to the east-shore

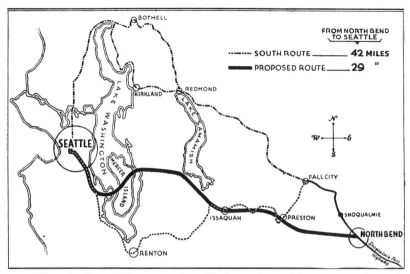

Map showing a bridge route rejected in favor of a straighter route to the north.

communities, but would also offer a better highway link between eastern and western Washington.

It should be recalled here that in the 1913 state legislative session, Miller had served on the Highway Commission which had opened the way for appropriation of funds for the first paving across the Cascades. At the time this project was a big step toward speeding communications between the two large economic areas of eastern and western Washington. That highway, while reasonably direct from Yakima to North Bend on the west slope of the Cascades, then lost itself and, by various circuitous routes, wound its slow way around Lake Washington into Seattle. It now seemed logical to Miller to link construction of a straightened cross-state highway with a Lake Washington crossing.

In view of these considerations, Miller envisioned greater benefits from the proposed crossing than those uppermost in the minds of most east-side residents.

Predictably, during the period of exploration, several factions formed within the groups discussing the project. Because no proposed route suited a majority, it was decided to initiate a study by an impartial and authoritative body which could recommend a placement to benefit all east-side communities.

There were a few problems to overcome, however, before this study could be made. At that time it was discovered that the County Road Commission was at odds with the State Highway Department, and that the two bodies which should have been working together to speed progress on the project were deadlocked in a bitter dispute.

Upon learning about this dispute at a meeting, Miller expressed the opinion that such a state of affairs was shortsighted and petty. The matter should immediately be put before the state highway commissioner, he said. The fellow who puts forth the ideas is often tagged to do the job, and Miller was asked if he would go to Olympia and call on the

179

The General Is Ill! We Don't Wonder After This

(EDITORIAL)

"The General" is off the track again! In a stupendous four-column editorial on the Mercer Island bridge in the Sunday Times, Mr. Blethen has figured out some very peculiar recommendations for aiding Seattle's growth and Seattle's business.

In condemning the lake bridge he says: "There is ground for belief that the best route from central Washington either would end in Tacoma or debouch somewhere between Tacoma and Seattle. It is perfectly possible that the state as a whole and the Sound as a district would profit more by a good Stevens Pass highway to the north (connecting up at Everett) and a Snoqualmie pass-Tacoma highway to the south."

"The General" believes that if we work hard to build up Everett and Tacoma, there might be some leftover profit for Seattle if we attach ourselves to the coat-tails of the other two.

Mr. Blethen also would take down the bars to Seattle's Cedar river watershed and push a new highway thru it to connect up Tacoma (not Seattle) with eastern Washington. He continues: "It is no longer necessary to lift one's hands in holy horror when the possibility of violating the sanctity of the city watershed is concerned. Nowadays our water is chlorinated.

"The Milwaukee railroad already crosses the watershed. Simple regulations to prevent picnicking, gas stations and the like, and any stops other than for emergency purposes would suffice to protect the area from contamination."

A note in the morning newspaper says "The General" is ill today. We don't wonder!

*   *   *

The Star takes issue emphatically with this silly attitude.

It is for Seattle first, last and all the time. It has campaigned for a Lake Washington bridge because it believes such a structure will bring thousands of people and millions of dollars into the city. That kind of business is what will make Seattle progress. Any other viewpoint is merely injuring Seattle.

The Star believes other Washington cities, too, should progress. That is why it has helped in the fight for the Narrows bridge, to give Tacoma a chance to tap its back country. But it does not believe that Tacoma or Everett or any other city would be so foolish as to expect to be helped by ——'s own expense. ...t frequently in

Seattle dailies expressed their views on the bridge in editorials and cartoons. This editorial is from the Seattle Star of July 18, 1938.

commissioner to see what could be done to break the deadlock.

He was not adverse to tackling this assignment and, on the following day, he visited the commissioner, Lacey V. Murrow (brother of Edward R. Murrow), in Olympia. Discussing the proposition of a Lake Washington bridge, Miller pointed out the difficulties he foresaw in working toward a goal when the two bodies, county and state, whose cooperation was essential, were set against one another. Murrow agreed, saying he thought that the factions at odds could resolve their differences. He was also heartily in favor of getting things moving on the bridge and eager to talk to Miller about it.

To begin with, Murrow asked Miller what his own ideas were as to the location of such a structure. Miller had not given this serious thought and, furthermore, did not pretend to be an authority on such matters. But, somewhat extemporaneously, he said he felt that the

Look Out, Mister!

Cartoon from the Post-Intelligencer *of June 24, 1938.*

bridge should do several things. First, he believed, it should tie in with the Snoqualmie Pass highway, which would necessitate the building of a new section of state highway from North Bend at the west base of Snoqualmie Pass to Seattle. Second, it should serve Mercer Island and the east-side communities and, third, it should terminate at a reasonably central spot in Seattle.

The two men moved to a large area map of the district, and it became evident that the section of highway Miller had proposed was the shortest distance between the two points under discussion. When Murrow placed a ruler from North Bend to tidewater, the east-west extremities, both men were surprised by the logic of the route.

One troublesome fact was quickly evident in that such a plan would call for a crossing of Lake Washington at one of its widest stretches, thus ruling out the construction of a traditional bridge. It was apparent

Miller Freeman purchased a controlling interest in the Bellevue American and gave the east-side communities strong support for the bridge.

that, unless this problem could be solved in some manner not immediately obvious, a less direct route would have to be adopted.

Not long after this meeting, Murrow began to visualize the possibility of a floating structure to connect the longest stretch over water between Mercer Island and Seattle. While this was a pioneering idea, it was not without precedent, and Murrow felt that it was entirely feasible from an engineering standpoint. Both men considered it an exciting concept.

Efforts on Murrow's part soon resolved the differences between the Highway Department and the County Road Commission and, with the political logjam broken, the proposition for a better link between eastern and western Washington seemed a distinct possibility. Federal funds were obtained to augment state highway appropriations and the project moved closer to reality. The Northwest community now began to take an enthusiastic interest in the proposed Lake Washington bridge.

Inasmuch as there were several possible highway routes other than the one Murrow's ruler had indicated, considerable controversy centered on which one was the most logical. Community factions on both sides of the lake entered the arena of lively argument on these issues. Soon, the Northwest press began giving the controversy full coverage and, by the time a decision was reached, most people in the area were well acquainted with the pros and cons of the several routes that had been under consideration—and most of them had strong opinions on the subject. (It is significant that, when all was sifted down to practicality, the route ultimately followed was remarkably close to the one discussed by Lacey Murrow and Miller Freeman.)

The routing of the interstate highway was not the only matter at issue, however. The type of bridge structure for the crossing was also

182

Harold L. Ickes, secretary of the interior, and Miller Freeman, frequent antagonists, pictured after Miller had shown Ickes the floating bridge.

hotly debated. Here, too, the press took an enthusiastic part in fanning the flames of argument.

Once more Miller's old adversary, Colonel (now Brigadier General) Clarance Blethen of the *Seattle Times,* disagreed vociferously with him and the other supporters of the bridge and highway project. Blethen rose to great literary heights in opposition to the route chosen and, most particularly, to the floating bridge. A "cause" was to his liking. The floating structure, he said, would *never* work.

With equal enthusiasm for a good fight, Miller girded himself to do battle. Miller decided he needed a literary ammunition depot in the form of a publication through which he could voice support for the favored highway route and the bridge. With this in mind, he purchased a controlling interest in a small east-side weekly newspaper, the *Bellevue American,* and, with deep enjoyment, gave the east-side communities a strong supporting voice for the project.

The battle lines were drawn. With the *Seattle Post-Intelligencer* and the *Bellevue American* giving enthusiastic support to the project, Blethen and the *Times* fought a heroic and sometimes lonely fight in opposition to it. The editorial jousting brought untold pleasure and excitement to the whole Northwest community which alternatively rocked with anger and glee over the strong editorial fare in which the papers indulged.

No one enjoyed the fight more than Miller who trained the slingshot from the *Bellevue American* at the cannon of the Goliath *Seattle Times.* The battle strategy brought back vivid memories to the *Town Crier,* the small newssheet that he had used in 1910 in support of the Lake Washington Canal.

While the giant construction job moved ahead with speed and efficiency, Blethen continued to warn of dire calamity for the bridge,

183

LAKE PONTOON BRIDGE

which he felt was structurally unsound. He predicted that the floating section between Mercer Island and the Seattle shore would break up in the first major wind storm. His graphic cartoons, showing broken chunks of concrete lying on a desolate shore, gave chills to some doubters in the community and provided great joy for others. The editorial contest became a semi-athletic diversion over which the pro and con teams rocked with violent feeling.

As the bridge neared completion, a cartoon appeared in the *Times* which was to give Miller deep and lasting enjoyment. For many years he had belonged to a small east-side poker group composed of old friends who called themselves "The Volunteer Firemen." General Blethen, while not a member, had known of the club and of its sacred tradition which was the passing of an authentic fireman's hat to each winner. Thus the *Times'* cartoon showing a bleak shore landscape, dominated by a tall spar bearing on its top a fireman's hat, was clearly the symbol of the impalement of Miller, the strongest advocate of the Lake Washington bridge.

The new bridge was completed in 1940 and, being the first structure of its kind, attracted considerable national attention. The dedication was a highlight in the Northwest, but an even greater event to Miller

BIGGEST THING AFLOAT

was Blethen's editorial appearing in the *Seattle Times* for June 30, 1940. The signed editorial was titled "I Go For a Ride." It read:

> "Here's where I eat crow," said Alice.
> "Crow?" queried the Walrus.
> "Crow," said Alice.
> "But why crow?" persisted the Walrus.
> "There are two reasons for eating crow," responded Alice. "One is because you have to, and the other is because you feel you should."
> The Lake Washington floating bridge is an unqualified success. More, it is an attraction for tourists, fully on a par with San Francisco's great structures. I almost may be justified in saying that because of its uniqueness, in the end it will attract more visitors and excite more admiration.

Thus, at the last, Miller and his old adversary came together in mutual enthusiasm. Perhaps the general adopted the only course open to him for the floating bridge was universally hailed as an unqualified success. The bonds were paid off years before the time anticipated and Miller, who was with Governor Langlie for the toll removal ceremony, had the honor of paying the last nickel to cross the bridge.

185

Miller Freeman pays the last nickel passenger fee to cross the floating bridge on July 2, 1949. Governor Arthur Langlie acts as collector, while Ex-Governor Martin, under whom the bridge was built, keeps a sharp eye on the transaction.

The long campaign was over and the victory was heartwarming to Miller. Driving back to his office after the impressive affair and experiencing a glow of satisfaction, the tireless campaigner said, "Now we must get started on a second bridge." While he was not active in the campaign for the Seattle-Evergreen Point bridge, planning for such a span had already begun and, largely due to the unqualified success of the first pioneering project, became a reality a few years later.

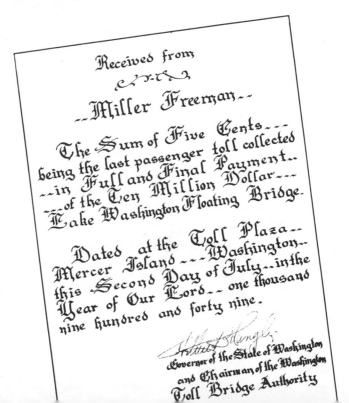

Received from

Miller Freeman

The Sum of Five Cents being the last passenger toll collected in Full and Final Payment of the Ten Million Dollar Lake Washington Floating Bridge.

Dated at the Toll Plaza Mercer Island Washington this Second Day of July in the Year of Our Lord one thousand nine hundred and forty nine.

Governor of the State of Washington and Chairman of the Washington Toll Bridge Authority

28
PEARL HARBOR and WORLD WAR II

J UST AS A RUNNER ADROITLY CHANGES PACE, so Miller was forced to do in September 1941, when he suffered a heart attack of serious proportions. After the first anxious weeks in a hospital, he returned home. It was evident he was on his way to a cautious recovery period and he accepted his forced inactivity, cooperating well with the authorities who had him surrounded and unable to do otherwise in any event. The period of rest was hard enough for a man of his natural energies but one of the bitterest blows came when he was told he could not play golf again. (It took a Dwight Eisenhower—and later a Lyndon Johnson—to publicize the newer medical theory that within reason a normal life, including exercise, could be pursued following a coronary.) This disappointment, on top of his curtailed business activities, required some pretty stern mental readjustment, to which, as he gradually recovered, he admirably addressed himself.

There was, however, considerable solace to him in the fact that he could carry on his voluminous correspondence, and the pace of his letter writing stepped up. It was an activity in which he could indulge without undue strain. Letters became increasingly a way of maintaining contact with his campaigns and his many outside interests.

While Miller gradually resumed an active life, the slowdown served, nonetheless, to mellow his approach and his outlook. He became increasingly philosophical, his mind alert, and his thinking tempered and sagacious. The Indian Chief perhaps came closer to his real self then. He was more often called "Big Chief" by his grandchildren and quite naturally assumed the role of leader of his tribe. He wore his Indian headdress on more frequent occasions, to the delight of the young ones. He was often to advise his friends: "If you want to live a long life get yourself a fatal illness and take care of it."

Suddenly, events took place which changed the course of United States history and altered the smooth flow of life for its people. War with Japan—and U. S. involvement in World War II—came three

8 Points of Approach
to the Problem of the Japanese in America

PROBLEMS stemming from the presence in the United States of hundreds of thousands of persons of Japanese blood—many of them maintaining allegiance to Japan—were pointed out by Miller Freeman, president, Miller Freeman Publications, in an editorial printed some months ago.

This editorial was read into the Congressional Record by Senator Homer T. Bone of Washington. It provoked widespread comment and numerous requests for elaboration of specific points of approach to the problem.

One of these requests for extension of suggestions as to procedure came from Assemblyman Thomas A. Maloney, member of the California legislature. His letter is reproduced in full herewith.

Accompanying it is Mr. Freeman's reply, establishing the principles upon which the Miller Freeman Publications take their stand.

YOU ASK me to express my views on what would be the proper procedure for us to follow relative to the Japanese question when the war ends.

America must find a sound and permanent solution of the problem. There are approximately three hundred thousand Japanese in the United States and Hawaii, of whom two-thirds are native-born, and therefore American citizens. The average age of the aliens is 58; of American-born, 23 years. They comprise a close-knit minority, in part truly loyal to this country, but shot through-and-in through with a web of treason woven and controlled in Tokyo.

Japan maintains that these people, first of all, are subjects of the Sun Emperor by virtue of their blood. America has granted them citizenship because they were born here. That is perfectly satisfactory to Japan, so long as the allegiance to Japan always is paramount.

Although some American Japanese renounce this duality of citizenship, in deed as well as in word, we know that others in their hearts regard themselves as Japanese first and fundamentally; and Americans only by accident and for purposes of expediency, and sometimes of treason.

The original Japanese immigrants were actually exported to Hawaii and the United States by the government of Japan in its deliberate program of establishing Japanese colonies in all the countries around the Pacific. From the earliest days, Japan has been working toward a grandiose program of Pacific conquest. Its strategy called for founding of colonies which would subsequently become strong-points from which to extend further infiltration.

Much that has long been understood by a few Americans is now revealed to all in colors which cannot be misinterpreted. We know the Japanese government has initiated, financed, directed and controlled concentrated Japanese enterprises. These have achieved the power through which this alien government successfully exerted tremendous leverage upon local governments, and even the Federal government of the United States.

Sound, just and lasting solution of the problem posed by the American citizens of Japanese blood, and perhaps of Japanese allegiance, can be found only through thoughtful attention of American leaders; unflinching, but not unjust, action by the American government; and sincere and selfless efforts of the Japanese Americans themselves.

In the very beginning, there should be an end of proposals to revoke the American citizenship of Japanese who, under our laws, have been born to it.

We can require them to prove themselves worthy of that citizenship, and publicly to accept its responsibilities; but there is no ground in justice for wholesale revocation of citizenship which we in our prodigality have freely given, with no questions asked. To revoke that citizenship now would be a blot on this nation which could never be erased.

I.

First step in any sound and permanent solution of the problem of our Japanese must be taken by them. They must cut themselves aloof completely from the control and authority of Japan and its Emperor. This renouncement must be from the heart, and must be such that it will be evident to all Americans, else there can be no credence or confidence in it among Americans who have come to know perfidy can be bottomless.

II.

Second, our federal and state governments must protect the loyal American Japanese in their renunciation of dual citizenship and alien control. Within their colonies, the Japanese who are loyal Americans live under the threat of fascistic elements controlled and directed by Tokyo.

III.

Third, we must expose and tear out the whole web of Japan's influence, propaganda and intrigue in which this nation has been enmeshed. Tight, deliverable blocs of votes can always be used to pander to venal politicians.

IV.

Fourth, we must make it impossible for Tokyo-conceived-and-directed enterprises to achieve control, often amounting to monopoly, over essential activities in our American economy.

V.

Fifth, the Japanese who would be loyal to the United States must take the lead in weeding out the fascistic, Japan-adhering elements among their brethren.

VI.

Sixth, there must be an end to unsupervised Japanese-language schools conducted in the United States and its territories by the Japanese government for the purpose of indoctrinating the American-born in the creed of dual citizenship, and of inoculating them against assimilation of true Americanism.

VII.

Seventh, Japan-controlled firms and institutions must sever their connections with the Japanese government. They must no longer be permitted to exercise strangling control over the Japanese population. They must never again be in position to influence public officials and legislative bodies at the behest of the government in Tokyo.

VIII.

Finally, these things must be done justly and with tolerance. There must be no witch-burning, no persecution, no rabble-rousing. This is a problem in the humanities. It must be dealt with accordingly in American principles of justice, albeit with a new awareness, and a determination that there is no place among American citizens for dual allegiance.

Yours sincerely,
MILLER FREEMAN.

Eight points of approach to the Japanese problem in America were given in Miller Freeman's editorial printed in March 1943 MFP magazines.

months after his heart attack, as Miller began to resume normal activities. These events served to push the trauma of his illness into the background and he now became absorbed in the multiple problems and immediate emergencies which faced all Americans and particularly those living on the West Coast.

On Sunday morning, December 7, 1941, the Japanese, without declaration of war, dropped bombs on Hawaii's Pearl Harbor, wreaking devastation on the Pacific fleet at a United States outpost. There had been a breakdown in diplomatic negotiations in Washington immediately previous to this event, but few people were prepared for what happened. Congress declared war on Japan on December 8, and on December 11 Germany and Italy declared war on the United States.

Stunned and unprepared, the United States reeled following the Pearl Harbor disaster. Many in West Coast areas were thrown into a state of near panic, and uncertainty and fear gripped everyone. Within hours, the military ordered blackouts of coastal cities, increasing public fear of attack. Questions haunting the people were "How strong is Japan?" and "How well can the West Coast defend itself in case of bombing?" No one knew the answers during the first days, and reports coming from the weakened stronghold in the Philippines were increasingly frightening as U.S. defenses there fell.

In Seattle, Miller was grim and quiet. Perhaps he was less surprised than most people by the nature of the unexpected attack. He had warned of Japanese aggression and had witnessed confrontations with them on many fronts and on many occasions. He had never claimed before the attack any prophetic powers to foresee the eventuality—nor did he claim any after it—but through the years his publishing field had given him ample opportunity to observe Japanese psychology. He did not trust the Japanese military which was virtually a dictatorship at the time, or the Japanese government. He believed too that the basic differences between Japanese and United States cultures made it impossible for them to deal as equals in the game of international politics.

Within weeks following Pearl Harbor, there were numerous proposals for punitive actions against Japanese aliens and citizens residing on the Pacific Coast. Miller deplored these proposals and resolutely declined to be associated with them in any way. He reacted in the same way to demands that U.S. citizenship of American born Japanese should be revoked and that these citizens, along with all other Japanese, should be deported at the end of the war. In an editorial published in the March 1943 editions of all Miller Freeman publications, giving eight points of approach to the problem of the Japanese in America, he said: "In the very beginning, there should be an end of proposals to revoke . . . citizenship of Japanese who, under our laws, have been born to it. We can require them to prove themselves worthy of that citizenship, and publicly to accept its responsibilities; but there

Homer T. Bone, speaking in the U.S. Senate, tells of Miller Freeman, his publications, and editorials on the Japanese question. At his request, Miller's "8 Points" editorial was printed in the Congressional Record.

is no ground in justice for wholesale revocation of citizenship which we in our prodigality have freely given, with no questions asked. To revoke that citizenship now would be a blot on this nation which could never be erased."

Actually, one of the first steps he took following the outbreak of war was the organization in Bellevue of a special committee to deal with the problems relating to Japanese residents of the community. Under his chairmanship, this committee saw to it that Japanese residents were treated justly and with humanity. A courageous, implacable fighter, Miller Freeman was ever a fair one.

Miller's attitudes on the Japanese question, before and after Pearl Harbor, often appeared in editorials and public statements. A speech by Senator Homer T. Bone of Washington, a Democrat, in the Senate on September 10, 1942 commented on Miller Freeman, his publications, and his views on the Japanese question. The speech, which was reprinted in the *Congressional Record* along with one of Miller's editorials, said at one point: "Without attempting to evaluate Mr. Freeman's views, because they speak for themselves, it may be said, whether one agrees with his party philosophy or not, that he is a very able and patriotic man. He has written an editorial which will appear or has already appeared in his Pacific coast publications. . . . Because it is an interesting and forceful editorial, Mr. President, I ask unanimous consent that it be printed in the *Record* as a part of my remarks. I am sure that all those who are vitally interested in the Japanese question will find it to their advantage to read it."

However, in December 1941, as war started, whatever his thoughts about past and future may have been, Miller wasted little time on pronouncements. There were many considerations of vital and im-

190

Why Border Barriers?

Removal of restrictive immigration barriers between Canada and the United States is being advocated editorially by the Miller Freeman group of trade journals, published in Seattle and San Francisco.

Referring to the recent action of the Pacific Northwest Trade Association in urging modification of border regulations, Pacific Pulp & Paper Industry and other journals of the Miller Freeman group declare that such an attitude was based on realism and common sense.

"After all, we in the United States and Canada are in the war together, and some day we will be solving the problems of peace together," the journal points out. There is no substitute for personal contact in maintaining the complete harmony and mutual understanding that are so necessary for both countries.

"To those fortunate individuals who have not been initiated into sidered necessary even in wartime. To those who have survived the ordeal it is a bitter memory of inconvenience, loss of time and often personal hardship —and to what purpose?

"Gas rationing, shortage of hotel, boat and train accommodation have discouraged most people from moving from place to place unless they have good reason for doing so. Most of these inconveniences are no doubt justified.

"But the snarl of red tape from which the border crosser must extricate himself is in a very different category. Obviously, there is good cause for maintaining an official record of those who travel in and out of a country. Obviously, it is necessary to provide the means of keeping out undesirables.

"But it is highly questionable whether a policy of deliberately discouraging Canadians from visiting the United States and Americans from going across the

The Victoria Daily Times *for November 10, 1943 refers to Miller Freeman's editorial urging modification of border regulations.*

mediate importance which took precedence over all others. The first question in the minds of military men on the West Coast was that of the loyalty of the Japanese population concentrated in California, Oregon, and Washington.

There were thousands of Orientals living in coastal areas and the highest percentage were American-born Japanese. The trustworthiness of most of them was not questioned. The danger of even a small number of disloyal Japanese, however, posed such a risk that in the minds of those charged with the responsibility of the protection and defense of the West Coast, a drastic step had to be taken.

Within weeks plans were made to remove all Japanese from coastal areas and to impound these people in relocation centers on lands away from the Pacific Coast, thus eliminating them from points of strategic military importance. The speedy evacuation of the Japanese from their homes required tough and decisive action. It was inevitable that in many cases the hardship of sudden dispossession proved cruel treatment; surely to the great majority whose loyalties to the United States were real this was the case.

While he approved the military necessity of the removal of the Japanese from the coastal areas for the duration of the war, Miller deplored unnecessarily harsh treatment of these people. It is evident that he was sometimes critical of the administration of relocation centers as imposing unnecessary hardships on the Japanese.

Miller Freeman believed implicitly, however, that wartime evacuation of all Japanese from the coastal area of the Pacific was essential to the safety of U.S. citizens and aliens alike. Testifying in March 1942 before the Tolan Congressional Committee investigating national migration, he endorsed this view.

The war dragged on as the United States seemed mired in an endless series of military engagements. While victories increased, an end to the hostilities seemed unpredictable. Even after the unconditional surrender of Germany on May 7, 1945, the war in the Pacific continued.

Miller accepted wartime reality philosophically, however. Long before others had conceded the fact of inevitable defeat for Japan, Miller read the news with optimism. He pointed to Japan's untenable position well in advance of the summer of 1945 and the dropping of the atomic bomb. A view beyond the present often seemed clear to him. Thus, at a time when most people still saw only the crushing problems of the war, Miller frequently talked about the years of peace that would follow it.

Miller Freeman was seventy years old when the war in the Pacific ended on August 14, 1945. The years of his greatest activity lay behind him, but the years ahead were to be in many ways the richest for him. Physical effort was necessarily limited but his contacts were kept alive at every level through letter writing. Correspondence became an increasingly important tool to keep him in touch with issues and campaigns which he continued to pursue.

During the war the issue of immigration barriers between the United States and Canada had become a concern of Miller's largely due to his membership in the Northwest Trade Association. That body was urging the removal of restrictive barriers between the two countries. Miller had long been critical of what he considered unnecessary bureaucratic regulations which slowed and hampered the traveler who went across the border between the two countries. He began applying pressure through his publications. The following editorial is typical.

> After all, we in the United States and Canada are in a war together, and some day will be solving the problems of peace together.
>
> To those fortunate individuals who have not been initiated into the mysteries, complications and confusions of border crossing in recent months, it is almost incredible that such conditions as actually exist should be considered necessary in war times.
>
> Obviously there is good cause for maintaining official record of those who travel in and out of a country. But it is highly questionable whether a policy of deliberately discouraging Canadians from visiting the United States and Americans from going across the border into Canada can be defended on any grounds other than those of blind officialdom.

Continued pressure on this front, accelerated by the necessity for closeness with a valued ally, soon brought about a relaxing of border regulations of lasting benefit to the two countries.

29
CAMPAIGNING for the REPUBLICAN PARTY

MILLER HAD SERVED AS A STALWART of the Republican party for many years. As a member of the Republican State Central Committee, a delegate to the 1916 and 1936 national conventions, and a vocal supporter of Republican principles, he was well known and generally conceded to have special stature in Republican ranks. His standing in the public eye made him somewhat removed from the straight party man. He had supported many nonpartisan issues for the benefit of all people of the state of Washington. The Republican party of the mid-1930s was admittedly "flat on its back" following the Landon defeat by Franklin Roosevelt. Miller had served on the delegation that sent Alfred Landon out against FDR in 1936 and realistically he had held out slim hopes for his victory. Nor was he particularly enthusiastic about the Republican party candidate. In any event, who could delude himself that the Republicans had a chance in that election year? The New Deal was in its heyday and the Republicans knew they had to look toward the future. The present was pretty hopeless for the old guard.

But, immediately after the debacle of 1936, the Republican bigwigs within the state of Washington began looking for strong leadership to guide them toward a 1940 comeback. Miller was asked, in 1937, to take the chairmanship of the Washington State Republican Committee. This automatically placed him in position to be chairman of the Washington delegation at the 1940 nominating convention.

Miller was then in his sixties and he was not anxious to increase his involvement in such affairs at that time. However, in view of the sad state of the Republican party, he answered that, if it was felt his leadership would be of value, he would accept the position with certain stipulations. These were, first, that he would serve providing the sentiment of the committee was unanimously in favor of his appointment and, second, that the duties of the National Committeeman and those pertaining to his position as chairman of the State Committee be kept separate and clearly defined as to areas of operation. This last stipulation came as the result of his observation that the two jobs were

WENDELL L. WILLKIE
109 EAST 42ND STREET
NEW YORK CITY

November 25, 1940.

Mr. Miller Freeman
Miller Freeman Publications
71 Columbia Street
Seattle, Washington

Dear Mr. Freeman:

I want you to know that your message touched me deeply. It conveyed to me not only your good will, but also a heartening faith in the principles for which I stand.

Sincerely,

Wendell Willkie sends a warm note to Miller Freeman in 1940.

frequently confused and were damaging to the effectiveness of party leadership. His qualifications were unanimously accepted and his big job soon began with preparations for the nominating convention of 1940.

In 1939, at the time Miller was stepping up activities on the political front in readiness for the National GOP Convention, he had expressed a popular viewpoint and was quoted in the *Seattle Times* on April 20, 1939, as follows:

> The American people resent President Roosevelt's own indulgence in the identical manners and language of totalitarianism as shown by his arbitrarily assuming our entry into a foreign war against the same ideology.
>
> President Roosevelt has reached the end of his domination of Congress. Courageous and patriotic leaders of his own party are deserting him.
>
> The people are aware that while Mr. Roosevelt is denouncing dictators, he himself is following their rules of conduct and using their manners and pronouncements. . . .
>
> Coupled with this swing away from one-man control, although not depending on it entirely, is an obviously favorable outlook for the Republican party in other ways. The popular opinion against vagaries of the New Deal so decisively shown at the polls last November has continued and grown ever since.

September 11, 1940

Hon. Miller Freeman
71 Columbia Street
Seattle, Washington

Dear Mr. Freeman:

      I have your letter of August 2
and appreciate more than I can tell you
your good invitation to visit you at your
home if I come to Washington during the
campaign.

      I just don't know yet where I'm
going to speak and won't know for another
two or three weeks. But if it should come
to pass that I go to Seattle, I will let
you know and will certainly look forward
to seeing you.

      With many thanks and warm regards,
I am

      Sincerely yours,

TED:AB   Thomas E. Dewey

Thomas Dewey writes to Miller during the 1940 campaign.

As 1940 approached, there was a sufficient crack in the Roosevelt armor for the Republicans to hold out good hope for a comeback. The feeling against the President's running for an unprecedented third term seemed to bode well for the party out of power.

Miller went back to Philadelphia in July 1940 as chairman of the Washington State delegation, pledged to support the nomination of Senator Robert A. Taft for president. It was generally conceded that he would receive the nomination, inasmuch as the powers within the Republican party favored him as the man to defeat Roosevelt. But a political surprise was in the making. For several months before the convention a ground swell of public opinion steadily built in support of Wendell Willkie, a political unknown. A lawyer from the northeast, Willkie was at that time president of the Commonwealth and Southern Corporation, a large utility company. A dynamic speaker, he had expressed himself in favor of individual initiative and the place of private enterprise in our society, a subject dear to the hearts of Republicans and one that seemed the emblem of a losing cause in the 1930s and early 1940s. Willkie's words struck fire to the suppressed embers of Republican ideals.

Another event put Willkie in the national limelight. Henry Luce of Time-Life Incorporated, who strongly supported him, ran an article about Willkie that swept the country and excited millions who desper-

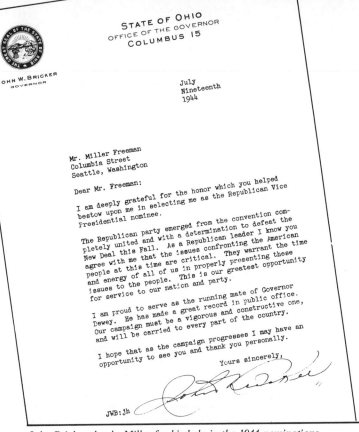

John Bricker thanks Miller for his help in the 1944 nominations.

ately wanted to see a change in Washington. With the strength and charisma of Willkie, the article implied, there was a chance of defeating the man in the White House.

As the delegates gathered in the steaming heat of Philadelphia in the summer of 1940, the Republicans had two clear choices for presidential candidate. The front runner, Senator Robert Taft, was an able man with many years of effective service to the party behind him. While his appearance was somewhat stiff and colorless, he was a man of out-standing ability. He was tagged as Mr. Conservative but his record in the Senate was one marked with work on many progressive measures. The Republican stalwarts considered him to be the outstanding choice to bring the country back to sanity.

The other man, Wendell Willkie, while not the party's choice, was being forced on the Republican hierarchy with increasing pressure from all parts of the country. And it was not hard to rally toward Willkie. He was a bull of a man with a shock of dark hair, an open, friendly manner, and a magnetic, rumbling voice. He did, in fact, catch the imagination of the general public with that hard to define quality called "charisma." But he had not held public office and did not fit the picture of an acceptable party candidate. And on this basis most delegates did not favor his nomination.

EARL   WARREN
Sacramento California

July 7, 1944

Mr. Miller Freeman
71 Columbia Street
Seattle, Washington

Dear Mr. Freeman:

Many thanks for your telegram
of June 27, 1944.

It is gratifying to know that
my keynote address met with your approval.
The task was one which I undertook hoping
that I might in some way inspire greater
unity of thought and action among all our
concerned citizenry.

I shall be happy if the speech
accomplished that result.

Sincerely,

Earl Warren

EW:aj

*Met your son recently and
enjoyed the visit with him.
Hope to see you during
the campaign.*

E.

Earl Warren pens a friendly postscript to his letter.

The convention began according to normal procedure. As the endless protocol got under way, however, an indefinable air of excitement rose from the onlookers in the galleries. The undercurrent of feeling which pervaded the vast audience could be likened to that stirred by the beat of distant jungle drums—the tempo gradually growing to reach a crescendo near hysteria. The onlookers, reacting to the excitement, took to a constant chant of "We Want Willkie—We Want Willkie."

The delegates on the convention floor determinedly disregarded the turmoil as much as possible and carried on their business. However, as the noise and interruptions increased, they showed more irritation. *They* were the people who had been duly elected or appointed by their party and charged with the responsibility of picking the candidate best qualified to lead the party—and to defeat the seemingly unbeatable Franklin Roosevelt. They had carefully weighed their candidate's qualifications and believed that Taft had a good chance of succeeding. They thoroughly resented the insistent pressure from the galleries and from the public at large, for they were by then receiving thousands of telegrams daily from all parts of the country urging Willkie's nomination by the Republicans.

The chairman of the Washington State delegation was among those who resented the intervention of outsiders not charged with duly constituted authority as were the official delegates. Additionally, the delegates were "party" people who could see very little about the man, Willkie, or his record, to qualify him for the office of president— little, they conceded, aside from personal attractiveness and ability to express himself well on the subject of Republican principles.

History takes over from here, however, for the pressures from Republicans all over the country, as well as many Democrats, disillusioned with Roosevelt, gradually broke down the voting blocks in the delegations pledged to Robert Taft; and to the wild joy of his supporters, Wendell Willkie was nominated—only to be defeated by Roosevelt in November 1940.

Wendell Willkie died several years after this event. Whether he had either the experience or the ability to provide strong leadership for the nation at war will remain forever an unanswered question. In the minds of many, including Miller, the Willkie boom was an example of mob hysteria which built out of thin air an untried hero but one who was desperately wanted by many Americans at that time.

Miller accepted the ultimate outcome with equanimity, albeit with considerable disappointment. However, along with many party people, he remained convinced that the most able man had not been nominated in 1940. He did not imply, however, that Roosevelt could have been defeated by Taft, for there were few then who could have so deluded themselves.

Following the election campaign and defeat of Wendell Willkie, Miller's term of office as National Committeeman for Washington continued. After the 1940 defeat, Miller, along with other influential Republicans, sought to strengthen the state Republican forces. He urged unity, where disunity threatened because, he said, only a united Republican party organization would be an effective force in the campaign of 1944 to which they must now look.

To the Washington State national committeeman, William Reed, he wrote in September 1941: "It appears to me that a continuation of the past chaotic conditions within the Central Committee will prevent the party from functioning constructively and militantly in forwarding Republican principles. We must unite all those citizens anxious to support the party and guarantee to the contributors to party funds that their contributions will be expended in the most effective manner."

A few days after this communication, Miller was asked to meet in Yakima, Washington, with Senator Joseph Martin, Junior, chairman of the Republican National Committee, Governor Langlie of Washington, William Reed, and other Republican dignitaries, to discuss and to mold policies of the party.

Three years later, in 1944, despite concerted Republican effort, the party saw another defeat for its forces. Franklin Roosevelt ran for a fourth term as the "indispensable" man and wartime President, and

198

he—not party disunity—once more spelled calamity for the Republicans. By then the issue of the number of terms a president should be allowed to serve was a national one. Along with many citizens, Miller considered Roosevelt's decision to run for a fourth term a flagrant abuse of power. Miller's policy, as always, was to take positive action and state the matter clearly in writing to the right sources, and on April 16, 1945, the following letter was sent by Miller to Herbert Brownell, Junior, chairman of the Republican National Committee:

> Dear Mr Brownell:
> I suggest that at the next meeting of the Republican National Committee, a resolution be adopted that the tenure of the office of the President of the United States be limited to two terms, otherwise, it is inevitable that the office may continue to be held for life.
> Sincerely yours,
> Miller Freeman

In January 1945, a tired and sick President had taken office, presumably for another four years. There were not many in either party, however, who thought Roosevelt would survive to complete his fourth term. He died three months after his inauguration and four months before Japan surrendered in August of 1945.

Harry S. Truman took the oath of office as President upon the death of Franklin Roosevelt in April 1945. Vice President Truman became a businesslike President, served three years, saw the dramatic end of World War II with his historic decision to drop the atomic bomb, and then faced election on his own in 1948.

This was the moment the Republicans had been impatiently awaiting. With Franklin Roosevelt gone and a man in office whom many considered a weak second to follow Roosevelt's strength, their chances seemed better than they had been for sixteen long years of political drought. Additionally, Thomas Dewey, who had run unsuccessfully against Roosevelt in 1944, was a tough political fighter. He was conceded excellent chances to defeat a Truman even if he could not vanquish a Roosevelt. This time it would be a different story, everyone thought.

Miller had been active on the sidelines when Dewey campaigned in 1944. He admired the ex-attorney general of New York State, and considered him an effective man and an able administrator. He came to know him personally following his defeat at the hands of Roosevelt, and his subsequent election as governor of New York. He strongly supported his future candidacy for the office of president in the 1948 election.

The New York State governorship, in view of the experience of his immediate predecessor, seemed a fine springboard for the presidency, and Miller was satisfied when Thomas Dewey was nominated at the Republican convention in the summer of 1948. Chances for the comeback of the party looked better than they had for many years.

As the campaign got under way, Republican organization was strong. Dewey had fine party backing and was an excellent propounder of Republican principles and an eminently satisfactory party man. Enthusiastic henchmen surrounded and guided him carefully with campaign strategy calculated to assure victory.

Miller watched from the political sidelines as the 1948 campaign started rolling. It very soon became evident that, strong as was Dewey himself, he had, nevertheless, conceded an overall campaign strategy control to a group of political "prophets" surrounding him. Miller was outspokenly critical of the careful and tight management of Dewey's campaign by this squad of political experts who guided his every word and move.

However, it could not be denied that Thomas Dewey, the able prosecuting attorney, seemed by all counts to be laying low the "little" man in the White House. Dewey's henchmen read the polls, were well satisfied, and advised Dewey months before the election that he had "a win" in his pocket and to "lay off and not rock the boat."

Miller's uneasiness increased, however, as the campaign rolled toward its conclusion. He was openly critical of the advice that Dewey was receiving, and was apparently accepting. During his campaign Dewey visited the state of Washington and went to Seattle for a large rally. Miller contacted those who were in charge of his appearance and asked specifically to see and visit with the candidate. He was told this was impossible because of Dewey's tight schedule. Specifically, Miller was prepared to warn him about overconfidence.

Admittedly, it did not take second sight to foresee the danger of the evident state of overconfidence in Republican ranks. Miller neared his seventy-fourth year then. His political observations, based on watching many campaigns, gave him ample background for fear. There was precedent for a political surprise under the circumstances if anyone cared to refer to campaign history. No one did right then, and least of all those who sincerely thought they were riding the tide of a great political victory.

What happened during the last weeks of the campaign has become historic. An overconfident Thomas Dewey held back his political punches and was defeated by a scrappy President Truman who campaigned like a prize fighter up to the final moment of voting. His last-minute whistle-stop campaign, with ringing speeches delivered from train platforms, tipped the scales in his favor. Dewey was defeated to the everlasting embarrassment of the pollsters and the bitter disappointment of all Republicans.

For a fifth successive time the Republican party reeled under the ignominious defeat at the hands of the Democrats. It seemed to many to presage the death knell of the party itself. And for the first time a note of discouragement crept into the old fighter's tone. Of all the Republican defeats since 1932, this was perhaps the one hardest for Miller to take.

VI
The Mellowing Years
1945-1955

30
A CHANGE of PACE

T HE SUDDEN DEATH OF HIS CLOSE FRIEND, William Calvert, greatly affected Miller. This was surely one of the deep friendships of his life. After this loss he wrote that he had nothing but the finest memories of William Calvert. And he continued: "Only last Sunday I was strolling with him through his orchard, and he said, 'Miller, these look like a lot of old gnarled trees, the apples are no good, but I love this orchard. It is filled with memories of the past when things were very hard. My Dad and I cleared this land by hard labor and planted all these trees. People worked hard in those days, just to live. It was constructive work. We thought of it as a place where we could go to the soil and raise something for ourselves.' And so it was." Miller also wrote:

> You know William Calvert had a lot of character. You may have wondered how people develop character. It comes, not from an easy, soft life but by meeting and conquering the problems of the times. The efforts of parents are often defeated by their desire to lift their children over the rough spots.
> William Calvert started life under great hardships. His people had met with adversity in the Middle West. He failed in the stationery business. He failed in the printing business. Finally, he took a failure—a small fish business—and built it into one of the finest concerns of the kind in America.

There may well have been a correlation between the loss of his close friend and a period of contemplation Miller seemed to experience at about this time in his career. It is a fact that the mid-1940s were for him a time of reassessment of his position in the publishing house. He began to look back over the years since his career had begun. He had joined the working force of his father's family as a boy of ten. He saw in his mind's eye the small child who began his day at six o'clock in the morning as he swept out the printing plant, built the fire, and straightened the office preparatory to the family working day. He recalled that as the boy grew he assumed errand-boy duties, next he learned typesetting at which he fast became proficient—so adept, he ruminated, that this job was increasingly assigned to him and became a grueling, boring part of his boyhood days. Finally, he looked back on the time when he assumed responsibility for all jobs that pertained to the publishing of a country paper. By his seventeenth year he was prepared to carry on without coaching. Considering his earliest beginnings, he had, in the fullest sense, learned publishing from the very floor of the printing office.

All of this was many years ago in the now dim past—a past and a boyhood lacking in the normal elements of family warmth and security; for his world, despite his father's good intentions, had been one of hard reality to which he had been toughened from childhood. Maybe, he now thought, when you had known nothing else, you did not expect too much from life; you expected only that which *you*, by your own initiative and ability, were able to milk out of it. Such thoughts as these, to which Miller had never before given time, now passed through his mind in clear perspective and sharp review.

He had started out on his own nearly fifty years before. Half a century was pretty much of a lifetime and it was time now, he decided, to pull away from the routine details of the publishing business. Why had he surrounded himself with able people if he was not willing to entrust to them full responsibilities? They had regularly proven themselves capable during his many absences. These key men were highly effective on managerial and editorial levels. Additionally, his three sons had joined the business in subordinate and learning roles and now should be given a chance to go ahead, he reasoned.

With this philosophy, Miller began to move purposefully onto a side position where he could maintain a watchful eye and retain final authority while allowing leeway for the strengths of the others to develop. This was a vital decision for a man of Miller's mold and not an easy assignment for one who had been in full authority for many years. However, he now addressed himself to the change with plan and purpose. He had set his course.

Putting into effect his avowed plan to pull himself away from office detail Miller now found more time to pursue other facets of community life closely connected with his home area of Bellevue.

The *Bellevue American* had served its valuable part in the Lake Washington bridge campaign. The small paper continued to be a stimulating side venture dedicated to the propounding of issues regarding east-side development in which he took increasing interest.

Looking ahead, Miller began to envision vast changes in the rural community in which, since 1928, he had made his home. With the completion of the Lake Washington floating bridge in 1940, the east-side communities had been brought many minutes closer to Seattle's center. While the war was going on, little actual growth took place; however, restless stirrings in real estate began well in advance of war's end. Boom development looked inevitable as peacetime economy returned.

The lure of real estate once more attracted Miller and he saw opportunity for the men who got in on the ground floor and bought property prior to the actual surge of growth. By the mid-1940s two of Miller's sons, Kemper and Miller, Junior, were becoming active in the east-side community of Bellevue. This area seemed the natural center of potential development in which the father and sons now took increasing interest.

In 1944 Miller had purchased approximately twenty-five acres of land in Bellevue, several blocks from the old main street of the town. In 1945 he sold this property to his sons and the three men pooled ideas for the development of a shopping center. While the concept of a well-planned and geographically defined shopping square was a new one then, there were, in fact, some centers which were proving popular and successful in eastern suburban communities. These Kemper visited.

With sufficient study along these lines to make a start, the groundwork was laid for the establishment of the Bellevue Shopping Square, with Kemper and Miller, Junior doing most of the leg work and making contacts necessary for a balanced development to provide the east-side community full shopping facilities. Miller watched with great interest and played a guiding role in the venture.

The admitted goal of the planned shopping square was to make it a one-place answer to all buying needs. Careful work was done to bring together a variety of shops with high-quality merchandise. Most of these contacts were made by Kemper who took a leading part in negotiations during this stage of the project.

Along with the well-balanced community of shops, both large and small, Bellevue needed a new bank, Miller was convinced—specifically, one located in the shopping square. This was a fine challenge to which he addressed himself with his customary enthusiasm. He began by gathering a group of well-known citizens from the east side to form a board of directors, each supplying modest capital. With a good start in that respect, he set about applying to the comptroller of currency in Washington, D.C., for a franchise to open the First National Bank of Bellevue.

Having advanced successfully so far, he was considerably shocked when he received, in due course, a letter from the comptroller stating that a new charter could not be granted for such a bank for reasons clearly laid down, which said, in effect, that Bellevue, according to federal standards, did not qualify, populationwise, for a second bank. Miller, with the rest of the directors, however, felt that in view of the growth projections for the Bellevue area the bank's establishment was entirely logical and the position of the federal comptroller was shortsighted and high-handed.

Application to organize the First National Bank of Bellevue, Washington, was filed in May 1946. This story in the Bellevue American *of May 23, 1946, gives details.*

Miller's hackles rose as he faced an old enemy—bureaucracy. He primed for battle with government authority, knowing well the most effective procedures to employ against it. First guns were fired as his letters began going to many top men in the state who had interests in Seattle and its environs. He made, as well, numerous personal contacts at all political levels. His strongest ammunition was in convincing all parties concerned that the predictable growth for the Bellevue area made the establishment of a second bank entirely logical and soon C. B. Upham, the comptroller, to his probable surprise, found himself under strenuous siege from that quarter.

Whether the comptroller of currency in Washington, D.C., became convinced by the barrage of argument or whether the political pressure became too great, only he could have then divulged. The upshot was, however, that on April 8, 1947, Miller Freeman received a telegram authorizing the bank's operation. The fight to establish the bank was won and Miller was in the banking business. With great jubilation he saw the doors of the First National Bank open in the Bellevue Shopping Square.

T.WA459 12 COLLECT=WUX WASHINGTON DC 14 519P

MILLER.FREEMAN= ǕV. MILLER FREEMAN PUBLICATIONS

BELLEVUE WASH=   71 COLUMBIA ST

:APPLICATION TO ORGANIZE FIRST NATIONAL BANK OF BELLEVUE
APPROVED. LETTER FOLLOWS:
=C B UPHAM DEPUTY COMPTROLLER OF THE CURRENCY.

Telegram dated March 14, 1947, reports approval of bank application. A later wire, on April 8, authorized the bank to commence business.

Miller took particular interest in the selection of a safe for the new bank. There must be a safe—who ever heard of a bank without one? However, for the Bellevue bank it must be a very special one. He hunted all around the state of Washington and finally found one that suited him. It was the cannonball type used in the 1880s and stood about six feet high. It pleased him to have this relic of childhood but it was not merely a toy. This fireproof safe held the bank records—and cash at night—for several years.

Miller was familiar with banking methods and procedures because he had, some years before, served as a founding director of the Pacific National Bank of Seattle which had been organized in the mid-1930s by William Calvert of the San Juan Fishing & Packing Corporation. In this capacity Miller had gained considerable insight into the inner workings of banks and the world of banking finance and he was cognizant of the pitfalls which his new bank faced as its doors opened.

It is significant to mention here that he always claimed a certain skepticism about bankers as a breed and now, in contradiction, chose to further associate himself with their kind. His attitude up to this time might be summed up by the words, "Watch out for bankers—they're after your hide!" Despite this fact it must be guessed that he had had, in actual fact, a subconscious yearning to become a banker and was now realizing a lifelong ambition.

The First National Bank of Bellevue made its way on a modest scale. Admittedly, independent banks with limited capital seldom proved themselves more than moderately good business propositions—and the new bank was no exception to this rule. After six years of financial struggle, in 1953, largely through the initiative of Miller's friend, Charles Frankland, Pacific National Bank president, the Bellevue bank was bought out by the Pacific National Bank of Seattle and became a branch of that large and stable organization.

At this time, Big Chief, the Yakima Indian, leader of the Society for the Preservation of the Cigar Store Indian, who had successfully emerged from this earlier campaign *without* having acquired a wooden Indian*, now confounded his family, friends, and the historians by commissioning a fine wooden figure of an Indian to be placed in full view at the entrance of the newly built Pacific National Bank of Bellevue. This, his signature, remained until after his death as a reminder of the North American Indian who had ended a happy life in Bellevue— perhaps, also, as a symbol of the danger of scalping which a man chanced when he crossed the threshold of a bank.

This incident is related in Part 7, "On the Lighter Side."

Standard Oil Company of California dedicates a marker at the site of the world's first service station, opened in Seattle in 1907. Miller, the station's first customer, stands with Joshua Green, Peoples National Bank, center.

31
LET US FORGET the PAST and LOOK to the FUTURE

ITH THE END OF WORLD WAR II, once more Miller's
thinking turned toward the long-range future of the
fisheries resources of the Pacific. In his view, the vast
north Pacific waters provided opportunity for much
reckless international competition which could ultimately endanger
the yield. The United States, Canada, and Japan were the potential
competitors with no existing treaties at that time large enough in scope
to control their activities in this extensive far northern area.

In September 1945 President Truman proclaimed the United States
ocean fishery policy, designed to open the way for unilateral action to
protect developed fisheries and for international conservation treaties.
One statement in the proclamation asserted that "under certain conditions a nation could declare areas of conservation in the high seas
contiguous to its coast."

Many fisheries people in the Pacific states became alarmed that the
federal government would use the proclamation to take over control of
ocean fisheries to the exclusion of the states. Quite predictably Secretary of the Interior Ickes, Miller's old adversary, supported the idea.
Many, however, saw potential danger from the assertion of federal
authority over areas heretofore considered to be under industry and
state jurisdiction. And, once again, Ickes and Freeman were set on a
collision course.

Miller felt that speedy, strong, and concerted action coming from
the whole West Coast fisheries industry was vital in this situation. He
believed that those within the industry, through their own initiative,
should take the necessary steps toward permanent fisheries' protection and conservation and thus forestall a federal move.

Soon after Truman's pronouncement, Miller called a meeting in Los
Angeles of representatives of the West Coast fishing industry. A large
and determined group gathered and came to quick decisions. The
meeting accomplished three things: It (1) formed a Pacific Fisheries

Congressman Thor Tollefson presents to Miller Freeman and Ed Allen, Halibut Fisheries Commission chairman, the pens used by President Eisenhower to sign a 1954 document implementing the fisheries treaty of 1952.

Conference as a federation of fishery unions and associations; (2) called for a reorganization of the Department of State to give the fisheries resource standing of equal importance in international affairs and concord; (3) created a committee to propose means by which the Pacific states might pool their interests for the protection and conservation of the Pacific fisheries.

Thereafter, specific and well-directed pressure from the industry brought about necessary state legislation governing fisheries protection and conservation. The legislatures of Washington, Oregon, and California passed laws to insure individual state controls, and by the summer of 1947, Congress had approved a three-state compact which clearly precluded federal intervention in state programs.

A satisfying result of this industry action was the establishment in the Department of State of a new office designated "special assistant for fisheries and wildlife," to operate as an auxiliary to the under-secretary of state. The first to hold the office was Dr. D.W. Chapman, a man long active in the Pacific Coast fisheries industry and acceptable to all concerned. Among the accomplishments during his term were establishment of a department policy to consult with the industry concerned before commitment to international understandings; negotiation of an inter-American tropical tuna treaty; and initiation of action for a tripartite treaty for conservation of the Pacific fisheries.

The Pacific Fisheries Conference, which operated so effectively to bring about these and other actions, had its genesis, it should be recalled, in the Joint Committee for the Protection of Pacific Coast Fisheries. This group, mentioned in an earlier chapter, had been brought into being in the early 1930s when the American salmon industry was threatened by the operations of the Japanese on Bristol

At the first meeting of the International North Pacific Fisheries Commission, Miller Freeman sits as consultant with John L. Farley, U.S. commissioner, and Milton S. Brooding, chairman of the commission's U.S. section.

Bay. Action by the Joint Committee had resulted in bringing sufficient pressure to force voluntary withdrawal by the Japanese.

A good many years had passed since that time. A long and bitter war with Japan was won. Now Miller's thinking was that Japan must become a partner with the West in many mutual considerations. Important among them would be the sharing of the Pacific fisheries resource rightfully belonging to all peoples. However, superseding all else in priority, he felt, should be the proper overall control of the industry to assure its perpetuation.

With the agreement of all elements in the fishing industry, the Pacific Fisheries Conference was dedicated to a broad concept of protection for the fisheries of the entire north Pacific and, significantly, it included Japan as a new partner in its deliberations.

It is expedient to telescope the period of negotiations in which Miller, conference chairman, played a leading role and which resulted in a treaty with Japan and establishment of a tripartite commission including representatives of the United States, Canada, and Japan. All parties were dedicated to the proposition of pooling scientific research on every aspect of the fisheries for the lasting benefit of a valuable natural resource of the Pacific.

The North Pacific Fisheries Treaty under which the United States, Canada, and Japan were to undertake the development of the ocean's fisheries on a sustained basis was signed in March 1952 and ratified in the spring of 1953. The principle behind the treaty was: A nation should abstain from entering a fishery that (1) has been under exploitation by one or more countries; (2) is being fished as fully as possible consistent with sustained yield; (3) is under administrative control designed to maintain it on a basis of sustained yield; and (4) is subject to scientific

Speaking before Congress on February 8, 1954, Thor Tollefson pays tribute to Miller Freeman and his half-century campaign for fisheries conservation through international treaties, research, and intelligent management.

North Pacific Fisheries Treaty a Tribute to Miller Freeman

REMARKS
OF

HON. THOR C. TOLLEFSON
OF WASHINGTON

IN THE HOUSE OF REPRESENTATIVES

Monday, February 8, 1954

(Mr. TOLLEFSON asked and was given permission to address the House and to revise and extend his remarks.)

Mr. TOLLEFSON. Mr. Speaker, in keeping with the thought that we should send flowers to the living I desire to pay tribute to a great citizen of the Pacific Northwest, who resides in my congressional district.

Activation in Washington this month of the International North Pacific Fisheries Commission crowns the career of Miller Freeman, Seattle industrial publisher, and his half-century campaign for the conservation of the world's fishery resources through the means of international agreements applying scientific research and intelligent management to the end of "use without destruction."

The North Pacific Fisheries Treaty, under which the United States, Canada, and Japan are undertaking the development of that ocean's fisheries on the basis of sustained yield is the third such treaty which has come into effect in large degree through the vision, faith, and efforts of Miller Freeman. All have grown in the pattern of the first, through which the United States and Canada in 1924 agreed to joint management of the Pacific halibut resource. Largely conceived and carried through negotiation to actuality by Mr. Freeman, the halibut treaty and the research and conservation achieved under it have stood for 30 years as the world's best example of achievement in the field of international fisheries conservation.

Some 20 years ago, the United States and Canada, again under the leadership and stimulus of this man, united their efforts to solve scientifically the perplexing riddle of the once fantastically abundant Sockeye salmon of the Fraser River. From virtual extinction, this run today is rebuilding into one of the rich natural resources of North America. What was virtually lost to men, through this treaty which Miller Freeman shepherded into being now promises to yield food and wealth to Canadians and Americans forever.

With the end of war in the Pacific, Miller Freeman undertook to stimulate thinking throughout the Pacific States to the end that a means might be evolved to prevent destruction of the fishery resources of the North Pacific through reckless international competition. Out of his suggestions grew the Pacific Fisheries Conference, an exceedingly interesting agency in which all elements of the fisheries, unions and owners, workers and operators, crewmen and scientists, unite their efforts to solve fishery problems of common concern. From its inception early in 1946, Mr. Freeman has been the modest chairman of this con-

ference, out of which has come the International North Pacific Fisheries Treaty.

This treaty raises a new concept of conservation. In it the three nations agree to pool their scientific research through the tripartite commission, studying the fisheries which they develop to the end that the crop can be harvested without impairing the future, and that the yield may be sustained at maximum levels. It goes even further in that the nations agree that: Where a fishery resource has been under development, is utilized to its full capacity, is under scientific study and management directed at its conservation, nations not previously engaged in the fishery should abstain from entering it.

Here is a breadth of common concept which has never appeared before in the field of international fisheries. It is a concept and an achievement which has grown out of the thinking and working of Miller Freeman for 50 years in the field of fishery conservation, in the sense which counts wise use as the very essence of conservation.

This man is a publisher, not a scientist, not a fisheries expert. He is the founder and builder of one of the leading industrial publishing houses of this country. His earliest memory is that of traveling through the mountains of Montana with a knock-down print shop carried in two covered wagons which served as well to bear and shelter the Freeman family.

His father was a Confederate soldier from Culpeper Court House, Va., who after the War Between the States chose the way of the West, where he published an unique newspaper—the Frontier Index—which moved with the frontier, west and west.

Miller Freeman was born in Ogden, Utah, 79 years ago. As I have said, his first memory recalls the journey as the wagons moved on to Butte. Then to Yakima, in my State of Washington.

As a very young man, Miller Freeman launched forth as an editor and publisher on his own on Puget Sound. In 1903 at Seattle he founded Pacific Fisherman, the first of his numerous industrial journals, most of them devoted to trial journals, most of them devoted to the natural resource industries. Some of them deal primarily with the Pacific region. Others, like Pulp and Paper, The Lumberman, Mining World, and The Log are national in scope; and all are international in reputation and respect.

A naval captain in World War I, Mr. Freeman has served my State for many years in many ways—and particularly in enterprises which required forward vision, faith, courage, and energy abounding. America's first, and still only, great floating bridge would never have come into being if he had not fought through to fulfillment the enterprise which the engineers conceived, but could not of themselves achieve.

Miller Freeman has made his mark and served his country well in widely varied ways. In this new treaty, with its wider concepts, he serves all mankind, for the Pacific—whose productivity the treaty protects—is one of Earth's richest reserves, with resources tha'., wisely used, can furnish man with food and wealth forever.

study to determine the point of sustained yield and how to maintain it.
A memorable event took place in Washington, D.C., following ratification of the treaty. The first meeting of the tripartite North Pacific International Commission, in early 1954, was inaugurated with a reception given by the U.S. Department of State at Blair House (temporary presidential residence during reconstruction of the White House in the Truman administration). Miller Freeman, who was accompanied to the capital by DeWitt Gilbert, editor of *Pacific Fisherman*, was the sole nongovernmental advisor to the United States delegation.

Miller was then seventy-eight years old and for fifty of those years he had been actively concerned with all aspects of the fisheries industry of the U.S. West Coast. He was a well-known figure to all who attended the meeting and, most particularly, to the Japanese gentlemen who were, for the first time, included in these deliberations. In view of his persistent and continued opposition to the Japanese on several fronts, he, and probably others in the delegation, wondered how he would be received by these people at the historic meeting.

Miller Freeman was asked to speak first. Perhaps no man could feel more gratification at this turn of events than the warrior of the Pacific who now saw the realization of a long-sought goal in this all-inclusive movement to assure the perpetuation of one of mankind's most valuable resources.

The room was hushed as Miller rose to address the assembly. He faced his Japanese audience with the same tough honesty that had marked his years of campaigns against them. He felt no embarrassment. He had fought for *issues* and not against *men*. Something of this spirit must have been appreciated by his long-time adversaries for they listened solemnly and respectfully. In essence, here is what he said to them: "You leaders of the Japanese delegation know that I have long fought against you. With your new recognition of your obligations to abstain from historic fisheries of other nations, already fully exploited and now fully protected, we now respect and accept you as partners in these deliberations designed for the benefit of all of us. You may expect fair and humane treatment from us as long as you yourselves are fair and open."

Iwao Fugita, the head of the Japanese delegation, came forward and with dignity and solemnity assured Miller Freeman that they held for him only the honor and respect which an honest man feels for a brave and worthy antagonist.

Perhaps, of all the events of a life packed with accomplishment, Miller felt at that moment that he had attained a heartwarming and significant goal. Surely the plaudits that followed this memorable meeting gave him great satisfaction. Praise came to him from the highest sources, but he appreciated most highly the acclaim expressed in the *Congressional Record* of February 8, 1954, by Congressman Thor C. Tollefson whose remarks are reproduced here.

32
WHAT'S in it for ME?

W HEN THE FIELD OF INDUSTRIAL MAGAZINE PUBLISHING developed into a new medium in the twentieth century, involving a fresh concept of service to industry, Miller hewed his own innovative codes from bedrock experience. He was one of the first to conceive that there were two major roles for this kind of publishing: (1) to knit together facts common to a particular industry and provide a forum for expression of mutual interests, and (2) through journal advertising, to provide a means of product distribution. Abiding by these simple and basic principles he had built a healthy business for himself which, by flying neither too high in good times nor too low in bad, had withstood the ups and downs of a constantly rising and falling economy.

By the time he had reached his last semi-active business years, he had seen more than a half century of publishing—thus, it was a sweep of an era on which he based his concepts. Bearing these thoughts in mind, perhaps the following incident becomes more understandable.

The president of a large association of East and Midwest business and industrial journal publishing houses—known as Associated Business Publications—visited the Northwest in about 1951. The association of publishing companies for which William K. Beard served as president included some of the nation's largest and most influential in the category of industrial magazines.

The West Coast had few publishing houses comparable in size to those of the East and Midwest members of the association. Part of the ABP president's job was to enlarge membership in the organization and thus spread the doctrines of sound, aggressive, and knowledgeable methods of journal publishing on a national scale for the benefit of the business as a whole.

The West had been considered by the business and industrial East as far-off Indian country. Western publishers were not put in the same league with the big-time eastern fellows. With these thoughts in mind, Beard looked to the West Coast for potential new members.

Beard had met Miller's son, William B. Freeman, who headed the San Francisco office, and interested him in the apparent benefits of membership in a national association of industrial journal people. That was as far as things had gone when the ABP president planned a trip to Seattle to meet Miller Freeman.

Miller had admittedly come a long way on his own. He had made his own rules in industrial magazine publishing and they had proved sound. He was known as a strong publisher, with his business tied closely to basic western industries. In his estimation he was keeping abreast of modern publishing trends and he felt no particular need to become part of an association dedicated to "educating" his outfit to better publishing. To sum up his probable feelings—he *had done* all right, was *doing* all right and had reason to believe he would continue to do so.

Despite his lack of enthusiasm, when Miller met Beard he readily liked the man. He invited him to tell his story over lunch at Seattle's Rainier Club, where he would ask Lawrence Smith to join them.

A fine expounder of the highest principles and policies of industrial magazine publishing, Beard stated his case well. He gave good arguments, all pointing clearly to the fact that publishing on the West Coast was still somewhat behind the times—a little "immature" as he put it—and could unquestionably profit from rubbing shoulders with ABP members who represented a broad national spectrum.

Miller listened attentively, enjoyed the visit with Beard while remaining noncommittal in regard to the latter's persuasive arguments. On the way out of the club after lunch, Beard pressed the proposition of association membership for Miller Freeman Publications. Making his final point, he said that such contact would greatly benefit the firm's West Coast business by bringing it into the family of nationally recognized industrial publishing houses—where it belonged.

Continuing to walk with Beard, Miller was quiet. There was one word in the presentation that raised Miller's hackles. Inadvertently used the term *immature* had been unfortunate. Miller had at that time published for fifty-six years. He was, in fact, publishing prior to Beard's birth. At seventy-six years of age, with a background of recognized accomplishment in industrial journal publishing behind him, he felt that neither he nor his journals warranted the term *immature*. What other publisher, he wondered, had offered services to an industry comparable to those *Pacific Fisherman* had given the Pacific Coast fisheries business? And was Mr. Beard acquainted with the facts concerning his own dedication to the development of treaties for the protection of the resource?

Miller cocked his head to one side, and looked way up at the tall man walking beside him and said, "Mr. Beard, what can your organization do for me?" Taken off guard and realizing that his sales pitch had not struck the proper chord, Beard replied, "Well, Mr. Freeman, obviously we'll have to show you more effectively than *I* did today."

The visit ended shortly thereafter but Beard did not forget the challenging question Miller had asked. It was a simple and basic question—one calling for simple, clear answers. As the association president's plane flew east his ideas were forming. In the most simple terms, what *were* the irrefutable benefits a publishing house would receive from membership in ABP? There were many in *his* mind, but some further step must obviously be taken to convince doubters like Miller Freeman. He began sifting, culling, and boiling to an essence his convictions about the benefits of ABP membership, testing each point against an obvious skeptic like the Seattle publisher.

By the time he returned to his desk in New York, Beard had in mind a pamphlet to be sent out to publishing houses throughout the country as a lure for membership in ABP. Its title was *What's In It For Us?* Miller may have been considerably mollified when, several months later, he received from Beard an impressive presentation triggered by the impact of his question. With it came a note thanking Miller for being the instigator of the idea which had been used as an association sales effort.

Significant was Miller's reaction with respect to the question of Miller Freeman Publications' membership in the association. While he personally did not see particular benefit in joining, it was typical that he made it clear to his sons that they should decide for themselves on the wisdom and merits of membership. And if they did decide to join, he added, they must "reach out and gain the benefits."

The younger generation opted to join. Perhaps it was this measure of willingness to reach out and to gain the benefits which effectively carried on Miller's concept of adaptability. His sons recognized that these were changing times with a vastly more complex set of publishing problems than had been experienced in the past. Thus, in the next generation, Miller's basic publishing principle came into play—a principle which he often expressed aptly with the simile: "Like a boxer, stay light on your feet." His sons did. Their decision was recognized as an important milestone in the continued successful operation of the publishing house.

33
GLIMPSES of a WAY of OPERATING

WHILE MILLER'S PERSONAL GUIDANCE of the daily activities of the business lessened during his later years, nevertheless, he went to the office daily. To him this was a part of a lifetime routine not easily abandoned. And while the business was carried on somewhat independently, he was always keenly aware of the tone and the health of operations on each magazine in the coast offices: at Seattle, Portland, San Francisco and, the last established, Los Angeles. On the overall picture of the journals and their earning power, he maintained a watchful eye. While he accepted the proven abilities of the members of his staff, there was little that he missed, particularly if something went on a tangent—or, he saw something of which he disapproved. Thus, within a reasonable framework, he allowed freedom to those who now took on the full responsibilities of an expanding business, while never completely taking his finger off the pulse of the total operation.

To those in his office he often repeated his principles and philosophies of publishing, gleaned from many years of experience. These truisms of Miller's became a kind of creed within the organization. All of them were simple, sound, and often repeated.

Miller had always been an eminently kind and fair employer. Office rules were laid down within a loose framework and were subject to change according to the logic of any given situation. His method of working with people was to *suggest* that something be done; he rarely issued a direct command. His attitude with his associates was that *results* were the primary criteria—provided high standards of office policy were adhered to. The man who pulled his weight was never faulted—but, for the man who was lazy, he had no use.

Often sharp in his assessment of any fellow who loafed on the job, he was noticeably forebearing when, on occasion, one of his

Pacific Fisherman's *Fiftieth Anniversary Number was published in August 1952.*

employees wandered off the path of regulation. The following incident is illustrative of this.

Walking up the streets of Seattle on a business call with DeWitt Gilbert one midafternoon, he chanced to look across the street to see an employee of the company emerging from a motion picture theater. The man did not see his boss, however.

Miller continued walking, but presently he turned to Gilbert and said, "Remarkable that some people have enough leisure time to go to the movies in the middle of a working day!" The incident was then closed. The batting average of that employee was good enough to warrant disregard of an obvious infraction of rules.

In the area of morals Miller's standards were high. There was no compromise in that category with his own friends or close business associates. At one time a man in his company with whom he and Bess were personally and socially friendly strayed from the fold and left his wife and child for another woman. The friendship ended—there was no compromise on moral rights and wrongs with those who were his intimates.

This was a rare incident, however, for it was one of his principles

The PRIVILEGE of PUBLISHING

PACIFIC FISHERMAN rounds out 50 years of publishing to the fisheries sincerely recognizing the privilege of being the reporter for a great and dramatic industry peopled with men of courage, of vision, of faith.

For truly this *is* a privilege, which we acknowledge humbly, but in pride.

The men of the fisheries are strongly individual, and they need be, for theirs is a field of risk and danger, be it at sea or in the marketplace. To have known these men and written their stories has been a colorful assignment, full of compensations. To have won and kept their confidence for 50 years is the richest reward an industrial journal can achieve.

In this knowledge we are humble. Of this fact we are proud.

IN 1920 we had occasion to publish a "Declaration of Principles," of which the crux and key was:

"*Pacific Fisherman* is an entirely independent publication. It has no alliance with any association, organization or special interest within the trade, nor any obligation to any interest, or group of interests, save the obligation to serve the permanent welfare of the industry as a whole, and its attitude is governed solely by that consideration."

That was written 32 years ago. It was true then. It is true now. It will continue to be true.

It has ever been our conviction as publishers that to serve best "the permanent welfare of the industry as a whole" *Pacific Fisherman* must have an independent position, from which it can raise an independent voice as intelligent disinterest dictates.

We feel this journal can be *for* the industry without being *of* the industry, and that it is better so.

THROUGH 50 years *Pacific Fisherman* has learned many things. One of the simplest, yet most significant, is that the technique of the reporter and editor can be applied to scientific research and scientific management of fish and of fisheries. In a word:

Ascertain the facts, free of pre-conceived notions;

Thoughtfully determine what they mean;

Act upon this analysis with vigor, determination and impartiality.

This approach produced results in halibut research, and solved the secrets of the Sockeye; but the method does more than produce results and solve secrets—it commands public confidence, wins popular support, and gets things done.

THERE will never be an end to the fisheries' problems. As solutions are found, new posers arise. None is more serious for the fishing industry of North America than that produced by mounting costs, which cripple the industry competitively and lay its markets wide-open to the products of low-cost countries.

Here is a problem for today and tomorrow as perplexing and demanding as any of the past.

THERE can be no compromise with conservation. To have a fishing industry, you must have fish; and if you use your fish wisely you can have them forever. This is *true* conservation—"wise use"—and to it *Pacific Fisherman* has been dedicated from its beginnings—is irrevocably dedicated today.

Miller Freeman

In Pacific Fisherman's *August 1952 editorial, "The Privilege of Publishing," Miller Freeman reiterated his belief that a journal for the industry should be able "to raise an independent voice as intelligent disinterest dictates."*

that business and social friendships should be separate. In his mind these relationships were fraught with potential pitfalls. Therefore, generally an employee's personal life remained his own business— unless it inserted itself into the area of his productivity or in some way reflected adversely on the high standards of the business. In that case it became the employer's business as well.

No crystal ball could better reveal Miller's operating philosophies than his Organization Manual—a revered office document. Through its wording and between its lines he tells much about himself and his own firm principles of living and of business. Omitting much of the specific detail of preferred office procedures, its general essence with respect to personnel standards is culled in the following paragraphs.

The Operating Manual

General Regulations: This entire organization must be built up by people who have a genuine taste for this work, who have talent, and who want to make a success of it, and will give the utmost to the enthusiasm and loyalty of the whole.

Relatives and friends of members of the staff will be given the most favorable consideration; however, no one shall be permitted to apply for a position unless it is clearly evident that that person has qualities making his services valuable to the business.

Personal Relations: It should be constantly borne in mind by those in positions of trust that this is an institution and that the actions of a single individual affect the welfare of the whole.

While we never have any disposition to interfere with a man's private affairs, our experience has shown that the people who are drawn into extraneous activities of any kind do so at the sacrifice of the business, by distracting their attentions and dissipating their energies.

No person is expected to do anything that he feels is against his principles.

We have no prejudices against liquor and do not wish to impose undue restrictions on our people. In view of the fact, however, that it is necessary to keep fit and clearheaded in contact with people, experience shows that it is well to keep away from it.

Members of the staff are not permitted to accept entertainment or favors from representatives of any concern from which we buy goods or to which we give business.

Do not take members of your family with you on trips for this company made for the purpose of securing business or editorial matter.

Christmas presents: Employees are not expected to make presents to superiors, nor are superiors allowed to receive them.

Care should be exercised in giving assignments to members of the staff, in order that they not be required to assume any unusual risk or hazard to themselves.

Deportment: At all times remember, "you are the journal." You are not under any obligations of any sort to anyone other than efficient business relations, fortified with polite, but firm refusals to anything not consistent with the good standing and good name of the journal and the business purpose of your presence.

This policy is intended to protect the individual as well as the business; to make it clear that he does not have to stultify himself or sacrifice his self respect, or to endanger his health, his own good name, standing, or efficiency by indulging in liquor or anything else; that he does not have to make himself a "good fellow" in order to secure business, etc.

The disposition of the writer has always been to place full responsibility and impose confidence on all occasions in the members of the staff. There is no desire to lay down restrictions in any narrow sense, or to even have the feeling that the personnel is under close scrutiny by the management.

The writer's belief is that our people should at all times keep in their own sphere. We are news gatherers, or soliciting business. At gatherings a wholesome relationship may be maintained, without stepping out of our role. At any gathering we are not canners, or lumbermen, or papermen. We are there for business purposes only.

All our rules are purposely to be interpreted according to circumstances in the discretion of the individual.

There are certain principles of conduct which, if violated, bring their own penalty in destruction of health, efficiency, and standing of the individual. Any such violations are contrary to the wishes of the business.

While recognizing the natural desire to sympathize with and shield any member of the staff who gets into trouble, it is the duty of every member in such case, where any person loses control of himself, to see that he is at once taken in hand and looked out for; and that the management be immediately notified of the facts, so that proper steps can be taken to look out for such individual.

The writer feels that a clear and full explanation and reiteration of these policies is an obligation owed to the members of the staff. If, in the face of these clearly defined policies, any member of the staff willfully and knowingly violates them, it is on his own responsibility and not that of the business.

The writer has no disposition to take disciplinary action against any member of the staff. If such emergency arises, the business will be forced to take such summary action as may be deemed warranted after thorough investigation of the facts. Such action will become necessary not only in protection of the business, but in behalf of the other members of the organization.

Members violating these instructions will do so at their own risk. If the case be flagrant, it may force dismissal from the business.

As the problem of conduct presents, at times, difficult phases, members of this staff are invited to discuss any points that may not have been made clear in this memorandum, or present any suggestions to the writer.

Safeguarding Information: It must be borne in mind that competition is becoming increasingly keen, and that while there are no secrets in our business, we must keep our operations to ourselves or be to a degree deliberately thwarted by our own lack of reserve.

Failure to observe proper care in such matters is evidence of inefficiency. Deliberate disclosure of plans or discussion of the affairs of the business is disloyalty and will be treated as such. It should be understood that this is a requirement not only for the good of the business as a whole, but for the welfare of all members of the organization individually.

Attitude of Members of the Staff: Equally important for the morale and welfare of the business is the attitude of members of the staff toward others in the organization. Disparaging comment or criticism of the conduct of the business or of individuals serves no good purpose. The fullest confidence is imposed in every member of this organization. In return one hundred percent loyalty is expected.

Personal independence was an ingrained part of Miller's being. Independent: no other word better describes his spirit. Thus, he jealously guarded his right to act, free from the control of others, protecting leeway to function according to his own instincts. Perhaps the western creed as expressed in the well-known phrase, "Don't fence me in," best describes his motto.

Accepting this fact of Miller's nature, it must be conceded that one of his greatest talents was his ability to lead campaigns, represent groups, act frequently as an industry voice—all while maintaining his personal independence. The way this was accomplished is significant.

As has been emphasized before, it was his code never to lead unless his leadership was solicited by a group and accepted under stipulations laid down clearly by him. If his guidance was desired under these circumstances, he willingly assumed leadership, provided there was unanimous expression of approval from all involved. Given such authority, his method of working within groups was in guiding by indirect suggestion. He seldom made adamant statements. The comments he made often pointed toward unavoidable conclusions, but he left their expression to others in the group. Once these conclusions were expressed, however, he was quick to take the initiative, to boil the subject "down to the essence," and point the way for effective action. *Action* was Miller's watchword.

At public gatherings Miller was not known as a silver-tongued orator. He was, however, a forceful speaker when occasion called for it. Then he made his points with clipped, pertinent comments, directed unalterably toward an ultimate goal. He spoke quietly, without fanfare, with simple words and abrupt force, for the express purpose of directing and encouraging thought and action. On this basis he was a highly effective speaker.

Notable contradictions to Miller's customary directness and brevity in addressing public gatherings were his often lengthy dissertations delivered to his family—a captive audience—at the dinner table. Here he lost himself in monologues, often punctuated with thunderclaps of laughter, as he recounted in lucid word sketches events pertaining to one or more of his pursuits. Endlessly absorbing to him—and most often to his listeners as well—these anecdotes sometimes precluded "give and take" comments within the group. But the sheer force of dedication to his projects had the effect of withering small talk. It lifted the sights of the listeners beyond the mundane events of daily life. With him each person seemed able to stand a little higher and look beyond the confusions of the moment to see the horizons.

Old man history must have smiled a little wryly when Miller said of his own father, Legh, "I never remember having a conversation with my father. A discussion with him was a one-sided monologue with responses neither expected nor tolerated." But here the comparison between father and son must end. While Miller was sometimes long-winded with his sons, he was all—and more than all—that an understanding father should be.

34
The STEEL IS TEMPERED

MILLER WAS DESCRIBED by one who knew him well and who had worked with him for many years as, "a very gentle and kind man, as well as a man of steel." The steel in him sometimes coated the inner kindness and misled those who were unacquainted with him. He could scare the oversensitive, for he sometimes sounded gruff, particularly when he was preoccupied in the pursuit of a specific goal. His manner of speaking then was direct and blunt. Directives were delivered with quiet force more terrifying than loud proclamations.

While he was customarily fair and considerate to his employees and to those around him, there were nevertheless moments of irritation and, more rarely, of anger when the atmosphere in his office was charged; the air crackled. But the larger the irritation, the more controlled his voice and manner became. While he might deliver clear, clipped, decisive words in sharp criticism, these occasions were rare and the sting somewhat softened because his voice remained at an even pitch. Those who watched his eyes and mouth could tell more about the state of his emotions than could be determined from the sound of his voice. At these times his steely eyes glinted and his large mouth was set in a hard line.

Conversely, his mouth could predict a change of mood to those acquainted with him. Often any change in the straight line was a weathervane to presage the onset of humor. A twist might warn of a sudden burst of laughter which could startle anyone unprepared— never the old acquaintance. To those who knew him well, these explosive outbursts were predictable and anticipated pleasures.

A revealing incident occurred with a young secretary, newly employed by the publishing house and as yet unacquainted with its owner. When Miller's youngest son became active in the business, there was occasional confusion in the use of the proper appellation for the senior and junior Miller Freemans. Miller firmly believed that his proper designation was Miller Freeman, while his son's was Miller Freeman, Junior.

Miss X, the new secretary, was asked by Miller to take a letter. At the end of the letter, under the space for the signature, she decided that it would be clearer to designate which Mr. Freeman had given her the dictation. On the bottom of the page she typed, Miller Freeman, Senior. She laid the letter on his desk for his signature.

Somewhat later the young lady was carrying on her duties at her typewriter when Mr. Freeman approached her, unsmiling. Very deliberately he placed the letter before her and said, pointing to the typewritten signature, "Miss X, I am Miller Freeman. My *son* is Miller Freeman, Junior." He then walked away leaving the letter on her desk and Miss X flustered and confused. Near tears, she appealed to De-Witt Gilbert, *Pacific Fisherman* editor, asking him what he thought Mr. Freeman wanted her to do. Gilbert calmed the girl and recommended that she retype the letter appending the signature according to Mr. Freeman's wishes. This she did and the issue was closed.

Retha Lysons (later Mrs. Ramon Gill) became Miller's secretary in 1949 to serve him until his death in 1955. She was a young lady cut to Miller Freeman's taste. She ably and quietly carried out a variety of secretarial duties and became as well a close personal friend of his and of Mrs. Freeman's. Miss Lysons had remarkable ability to understand her employer and, with continued association, learned to predict his moods with real talent. Her major job was getting out her boss's ponderous correspondence.

Sending out letters with long lists of carbon copies to any and all who would be interested in the subject under discussion became a way of life for Miss Lysons. Miller's correspondence with congressmen and senators in Washington, D.C., plus those in his own state, became so voluminous that some in the nation's Capitol affectionately referred to him as "the Washington Correspondent."

In 1955 Miller approached his eightieth year. Having suffered a second heart attack three years before, his activities were further curtailed. He had his good days and bad days. Miss Lysons became an expert interpreter of the subtleties of the state of his health and his temper—and she adjusted to them. She had her secret indicators to help her. Here Miller's hat played an important role. She found that there were refinements in the tilt of his hat indicative of the state of her employer's mood and health. She watched these carefully and found that when he was in high gear and fine fettle, his hat was on askew, either cocked over his eye at a rakish angle, far back on his head, or just plain crooked as was normal. The signal was "go" on these days.

There were other, rarer days, when his hat sat firm and straight over his eyes and she learned these were his bad days. She knew the red light was on, the storm warnings were up and she would do well to tread lightly. On these occasions he was apt to bark—but he did not bite.

As she knew them better, Retha Lysons often stayed with the Freemans in their home. It was easy then to confess to them that, at first, her employer had scared her—and still did sometimes. Mrs. Freeman smiled when she heard this and said, "Miss Lysons, when Miller gets that way, you just say 'boo' to him." Miller exclaimed ruefully, "Oh, Mother!" as if a guarded secret had been given away.

Not long after this exchange, on a day when his hat sat straight, he was pressuring people on all sides to everyone's exasperation. Finally, having reached the extent of her patience, Retha Lysons looked at him, bolstered her courage and said, "Boo." In her words, "That dear man looked at me with those eyes of steel, then a smile slowly appeared. That was the influence Mrs. Freeman had on him—he did so love her and respect her opinions."

Bessie and Miller Freeman in 1952.

35
'KEEP to the BASICS, BOYS'

B EARING IN MIND the lack of a close relationship with his own
father or of understanding parental guidance, it becomes
more significant that, with his three sons, Miller became
dedicated to a policy of wise teaching and direction. During
his sons' early years he patiently and persistently exposed them to
enunciations of his own philosophies. He reiterated his wise principles
of living and of business procedures by repetitive stories illustrative of
the points he wished to emphasize.

It is safe to say that there were times in the boys' youth when their
father's talk had less meaning than in later years. But through repetition
his basic concepts became solid foundations on which to rely as they
grew. His clearly delineated postures and attitudes became an ingrained part of their thinking.

As his sons entered the publishing business, he regularly sought to
give them experiences that would illustrate proven principles. He
watched them closely, guided, and suggested. He customarily avoided
adamant directives. Instead, he pointed toward logical deductions.

On rare occasions he could be sharp and critical of them. It appeared, however, that he regretted these times. He realized it was his
own urgent desire to pass along the benefit of his experience that
sometimes made him overanxious and irritable.

His pattern was to bring his sons into contact with his friends and
associates, either on a business level or pertaining to a particular
campaign. Thus, his sons often had the opportunity to meet men of
stature and proven ability.

Additionally, the boys were constantly kept apprised and cur-
rently abreast of their father's activities by clearly defined reports.
Letter writing, always an important part of Miller's mode of operation
in business dealings, also played a vital role in the guidance of his sons.

The letters to his three sons, William, Kemper, and Miller, Junior,
typed by him using the hunt and peck system, encompassed the events
of the often tumultuous years between 1932 and 1953. They included
the period of the deep economic depression which followed the 1929
stock market crash, and later the New Deal years under Franklin

Roosevelt, with the eruption of war in Europe and its spread to the Pacific. They covered the eventual victory and the years of reconstruction. The many paragraphs he wrote define wise business policies, guidelines for sound conduct of personal life, and philosophical vignettes—all gleaned and sifted to an essence from the experience of a life lived to full richness. To his sons he wrote:

YOU MUST TAKE my comments with equanimity. The greater your responsibilities the harsher the criticism. You will be criticized sharply and sometimes, you will think, unjustly. But, right or wrong, you should welcome such criticism as the shortest road toward your own success.

KEEP YOUR BUSINESS to yourself. Do not answer leading questions which may be suddenly and ingeniously launched against you. In plain words, keep your mouth shut. Do not even intimate the condition of your business or personal affairs to anyone under any circumstances—relatives, bankers or anyone else.

IF YOU WILL KEEP on an even keel, attend strictly to business, refrain from having your energies drawn down by extraneous matters, *keep your own confidence strictly,* and finally are not swayed by other minds or other environments, you may look forward to your future with considerable assurance. But when things look wonderful, *look out.*

WHAT NOW SEEMS to me an exceedingly interesting and, in some respects, amusing phase of my own experience, as I look back at my earlier days, is that, in my ignorance I was so intent on my work with my mind fixed solely on the main objective, I didn't realize a lot of people didn't like my ways or the cut of my jib; so I escaped even worrying about what people thought of me.

YOU WON'T LEARN half as much from success as from adversity. The character you develop will not come from lucky breaks but from overcoming problems.

IT ISN'T COURAGE, as the term is ordinarily used, but fortitude that meets the ups and downs of life. Fortitude, as Webster defines it is to: 'Bear pain or adversity without murmuring, depression or despondency; passive courage; resolute endurance; firmness in confronting danger or enduring trouble. Fortitude is the guard and support of other virtues.'

I NOTE your remark that so many problems are confronting you simultaneously you are getting dizzy. Now, you are beginning to realize what made your poor old Father so irascible at times. That's what made him permanently cross-eyed.

TAKE IT EASY. All the more reason why you should operate on a slow speed just now while we are going through this blind reconstruction fog. Let's let the atmosphere clear a little.

THIS IS A BUSINESS that requires a pretty steady mental balance and a philosophical viewpoint at all times.

I WANT you to get fully in your mind this thing of control of your own situation. Maintain serene self confidence, and at the same time be humble as dust. 'Be bold, be ever bold, but not too bold' and always sit with your back to the wall.

THE OBJECT of running a business is primarily to make a living and insure a reasonable independence. Anything undertaken in the future should be first with the idea that this intrinsic position be not jeopardized.

WHAT WE as a family need to be thinking about is a balanced life, within our abilities, and mindful of our limitations.

I HAVE ALWAYS had to meet competition. I have noticed that by going along about my business, cultivating my own sphere of activity, I have always gotten along all right. We are always competing and being competed against. I have nailed a good many hides to the fence myself, primarily by being a little more industrious than the other fellow.

WE CAN'T DO EVERYTHING. I don't think these fellows who strive to be big, bigger, biggest, are any happier than we are. It is wholesome to strive. Let's direct our striving first to keep in good shape, ready to take on anything within our normal sphere.

THE TRUTH is that we are all just ordinary people, and shouldn't kid ourselves about extraordinary capacity. All I have ever had is a capacity for hard work, sufficient to overcome my deficiencies.

IT IS AN ASTONISHING FACT—one I never fail to marvel at—that there are reverse currents in human nature that make it difficult for one generation to transmit either businesses or estates to the next generation. What interests me as a vocation may be repulsive to you fellows. But that's what makes the world go 'round, and gives the fellow of ambition a chance to struggle up to the top. All around you, you can see heirs throw away their birthright and their patrimony. Like the passengers in elevators, some are always going down while others are going up; or like the log booms that continually pass in and out of Lake Washington. It sure make things interesting.

On the subject of education Miller wrote to one of his boys then in college:

NOW, GOING TO college is a business, so far as you are concerned. It is your job to get all you can out of it, as a return on the money and time you put into it.

IF YOU would only reverse the picture you would know that every instructor wants to impart to his students all the knowledge possible, and that he is proud of the students who later become successful.

ANOTHER DELUSION that seems to be rather prevalent is that students can kid the professors, or put it over on them. The fact is they never do. The student never has a chance to fool the professor, because he knows all the characteristics of the young men. You seem to even forget sometimes that your Dad was once a youngster.

NOW WHAT I am trying to tell you is that you should pay no attention to what anybody ever said against getting on a frank, intimate basis with as many of your professors as possible. Particularly never try to shape your course by what the crowd thinks or says. For myself, if I could, I would go around ringing doorbells at the homes of the capable instructors and, if I got stuck, I would certainly go to them and talk things over. All they could do would be to throw you out, which would be good for you.

228

It has been recorded that Miller was Republican national committeeman for Washington and chairman of the delegation at the time of the Philadelphia convention when Wendell Willkie was nominated in 1940. His attitude at the time of the election and defeat of Willkie at the hands of Franklin Roosevelt is typical of his philosophical bounce. Three days after the election he wrote:

THE ELECTION IS OVER. We should adjust ourselves accordingly.

THE WRITER, in looking back over many years since boyhood, has seen the country pass through many crises over which bitter campaigns were waged.

THE WRITER urges you to adapt yourselves philosophically to the world you live in. Hold steadfast to your opinions and ideals.

FORGET POLITICS and turn to your private business. Maintain at all times a constructive attitude. You will find a lot of people discouraged, throwing up their hands with a defeatist complex. Don't be influenced by their viewpoint, but get in and concentrate on your own work.

In 1944, at the time of the election of Franklin Roosevelt for a fourth term, the attitude of most Republicans in the country was of deep and hopeless depression. Miller wrote:

WHATEVER we may have thought about it, most of the people who went to the polls yesterday voted to keep the New Deal in.

MY RECOMMENDATION is that the fact be recognized that the New Deal is returned to power by the will of the majority of those who voted yesterday. Nothing is to be gained by continuing any discussion about it. It is imperative that we do not be distracted from concentrating on our own publishing business, being good reporters and interpreters of the happenings in the fields of our various journals.

At the time of the attack on Pearl Harbor, Miller directed these words to his staff:

THE ATTACK upon the citizens and defenses of the United States by the Imperial Japanese navy and air forces Sunday morning means that we are at war.

FROM NOW ON the entire effort of the American people will be directed toward the end that this war result in victory. There will be an all-out fight for our very existence that will affect not only our business but each and every one of us in many ways. No one can foresee all the effects or the ways in which we will be forced to adjust our affairs in the light of war conditions.

THERE WILL BE a great deal of confusion and undoubtedly we will have to withstand some severe shock. I want to urge that we all remain calm and continue our duties in the business without any slackening of effort. For the time being I construe that to be our most loyal course of action.

On January 11, 1942, he wrote:

I DON'T THINK the war will last ten years. Germany is on the defensive, and while Japan is now putting on a great show, she is extending herself all over the map. She won't be able to maintain her lines of communications.

Miller's thinking ranged over wide areas and here he talks about the Bible:

THE ARTICLE you sent me is curiously correct in picturing my own reaction to reading the Bible. It is interesting to old men because it pictures vividly all the old-age characteristics of human nature with all of its foibles, vanities, and weaknesses. From these are made the deductions of conduct and standards of practices of the sages of a race that throughout all its history has faced tragedy and persecution, largely of its own creation.

TO YOUNGER PEOPLE, the Bible is dry, a good deal of it a muddle. But that's human nature. There are a lot of highly entertaining stories of adventure and romance in it. I like the yarn about Joseph, and also the great epic of Moses and how he led his people out of the wilderness and laid down for them a pretty fine set of precepts.

ANY EDUCATED MAN should know the Bible. It is an example in the power of simple description, which is our business.

THE FUNDAMENTALS of the Bible make standards of practice that can't be beaten.

On sound general business policies his comments ranged widely to give a picture of Miller's thinking on a variety of management problems:

BEING AN OWNER does not entitle one to be a lone wolf. He must be 100 percent responsible to the requirements of the business. He must fulfill the obligations of his position as faithfully, promptly, and efficiently as his abilities and capacities permit. No person, beginning with the writer, can avoid being fully submissive to the disciplines of the business.

DO NOT ENCOURAGE your friends to come to the office, dropping in for purely personal visits. Friends worthwhile will be too busy. The others don't count anyway.

STANDARDS OF TREATMENT of visitors are exceedingly important. Be at all times courteous, but keep your callers strictly to the limits of their business, and let your conversations and attitude always be on the basis of the welfare of your own business.

I NEVER ENCOURAGE talebearers about others of the force. I think you know that I know pretty well the human characteristics and the faults of our people. A lot of things of a minor nature I don't show any evidence of seeing.

I HAVE ALWAYS FOUND that I could get along all right if I recognized realities and adjusted my overhead to suit changing conditions. This applies both to the business and to personal overhead. I have never deluded myself with the policy that superficial showoff and glamorized promotion are good for business. Maybe that philosophy is subject to challenge. Maybe not. I don't believe in miracles, either in this business or in cigarette advertising.

Once he wrote a comment about one of his publications in typical manner:

ITS EDITORIAL MATERIAL is very good. In quantity it is ample and features excellent.

NOTWITHSTANDING my injunction, they persist in tinkering with the makeup by running special boxes on many pages, thinking that this is the way to emphasize certain items of news. In my opinion, this shows a poverty of mentality and is a mere subterfuge employed by editors lacking in the qualities necessary to produce a journal filled in itself with immediate information and which could just as well be emphasized by plain headings and embraced in the usual run-of-the-mill makeup.

On editorial objectivity he commented:

UNDERSTAND that it is important that you adhere strictly to sound principles in treating the news fairly and without bias. You must guard yourself against allowing the journals to be guided by political or partisan points of view.

In a time of crisis, he said:

MY POLICY has always been to make whatever I undertake work—or to abandon it. It makes no difference how alluring a prospect may be, if it is found to be unprofitable, get rid of it. Take the losses and devote your energies to something worthwhile. Don't be self conscious about it or be deterred by any thought of impressions that others may have of your retrenchment. They will be all too busy with their own troubles even to think about yours.

And finally on the subject of flexibility:

I WANT TO CALL your attention to the fact that I do not go around, and never have, giving hard and fast instructions; but in all cases and with everybody, no matter how humble their position, I present my views to them with the thought that if they have the opportunity in turn to express themselves and to test out in actual practice their workability, we shall come to the best conclusions. You do not have to argue with anybody as to the soundness of your principles when you can show that you can go out and apply them successfully yourself.

MAINTAIN YOUR FLEXIBILITY of mind. Nothing courts disaster more than taking a rigid position. You have to be light on your feet, as a boxer.

An example of Miller's flexibility lies in a brief incident which tells much about his personal and business philosophy. One day he walked into the office of *Pacific Fisherman* and suggested that something be handled in a certain manner. The young man to whom he had made the suggestion was comparatively new, but he had studiously read the gray-backed manual of Miller Freeman Publications' practices, so he replied:

"I'm sorry, sir, but that is against the rule." And he explained how it was.

"Oh, I see," Miller said, starting for the door and then turning back abruptly, he asked, "Who made that rule?"

"You did, sir," said the young man.

"Well, young man, in this business rules are flexible things. We have only one rule which must *never* be broken, and it is: Any rule is to be broken when to do so is intelligent and serves the best interest of the public and of this business."

CHARACTER · QUALITY · AMERICA FIRST · ACCURACY · ENTERPRISE

Seattle Post-Intelligencer

TRUTH–JUSTICE 14 * Seattle, Tuesday, August 31· 1954   S   PUBLIC SERVICE

A Lesson Is Here

THE NEWS said this: there is a record catch of halibut in this year of 1954. It was news indeed, and good news at that.

But achievements of the International Pacific Halibut Fisheries Commission run well beyond this record catch of halibut—this season—as a result of the program fostered by the cooperative enterprise of Canada and the United States.

Record catches are always welcome—but here is one made not at the expense of the future, but rather by accomplishments of the past. And the real accomplishments of the halibut commission can never be measured in pounds of fish alone, nor in dollars.

Obviously, the attainment of this commission—over 30 years—has been this: a great resource, conserved and rebuilt.

Less apparent, but of broad importance and bright promise, are two bases on which have been builded other international undertakings in the field of fishery conservation.

TREATIES seeking to safeguard the fisheries of the Northwest Atlantic, the sockeye salmon resources of the Fraser River System, the tunas of the tropical Pacific, in fact all the fisheries of all the North Pacific today are founded on these two principles which, now, are the prime factors of the halibut program.

And what are these principles? They are so simple as to seem obvious in the light of hindsight.

But if they had not been proven in basic, dedicated research—plus hope and faith — on the halibut banks of the Gulf of Alaska, the cause of fishery conservation would be back at its blind beginnings today.

The two principles—so vital to all of us now in this great region—are these:

FIRST—That international cooperation in the conservation of a fishery resource of the high seas can succeed whenever

sound, objective, hopeful research determines truths which intelligent men may accept as basic for the protection of a great resource which one nation must share with others.

Second — That determination and measurement of reasonable utilization consistent with sustained yield (and this has so well applied to timber here, as it has to fisheries) is the heart of the biological problem of ocean fishery conservation. Take more than the measure of reasonable utilization and depletion sets in. Take less, the resource rebuilds itself.

Simple? Yes, simple now.

Yet back in 1924, international fishery conservation and research was as blank and bleak as an Aleutian fog. And there, against this blanket of gray ignorance, the halibut commission's work began.

Who did it, who began it all?

THE FIRST commission was composed of Miller Freeman, Henry O'Malley, J. P. Babcock and W. A. Found. Dr. W. F. Thompson of our great University of Washington was the first director who planned and carried through that first faltering decade of study and thought. Edward W. Allen has served the commission continuously since 1932; and H. O. Dunlop, present director of the commission, was charter member of the staff—as was Dr. Richard Van Cleve, today director of the University's School of Fisheries.

Of course there are more who should be named—for the alumni of Dr. Thompson's early staff all rank high now among men of science who grapple these days and nights with the great problem of oceanic conservation. He is a great teacher, and the works of a great teacher are forever multiplied.

So, as we said above, the achievements of the halibut commission are counted not alone in pounds of fish, nor in dollars. Nor yet even in jobs created, and families sustained, over the years.

Such achievements are counted most of all in the minds of men.

And in the principles which guided them.

Basic Pattern

TWO POINTS of fact loom high out of cloudy complex of the 10 million doll claim of Neah Bay's Makah Indian tr for loss of treaty rights as result of internatio conservation of the halibut and sockeye salm

These points may be examined and apprais without in any way undertaking to prejuc the Makah case; and they should be so examin because they affect not only the Makahs the well-being of every other man and wom in the coastal region of the Pacific Northwe British Columbia and Alaska.

Fact 1: If the United States and Cana had not entered into the halibut and socke salmon treaties in 1924 and 1937, these spec by now would be on the verge of commerc extinction.

Fact 2: Knowledge gained by scienti research made it possible to reverse depleti and restore abundance without restrictic crippling to the economy of the fishing indust.

AS MILLER FREEMAN testified at t Makah claims hearing, the downwa trend of depletion was sweeping t halibut and sockeye salmon into the sorry co pany of the sea otter and the buffalo. And knows, for he was perhaps the first to se the trend, and to recognize that only by tre could international competition be convert into international conservation. Convinced the danger, and that it could be countered, never left the fight until it was won.

It is fascinating that as the scientific searches of William F. Thompson, his staffs a successors, produced knowledge of the halib and the sockeye, they also found ways by whi the resources could be restored without inju to the industry, and actually without reduci the fishermen's catch.

How could this be? Very briefly, thus: In the case of halibut, by regulating the ti and place of fishery in such a way as to all more fish to reach spawning age. So regulate the fleet was able to continue its rate of catc while the decline in abundance was revers and the depleted population was rebuilt. Th process began about 1934. Twenty years lat the 1954 halibut catch was the largest in histor.

SOCKEYE RESEARCH showed that it ha been a mistake to blame depletion who on overfishing, that many escaping socke failed to spawn effectively because they we delayed or blocked at Hell's Gate. The answ was: fishways at Hell's Gate, supplemented regulations designed to make the catch fr the surplus of strong races, while permitti the escapement of prime spawners bound f barren or seriously depleted tributaries.

The sockeye treaty became effective 1937, fishways were finished in 1945, and abo that time regulation began.

The catch in each of the last four years h broken long standing records for its cycle—and that of 1954 was the largest catch of any ye since 1913.

These are achievements which affect t well-being of all men, for they carry a less with application to other resources and oth problems.

First find the facts. Then act on the intelligently.

36
NOT BAD for an UNEDUCATED MAN

FTER MILLER SLOWED his activities and mellowed, he paused more often to reflect on a full-paced life. Introspection had not been a habit of his but, with the years of activity piling up behind him, the cumulative weight of his accomplishments made him pause more often to assess his life. Inevitably, he experienced feelings of pride and satisfaction over acknowledged success. Some of these clearly expressed tributes to his effectiveness had touched him deeply as they came his way.

Perhaps one in particular had impressed him with a real sense of pride as well as a touch of waggish humor. When he was awarded an honorary degree from Whitman College in Pullman, Washington, he reflected on the giant step he had taken from the one-room Ahtanum school to this newly exalted position in the world of higher education.

Whimsically, he recalled the story he had often told apropos of his brief education. To the enjoyment of everyone he explained that when he reached the fifth grade he suddenly learned the principle of compound interest and immediately said, "How long has this been going on? Let me out of here!"

To a relative, he wrote:

> I've been under a very great strain during the last month, having submitted my examination papers to Whitman College. I've just received the news that I've passed and that they are going to give me a degree. I don't know what kind of a degree they are going to confer on me, in fact I think they are going to find this a sticker, even though in my one winter term in school I did spell down the whole school in a spelling bee.
>
> Anyway, as you know is always the case with us College fellows, I'm all exhausted and must get away where I can rest my mind from

---

Editorials in the Seattle Post-Intelligencer *on August 31, 1954, and June 30, 1955, attest to the success of the halibut and salmon treaties in restoring and conserving the fishery resource of the Pacific Northwest. Both editorials refer to the part played by research in determining facts on which to base intelligent action.*

the terrible stress I've been going through.

We are going to have the house all decorated for you in our college colors. I have been practicing the old college songs with my fellow alumnus, Mr. Nard Jones.

I wear my dressing gown around the house now with a mortar board hat practicing the steps for the big day when I march in the procession at Commencement.

I have not been to Walla Walla for some years. At times I have wondered when I would be going over there to reside in another very classy institution together with many of my prominent banker, bootlegger and business friends. (Re: the penal institution there.) I have reflected so much on this I'm going to be very careful in the Commencement parade not to put my hands on the shoulders of the dignitary in front of me and fall into lockstep.

Despite this touch of humor Miller honored the educational process. As he sat on the college platform in eastern Washington that hot June day in 1934 to receive this honor from the hands of his friend, Dr. Stephen Penrose, Whitman president, he must have wondered at the varied ways by which men went about attaining acknowledged educational success. And he surely smiled inwardly as he recalled that his friends, trustees and overseers of the college, had told him he must respond to the president's award in Latin. It was regrettable that he had worked so hard on his acceptance speech in Chinook Jargon, the language of the Northwest Indian, and to his disappointment was not asked to deliver it after all. It would have begun, "My Tillicums."

As the speakers on the platform droned on, his thoughts ranged far back to his beginnings. For him, the earliest recollections at the age of four had been sudden tragedy with the loss of his mother, which was followed by a period of terrifying confusion. From that point, his educational route had begun with four years at the Catholic boarding school, followed by a short winter semester in the one-room Ahtanum school. This period saw him doing hard work for a child, combining strict disciplines with training in manual skills learned at the Tanner ranch through absolute necessity. Returning to his father's home, his had been a pioneering childhood of harsh reality in an environment dominated by a Spartan father to whom sternness was a prideful code. Despite these early vicissitudes, Miller now thought, that small boy must have assessed wisely, judging and separating the important from the unimportant and somehow adapting to his life and his hard world on his own individual terms. Later, it was true, he had broadened his education on his own initiative with omnivorous reading. But what he had acquired, and for which he was now receiving acclaim, was of his own making, forged by the events of his youth and by his adaptation to these particular circumstances.

At a later date another compliment that he greatly valued came to Miller from an educator. He had sent a file of correspondence to Dr. Russell Blankenship of the University of Washington English Department, himself a brilliant writer and talker. In returning the correspon-

Three Freemans celebrate their birthday on July 20, 1955. Twins Neal, left, and Miller III are thirteen years old. Miller Freeman gets ready to cut his eightieth birthday cake.

dence, Dr. Blankenship opened his letter as follows: "I want to say in the beginning that I frankly envy you your really fine ability to express yourself. Of all the writers represented in the file, you use the best English. Your style is direct, clear, and forceful. No writer can reasonably ask for more."

One day in the summer of 1955, shortly before his death, Miller gratefully accepted one of the most valued compliments he ever received. He was in the company of Robert J. Schoettler, Washington State director of fisheries, and DeWitt Gilbert, editor of *Pacific Fisherman*. All were involved in discussion with Governor Arthur Langlie on the attitude of the state of Washington with respect to proposals for a possible extension of the sockeye salmon treaty to include pink salmon as well.

As the discussion concluded, the governor turned to Schoettler and Gilbert and he said something like this: "You know, if Miller Freeman had never done anything more—and of course he has done a great deal more—for the state of Washington than the services he rendered in conceiving and carrying through into effectiveness the halibut and sockeye salmon treaties, his contribution still would be one of the most important as well as the most unselfish and lasting of any made by any individual to this state in its whole history."

235

Miller's comment following this compliment conveys its meaning to him: "Spoken as they were, with evident sincerity to a group of only three men, by a man of Governor Langlie's position and principles, the words touched me deeply. I pass them along because only four men heard them and they are not elsewhere in the record. Perhaps I may be pardoned for being proud of them."

It is seldom that a man is afforded the opportunity to savor a time which can rightfully be called his "moment of fulfillment," when family, friends and associates pay warm, unstinting tribute to his accomplishments. But Miller was so honored as he reached his eightieth birthday on July 20, 1955. Surrounded by his large family at a birthday dinner in his home, "Big Chief," the "full blooded North American Indian, born on the Yakima Indian Reservation" took the spotlight and glowed with deep satisfaction as he received the plaudits from his tribe and from the many who had wished him well.

Among the many messages Miller received from friends and associates as he reached his eightieth birthday was a letter from Albert Wilson, editor of *Pulp and Paper*. This letter struck a particular chord of appreciation, and Miller's answer is perhaps a proper summation of a major theme of his life. Therefore his reply is reproduced.

Following his eightieth birthday, Miller Freeman tells Al Wilson of his pride in receiving Wilson's "warm expression of goodwill and regard."

Dear Mr. Wilson:

I have received a good many letters and telegrams congratulating me on arriving at my 80th year. I am particularly proud of your warm expression of good will and regard dated July 16th. You have emphasized my "intense and never-ending defense of the dignity of the individual man", and have stressed that this has characterized so many things that I have done. I am not only highly pleased but feel quite humble that you have recognized this trait, which has been consistent throughout my entire career. I hope and trust that this fundamental principle will be kept in mind and maintained by the members of the staff of the Miller Freeman Publications. If you feel so deeply please endeavor to pass it on to other members of the staff so that they may uphold it in turn not only among their fellow workmen but those with whom they come in contact.

Sincerely,

Miller Freeman

VII
On the
Lighter Side

37
INCIDENTS in a BUSY LIFE

N THE TELLING OF MILLER'S YEARS of nearly perpetual activity on many fronts, an emphasis on his business life, in combination with his multiple side activities, appears to take precedence over all else and to convey the picture of a man of restless, single-minded action. This he surely was. But to provide a balance, to leaven his attitudes and, inevitably, the pace of his career, an element of deep humor combined with innate humility played its vital role. These qualities of humor and humility modified and enriched a life, which, like a flame, might otherwise have burned with undue intensity. Despite his continual activity, he took time along the way to enjoy and to savor the richness life offered.

To see Miller in proper perspective, random glimpses, observations about him, incidents that occurred during the years of his greatest activity must bring him into better focus. Thus, it seems justified to recount a few personal glimpses that did not fit naturally into the continuity of this narrative.

The Crooked Hat

Until the 1950s, the white collar worker and executive regularly wore a fedora to work—or, in fact, whenever he went out. It was a part of the uniform of the day—as well as a badge of respectability.

There were refinements to the wearing of a hat. If a man wore an expensive hat, well placed on his head, he was assumed to be a successful man. Conversely, if a man had lost his job and his hopes, his hat mirrored his battered pride. It might be old, worn with limp dejection or a jaunty tilt, but it told a subtle story.

Successful executives had a certain way of placing their hats carefully on their heads to make a straight line across their foreheads, directly over their alert, intelligent eyes. Thus, properly hatted, they were recognized as men of substance.

While Miller was known as a leading citizen in his community, he was seldom seen with his fedora on in a manner commensurate with his stature. He did not *put* a hat on—he threw it on. If the first shot was good and the angle happened to be correct, that was lucky chance.

Because his percentage of bullseye shots was notoriously poor, he was often recognized from a distance by his crooked hat. Thus, the picture of Miller on the streets of Seattle was of a short, rather slim figure, neatly dressed and otherwise well-groomed—with his hat on sideways.

The Case of the Improvident Doctor
Golf was one of Miller's diversions before 1941 when his first coronary occurred. One of the highlights of each year was his trek to Victoria, British Columbia, with a group of friends for a stag weekend. The assemblage included a lawyer, a doctor, several merchants, and Miller, a publisher. All were pretty well-off financially, except Doctor Ford, who did not seem to care much about having a lot of money anyway. He was held in affectionate esteem by these friends, most of whom were also his patients.

Doc belonged in the category of the old family doctor who tended the ills of his friends, their wives, and children. He came willingly to the bedside of a sick patient at any time of day or night, according to the custom of his even then fast disappearing kind. As times changed and his friends became more affluent, he never remembered to raise his rates and never hurried people to pay their bills. He plugged along contentedly on a modest income.

With his hat on at an angle, Miller Freeman was in fine fettle.

On one annual outing Doc came in for a good amount of ribbing on this score—and the others on their weaknesses as well. In the club locker room one day after a round of golf, the lawyer, whose sharp tongue had flayed many on the witness stand, fell to berating the benevolent doctor. He said, "Why don't you get on to yourself? Why don't you make yourself some money? Why do you go on charging people what you used to years ago? Why don't you jack up your fees where they belong like modern doctors do? Why do you go on working for peanuts? Why don't you charge what you're worth?" As usual, the doctor smiled good-naturedly while this monologue continued.

Miller listened thoughtfully, saying nothing. Presently he pulled a checkbook out of his pocket and began writing. Finally he said to the lawyer, "You know, what you've been saying to Doc has set me thinking. *You* know he doesn't charge enough because he doesn't charge *you* enough. And you've made me realize that he has been mighty easy on his charges to the Freemans."

He handed the doctor a check, saying, "That's for one thousand dollars."

Turning to the lawyer he said, "I'm giving it to him as a means of making up for some of the mercy he's shown the Freemans over the years." Then Miller leaned forward and, looking the lawyer squarely in the eye, he added, "I'm sure you will want to do as much."

Spoofing the General

In the heyday of profit-taking late in the 1920s, Miller's friendly adversary of the *Seattle Times*, General Clarance Blethen, moved to the east shore of Lake Washington not far from the homes of Miller and his close friend, Will Calvert. Blethen had built largely and lived in gracious luxury along with many of his neighbors on Medina's Gold Coast, as that east-shore area was then called. However, he went one step further in grandness of living style by acquiring a large and excellently appointed yacht which he tied at the dock below his fine home and manicured lawns.

It became Blethen's custom to commute to Seattle, four miles across water, aboard his yacht, often running parallel to the scheduled ferry which carried many of his neighbors to the Seattle side of the lake. His impressive craft was well crewed by uniformed sailors. The ritual of his boarding in the morning, surrounded by smartly saluting attendants, became the subject of much discussion—and a delightful diversion as well—for the residents of Bellevue. Miller, more perhaps than anyone, enjoyed his friend's display of ostentation and joshed him good-naturedly on this score.

Will Calvert lived directly across the entrance to Meydenbauer Bay from Miller's home. The two often signaled with flags on special occasions and often enjoyed communication by rowing between their homes.

One Sunday morning at about the time Blethen usually began his spectacular voyages, Miller left his own dock aboard his rowboat with several young men sporting vestiges of tattered seamen's uniforms. A length of ancient carpet was rolled up in the bow. In the stern, in military dignity, wearing his old and misshapen officer's cap, Miller sat issuing clipped orders to his crew. The battered entourage pulled slowly across the water, tied up at the Calvert beach, all the while alerting its host with a series of shrill police whistles.

The Calverts, young and old, gathered at that moment for breakfast, streamed down to the shore to receive these unexpected dignitaries. When the audience had reached sizable proportions, Miller's ragtag crew stepped smartly on to the shore, unrolled the faded red carpet, lined up and came to stiff attention. Miller, the stern-faced admiral, stepped ashore and strode the carpet to the lawn in proper military fashion. No further explanation was needed for anyone there—and two old friends enjoyed a good laugh.

The Society for the Preservation
of the Cigar Store Indian

The story of Miller's part in establishing and leading the National Society for the Preservation of the Cigar Store Indian belongs in the list of his more publicized, if less important, accomplishments. Here once again we see him running true to his purposes when he worked for the conservation of a kind of national resource—more exactly an historical timber resource.

This new venture began during a visit to New York City with an invitation to a luncheon meeting of the American Tobacco Institute. Reasons for the invitation are unfortunately obscure. However, during the course of the luncheon, Miller was called on to make a few remarks and, in so doing, casually suggested that the institute initiate a campaign for the preservation of the cigar store Indian which, he recalled, during the 1880s and 1890s had stood prominently in front of every cigar store across the land. He deplored the fact that these relics of Americana were fast disappearing from the national scene, and said he felt that some effort should be made to preserve this form of art. What better group, he asked, could lead such an effort than the American Tobacco Institute? The tobacco industry, he pointed out, had originally spawned and popularized these wooden figures. Having said these words in casual jest, he sat down. But the man from the West had posed an intriguing idea.

With enthusiastic imagination, two young and eager advertising men for the tobacco industry summarized his remarks for the press. Fortunately for them there was little news of particular import on the national scene that day. The United Press willingly sent the item flashing across the country.

Miller, amused and surprised by the publicity, soon returned to the West Coast. By the time he arrived home he had nearly forgotten his words. But the two young advertising men did not forget the incident

At Terre Haute, Indiana, an injured cigar store Indian is wheeled into the hospital by Dr. Anthony W. Pendergast and an assistant.

Cigar store Indian rates place in fashion display of Bergdorf Goodman.

and, finding they had created a sensation, proceeded to build up the story to great proportions with continued press releases.

To Miller's surprise, letters began arriving from people in various parts of the country commending him on his desire to preserve this valuable symbol of Americana—the cigar store Indian. While a little taken aback by the national publicity his remarks had spawned, he nevertheless began to relish the incident and its growing repercussions. The national press readily joined in the fun, and the whole waggish idea became a happy countrywide diversion.

At some point during the publicity following his appearance before the Tobacco Institute, it was suggested that Miller become president of the organization for the Preservation of the Cigar Store Indian. Considering the fact that the position did not entail a swearing-in ceremony or other weighty official duties, Miller joined readily in the gag and accepted the appointment, suddenly finding himself the father of a national movement.

Thus, Miller, the Yakima Indian, became a sort of clearinghouse for matters dealing with the subject of the wooden Indian, who, it seems, had been hiding in frightening numbers in dust-covered obscurity in basements and attics all over the country.

With this rebirth of interest in their existence, people who harbored these monstrosities, inherited from their forebears, suddenly took enlivened interest in them. For any one of a number of reasons, these people wrote to Miller Freeman to discuss their ownership of one or more of the carved figures.

The president of the "association" found that the people who wrote to him fell into one of four categories and he filed their letters accordingly. In the first category were those few who had an honest interest in Americana and in the wooden Indian as a part of that interest; in the second, publicity agents for the tobacco business; in the third, a few who enjoyed the diversion and treated it as a harmless gag. The fourth, and by far the largest, category included those who had reluctantly given attic room to the wooden figures for many irritating years and were more than anxious to find a market for them.

Miller's file of correspondence grew to include letters containing intricate descriptions of particular Indian figures and enclosing many photographs of finer specimens. He became acquainted with voluminous facts about the great variety of replicas which had stood at the doorways of the old cigar stores.

With tongue-in-cheek, Miller suddenly became an authority on this form of art, all the while heartily relishing the absorbing diversion. The episode, lasting many months, became a form of recreation for Miller, laced, nevertheless, with a certain amount of danger from which he fortunately emerged unscathed. In actual fact, he did not want and never bought a cigar store wooden Indian for himself. He did, however, have a fine wooden carving of an Indian placed at the entrance of the Pacific National Bank of Bellevue, as recounted earlier.

A Dash of Color for Big Chief

It was noted earlier in his story that in his youth Miller liked bright colors and, specifically, tended to admire daring pattern in the choice of his first business suit—admittedly an unsuccessful venture. For many years this leaning toward colorful dress was kept under control with loving and careful guidance by his wife. Nevertheless, as he grew older, and somewhat harder to manage, he broke from control periodically and stealthily escaped to buy red shirts in a day when they were not as socially acceptable as they are now.

On the Fourth of July, which was a day of picnics and celebration at his home, Miller regularly wore his red shirt, adding his old bowler hat and carrying an American flag. This attire added a great note of festivity to the day and brought him into close partnership with the younger members of the family.

After this breakaway in his Fourth of July shirt, Miller ventured a step further toward Indian tradition when he bought an Indian chief's full-feathered headdress. It was a fine piece, immensely colorful, with feathers falling well down his back. He wore it on special occasions and often spoke words in the Chinook tongue. This outfit was worn more frequently with the arrival of increasing numbers of grandchildren. Surrounded by a wholly admiring band, he was a figure of tremendous impact with the toothless set, and it was not long before he became known as "Big Chief" by the gang and, as such, the true leader of his tribe.

Halo Kumtuks

Chinook Jargon was Miller's second language. This jargon was originally employed as a means of communication among Indian tribes of Oregon, Washington, British Columbia, and Alaska and the people of various nationalities who came to the Northwest from the 1880s on. Emerging from many tribal tongues, in combination with English and French, it was a language finally developed of necessity for use by the fur traders, those in commerce, the missionaries, and travelers.

While it is largely lost today, at the time Miller was growing up, and

Another tribal pose: Miller Freeman with Jimmy Swinnerton, well-known artist and cartoonist, enjoy themselves during a desert holiday.

well into the twentieth century, people of the Northwest quite naturally interspersed Chinook Jargon into their talk. Often heard were words such as *klootchman* for "woman," *wawa* for "talk," *potlatch* for "gift," *tillicum* for "friend," *skookum* for "strong."

On one occasion, meeting an old Indian in the Palm Springs area, Miller said a few words to him in Chinook Jargon. The man listened stoically, staring unsmiling at this queer customer who had so addressed him, and finally answered in his native tongue, fast and indistinctly, so that Miller could not follow the comment. The latter respectfully responded *Halo Kumtuks*, meaning, "I do not understand." The Indian viewed this intruder with considerable disdain and said, "I knew it all the time." The Yakima Indian recoiled in hurt. He had reason to expect more solicitous treatment from this desert brother!

North American Indian Takes a Cruise

In 1939 Miller and Bess took an extended trip to South America on the luxury cruise ship, *Nieuw Amsterdam*. On board were many people of note, including a large representation of those registered in the social *Blue Book*.

The trip proved to be a stimulating diversion and a thoroughly enjoyable eye-opener to Miller. With the exception of short trips to Canada and Mexico, he had not previously traveled out of the United States. This was in all respects a de luxe cruise representing a sophisticated form of travel he had not before encountered. The glitter and affluence of the passengers provided him with great opportunity to spoof "show" and ostentation in a good natured way—a sport he shared with many on board.

The Yakima Indian was dazzled by statistics regarding the liner with its 601 passengers and 800 crew members. (These statistics were so reported by him.) The guests on board were dressed appropriately for every hour of the long lazy days and, according to him, the diamonds worn by the ladies were so large and brilliant that it was necessary for the passengers to wear dark glasses day and night to protect their eyes.

Memos sent by him while aboard ship read as follows:

"Our stateroom practically on water-level. Looks like might fish out of porthole."

"Seated at table with dignified publisher of Lawrenceville, Kansas, *Union Journal*. In ten minutes learned Mrs. Simon, publisher's wife, is eligible for Daughters of 1812; that Mr. Simon's grandpappy was scalped by Indians."

"Told we are now entering tropics. First sign, many women's big toes sticking out of their shoes."

"Everybody except us has deck chairs. We decided to wait and see whether we really wanted them or maybe could sit in someone else's when they're not looking."

It was customary for Miller to talk easily with strangers and, strolling the decks, he became friendly with many on board. One of his and

246

Bess' happiest associations was with a fine southern lady named Mrs. Bellengrath. She shared with her new friends a hearty sense of humor about much that went on aboard ship. In one of his more confidential conversations with this lady, Miller sketched some of the interesting history of his early life—not leaving out, but greatly embellishing, his close relationship to the North American Indian. Mrs. Bellengrath was of a broad turn of mind and felt that this dramatic bit of information greatly enhanced her new friends. It was not long before the story spread, however, and the ship's passengers knew that there was a full-blooded North American Indian aboard the liner—one who had been born on the Yakima Indian Reservation.

The episode added great sparkle to the trip with many people making comparisons between North American Indians and South American Indians whom they were seeing at the time. With the suntan he gained on deck, Miller was better able to convince all concerned that his claim had a distinct possibility of being true. That many of the passengers took his statement seriously is certain, and that many more enjoyed carrying out the jest, whether true or not, is fair to say. Surely the Yakima Indian enjoyed the gag more than anyone else.

Incident of the Seattle Social Register

At Miller's office one day the telephone rang and a pleasant voice at the other end of the line said, "Mr. Freeman, I am calling from the office of the Seattle *Social Register* and wonder if you would supply me with up-to-date information for our *Blue Book*?"

Miller's interest immediately picked up. Sounding deeply regretful, he replied that he was very sorry that he was not really eligible for such an honor. The young woman calling insisted on knowing why this was the case. (At this point he signaled his son, Miller Junior, to pick up the phone in the adjoining office so that he too could enjoy the fun.)

Continuing his conversation with the young lady, Miller told her, confidentially, that he was born at Fort Simco, on the Yakima Indian Reservation and was a full-blooded North American Indian. At the other end of the line there was a moment of shocked silence, punctuated by an audible intake of breath. The young woman then said, "Just a minute, please, Mr. Freeman." It was obvious she was covering the mouthpiece and conversing with her superior. Coming back on the line after several awkward moments, she said, "We are sorry, we didn't know. We will keep what you tell us confidential. But I just want you to know that I have no racial prejudice whatsoever and I think most highly of our American Indians. After all, *they* are our First Families."

The Palm Court of the Palace Hotel

Miller often visited in San Francisco and took great pleasure in calling on business acquaintances of many years' standing. Frequently he saw Isadore Zellerbach in regard to paper orders, and he was always

247

gratified when the latter commended him upon the fact that he regularly qualified for the discount because of his prompt payments. On one memorable occasion he visited with Herbert Fleishhacker, Senior, and, upon asking, received a loan of $20,000 with no collateral required. It was evident and immensely satisfying to him that he was generally recognized as a good financial risk by those in banking circles.

A highlight of his San Francisco stay was always a lunch at his favorite haunt—the Palm Court of the Palace Hotel—where he would look immediately for a friend of many years. This old friend was the little man who circulated the dining room selling cigars from a box suspended by a strap around his neck. Miller would promptly accost him with two questions. The first was: "Do you have any Flora del Yakima cigars?" Greeting an old friend with a broad smile, the cigar seller always deeply regretted that he did not carry that brand. Then, expectantly waiting, he was poised for the next question: "Well, if you don't have those, do you have Juan de Fucas?" The same regretful reply was invariably followed by laughter. There were, in fact, no such brands; nor had there ever been.

As the years piled up, the same routine had been often repeated. It never took long after Miller's arrival for the little cigar hawker to spot his friend across the many tables and, with a wide smile, to make his way to him in order to once again enjoy the old repartee.

Miller's Birthday Tea

Miller tended to be scornful of social events. Therefore, when he inaugurated the institution of a tea party to honor his own and his twin grandsons' birthdays—which fell on the same day—the event was notable to those who knew him well. Not only did he enjoy the affair on its first occasion; it became a yearly event of the east side, participated in by his many friends with waggish humor and considerable enthusiasm on his part. Beginning as a modest affair, this male tea party burgeoned after its tenth year to include around one hundred guests.

Miller was interviewed about the event which had become noteworthy in his community and he was quoted as saying, "It's a man-sized job arranging the house and decorating the tables for the large tea, but Mrs. Freeman handles it very well. I send out the invitations."

The Seattle Times society reporter described one party in her column as follows: "Pouring at the tea and coffee urns at the annual party last week was Mr. D. K. McDonald, wearing his handsome red sports jacket which he reserves for such notable occasions as Captain Freeman's tea and Christmas, and also, Dr. Thomas Mesdag, in a tan sports coat of imported wool and wearing a contrasting boutonniere. Spectacular were the open-crowned garden hats worn by these bald headed assistants who presided at the tea table. In place of flowers, the table was decorated with a huge cake in his honor, and two smaller ones on either side, belonging to his five-year-old grandsons."

248

38
EXCERPTS from CORRESPONDENCE

ILLER FREEMAN'S VOLUMINOUS CORRESPONDENCE with his family and friends revealed his sense of humor and his enjoyment of life. Sometimes he enclosed a clipping with a brief comment attached. Often his message was penned at the bottom of a communication he received and wanted to share with a correspondent. Excerpts from a few typical examples will indicate the flavor of his informal letter writing.

In the *Spokesman Review* of August 1939, appeared the picture of five studious Republican gentlemen—among them Miller—listening attentively to a speaker. Sending a clipping, he wrote:

"Terribly sorry that pressing matters vital to the welfare of nation prevented me from getting home in time to speed you and yours on your way. If you will carefully scrutinize the countenances of the gentlemen pictured herewith you will note the strained, bewildered expression on each, except that of this writer whose mind is a complete vacuum."

The following are typical of his notes to relatives:

"I am sending a copy of the invitations sent out by J.H. Bloedel, to the members of the Northwest Senior Golfers Association, in which note the likeness, costume and title all verify that this writer [whose likeness was cartooned] is a North American Indian. As a matter of fact, I am leaving here in the morning for Vancouver Island where both the 'Boston' and the 'King George' Indians will have a powwow. I will *hyak klatawa* on the 9 o'clock boat for Victoria, *hyu mamoose potlatch ilahee* Empress Hotel for the ensuing *nenase* days. A *skookum* time will be had by all."

"Mother has been working very industriously on a sweater for me, but something went wrong with it and in an outburst of rage [one of his wife's least likely reactions] she ripped it all out. I expect she'll give me a ball of yarn and a pair of knitting needles and tell me to knit my own sweater."

On his birthday, the following:

"Waking up this morning on my sixtieth birthday, I oiled my creaking joints and tottered downstairs, munching my breakfast with my toothless gums. When I got the remembrance from dear you and yours I perked up and now think I will last through the day."

At a time when a member of his family had purchased a lot and was preparing to build a home:

"About the lot. Yes, of course I want to examine it, inspect it, cock my eye at it, clear my throat and deliver myself of my expert opinion. I don't know what kind of an opinion it will be; but that won't make a bit of difference, it will make me feel much better. Then, there will be a whole lot of advice about the house. So get your ear muffs and adjust your shock absorbers. In my younger days, I had to stand for a lot of guff my elders thought was good advice; that is, I heard the noise they made but never paid any attention to what they said. So, believe me, I have to get even. Never mind, after a while you'll be doing the same thing yourself; in fact, the time will come when you will be so full of advice you'll just bust if you can't make the youngsters stand still long enough for you to deliver it."

Penciled at the end of the letter:

"Don't give up, looks like business might get worse."

At the time of the 1936 Republican Nominating Convention, Miller was asked by the National Broadcasting Company what talents—such as singing, playing instruments, and so forth—any of the national delegates or alternates from the state of Washington might have. They evidently intended to put a show on a national hookup during the convention at Cleveland. At the bottom of the original letter of request, he wrote:

"Dear Mary; I have replied that this is a Republican Convention, that all the entertainers are in the Democratic party.

Private and confidential: Leaving here disguised as a Yakima Indian for

Invitation to Northwest Senior Golfers Association banquet carries a cartoon of Miller Freeman in Indian dress.

SENIOR GOLFER
Chief RAIN-IN-THE-FACE

entrusts me to invite you
(AT MY OWN EXPENSE)
to a BREAKFAST-POTLATCH *at the*
Empress Hotel, Victoria
Sunday morning, August 13 at 8:30

GIVES GIN FIZZES, HIGH BALLS,
EVERYTHING!

Cleveland and way points, June 1. All's well with Ol' Chief Salal on the trail.''

An element of stealth attended Miller's often unexpected use of his Indian myth. Thus, Mrs. James T. Urquhart, Washington's Republican national committeewoman, was surprised to receive the following telegram at a dinner in her honor which Miller was unable to attend. It read:

April 9, 1940

Mrs. James Urquhart,
Republican National Committeewoman
Gowman Hotel,
Seattle, Wash.

NIKA KLOSHE KOPA TUMTUM YAKIMA KLOOTCH-MAN DELATE HYAS KLOSHE NESIKA KONOWAY TILLICUMS YOUTL HYU MUCKAMUK KOPA SITKUM SUN MAHMOUK TAMAHMOUS KLOSHE NANITCH SPOSE KLATAWAH YAHWAK PE NIKA CHACO KAHWA DELATE WAWA ISKUM KUMTUX MIKA CULTUS TENAS MAN.

TYEE AHTANUM KEHLOKEE

Translated, it read:

GREETINGS TO MY MAGNIFICENT AND WISE WOMAN FRIEND FROM YAKIMA, FOR WHOM WE ALL HAVE THE GREATEST ADMIRATION. WE ARE PROUD TO HAVE YOU HONORED AT A FINE DINNER WITH MANY CHIEFTAINS AND MEDICINE MEN. WE REJOICE THAT YOU HAVE COME HERE FROM AFAR TO JOIN IN THE FEAST AND TAKE PART IN ALL THE BIG TALK. YOU KNOW THAT, ALTHOUGH ABSENT, I AM YOUR DEVOTED BUT UNWORTHY FRIEND.

MILLER FREEMAN
THE "AHTANUM MOOSE"

As a member of the ultraconservative Rainier Club, Miller received a lurid poster advertising the club's annual Hi-Jinxs. A cartoon visualized cannons exploding and the roof being blown off the sedate building by the exciting events to come. He reared in stiff-necked indignation and wrote the following letter to the club manager with carbon copies to members of the board of directors who were the Messrs. W. C. Dawson, Frank Taylor, Lester Baker, Edward W. Allen, Volney Richmond, Alex Peabody, and Samuel Barnes.

November 15, 1943

Dear Mr. Bowen:

I note that you say in your reply to me dated November 11th that you will present my letter of November 8th to the Trustees of the Rainier Club.

In the meantime there has reached me in the mail a lurid

251

circular picturing the Rainier Club being wrecked by the Hi-Jinx to be held on November 23rd.

Perhaps the best way out of its difficulties would be to complete the transformation of the Rainier Club by introducing slot machines, pinball machines and jukeboxes at all convenient spots. Also, there is a good deal of waste space in the living room and library that could be put to use by introducing a jive band and having dancing every evening. Neon lights at both the main entrance and the ladies' entrance would help attract the passing trade. I am sure if you had a lottery or drawing once a month it would bring in a good deal of additional revenue.

It might even be possible by these means to raise enough money to subsidize the Rainier Club proper to get out of its present quarters and find a more modest and economical location elsewhere.

I am offering these suggestions in the hope that they may be helpful to the Board of Directors.

Very Truly Yours
Miller Freeman

To an old and dear friend, Dorothy Rogers of San Francisco, he wrote in 1943:

Dear Dorothy:

I have heard that you are now engaged in peddling Wendell Willkie's book, *One World,* from door to door. It's a great work. If you hear rumors that he's going to be candidate for the Republican nomination for President, be sure to let me know. There are a lot of people who supported him last time before they knew he was such a liberal that will oppose him now that they know where he stands. On the other hand, now that he has declared himself I might actually support him. No kidding.

(This is significant in that, as Chairman of the Washington State delegation at the 1940 Convention, Miller was not enthusiastic about Willkie's nomination. Willkie died soon after this communication.)

To Nard Jones, a well-known writer and business associate who had written in regard to an issue that disturbed him, Miller replied:

Dear Mr. Jones:

Copy of your letter to [Senator] Neuberger received. Why bother? You know the man is a professional troublemaker. His stock is muckraking. My advice to you is forget and not be so damn serious all the time. All these things, of course, are a matter of judgement and my idea is just to be helpful to you and encourage your own peace of mind in this turbulent world.

Epilogue
A LAST CAMPAIGN

I N THE SUMMER OF 1955, Miller was planning a fall trip to Washington, D.C., to launch a new campaign designed to put federally held lands to productive use. Again, his often repeated theme guided him in a desire to see these areas, then locked up and lying idle, put to beneficial use. As he celebrated his eightieth birthday, he prepared to visit the Capitol by sending letters to persons he planned to see there regarding this project. But this trip he never made, for his last campaign ended before it began with his sudden death on September 17.

Miller had contemplated two trips that fall. Following the signing of the North Pacific Fisheries Treaty of 1954, he had persistently been urged by members of the Japan Fisheries Association to visit Japan. He seriously considered making the effort to go and had carried on considerable correspondence with men in the association regarding plans for such a trip.

Two factors made him decide against going to Japan. Primarily, he had become interested in his new campaign and, additionally, he considered that the long flight across the Pacific would be a strenuous one. He took neither trip but his thoughts were in high gear on his new program when he suddenly went to sleep.

In 1962, seven years after Miller's death, his son William Freeman, then president of Miller Freeman Publications, having increasing business in Japan, planned a visit to Tokyo. When this fact was known to the industry people in Japan, he received the same cordial invitations from the Japan Fisheries Association which his father had earlier received.

From the moment of his arrival in Japan, William Freeman was accorded the utmost courtesy by all members of the association. A final dinner at one of Tokyo's finest restaurants honored him and brought together the most distinguished and important men of Japan's largest industry. In the best tradition, superb food was served, while lovely geishas hovered beside each guest, filling and refilling sake cups

William B. Freeman, photographed with directors of the Japan Fisheries Association during his visit to Tokyo in 1962.

as they emptied, while heavily powdered geishas performed a ritual dance.

According to Japanese custom, during the meal, all remained seated on the floor behind low tables. As the meal ended a ceremony began. In turn, officials of the association came before the group, still kneeling, to speak for the organization to Mr. Freeman. While they addressed William Freeman, each man paid an added tribute to his father, Miller Freeman, with words carefully chosen and slowly spoken with great sincerity. The stillness in the dimly lit room added emphasis to these moments. All who were listening were keenly aware that these elder statesmen of the industry were saluting a man whose country had recently humbled theirs in a long and agonizing war; who had himself persistently, for many years previous to this event, fought Japanese aggression to protect the interests of his country on the issues of immigration and of invasion of the fisheries of Alaska and Canada. These facts were well known to all there.

Cognizant of this, these Japanese were proving themselves big men as they paid respect to one who had been a tough fighter, their persistent opponent—but, above all, a fair and magnanimous one in victory. He had, when the battle was won, actively urged Japan's inclusion in a partnership with the West. He bore no bitterness toward them. This they knew. For this an ultimate tribute was paid to Miller Freeman that night in Tokyo.

Elizabeth Wright . . .

The author of Miller Freeman/Man of Action,
*is the daughter-in-law of the protagonist,
one of the West's early industrial journal
publishers. In private life she is Elizabeth
Wright Freeman, who married Miller's
eldest son, William B. Freeman, in 1929.*

*A native Californian, Elizabeth Wright was educated in the state's
public schools, then spent two years at Miss Ransom's School for
Girls in Piedmont. She entered Mills College in 1928, but her
studies there were soon interrupted by marriage.*

*The mother of five sons, and active in local civic and political
affairs, Elizabeth Wright Freeman had little time for writing, her
avocation, while her children were growing up. Nevertheless she
was fascinated by the history of her husband's family, whose
publishing activities began soon after the U.S. Civil War. A few
years ago, she began to delve into old scrapbooks, letters, and
other mementos. As a result, she decided that the story deserved
a wider audience and fuller treatment than was given in the brief
Memoirs written for the family and a few intimate friends.*

Her first book, published in 1973, was Independence in all Things/
Neutrality in Nothing, *the biography of Legh Richmond Freeman,
native Virginian, who followed the emigrant trail to the far West.
Moving his press by wagon from town to town in the wake of the
builders of the first transcontinental railroad, this pioneer
journalist and publisher established a reputation for colorful,
often volatile, prose that outraged many of his readers.*

*In this second book, she tells the story of Miller Freeman, Legh's
third son, who started his career in his father's printshop at
the age of ten.* Miller Freeman/Man of Action *is the biography
of a publisher who turned away from his early interest in farm
journals to found an industrial magazine publishing house and
devote more than fifty years to its growth and the development of
the industries it served. Believing his obligation was to
those industries as a whole, not to special interests, he fought
independently for fisheries treaties, fair and realistic immigration
laws, harbor and highway improvements, and conservation of natural
resources on the "wise use" principle. His story brings in much
of the history of the Pacific Northwest, and particularly the
Seattle area, during the years between 1875 and 1955.*

*Elizabeth Wright Freeman and her husband now divide their time
between homes in Moraga (Contra Costa County), California
and Borrego Springs in the California desert.*